D1606109

SANCTIFIED SISTERS

Sanctified Sisters

A History of Protestant Deaconesses

Jenny Wiley Legath

NEW YORK UNIVERSITY PRESS
New York

NEW YORK UNIVERSITY PRESS
New York
www.nyupress.org

This publication is made possible in part from the Barr Ferree Foundation Fund for Publications, Department of Art and Archaeology, Princeton University.

References to Internet websites (URLs) were accurate at the time of writing. Neither the author nor New York University Press is responsible for URLs that may have expired or changed since the manuscript was prepared.

Library of Congress Cataloging-in-Publication Data
Names: Legath, Jennifer Anne Wiley, 1975–   author.
Title: Sanctified sisters : a history of Protestant deaconesses / Jenny Wiley Legath.
Description: New York : NYU Press, 2019. | Includes bibliographical references and index.
Identifiers: LCCN 2018059693 | ISBN 9781479860630 (cl : alk. paper)
Subjects: LCSH: Deaconesses—Protestant churches—History.
Classification: LCC BV 4423 .L44 2019 | DDC 262/.14082—dc23
LC record available at https://lccn.loc.gov/2018059693

New York University Press books are printed on acid-free paper, and their binding materials are chosen for strength and durability. We strive to use environmentally responsible suppliers and materials to the greatest extent possible in publishing our books.

Manufactured in the United States of America

10 9 8 7 6 5 4 3 2 1

Also available as an ebook

Dedicated to the memory of my mother,

Betsy Marshall Wiley,

who had a diaconal heart

CONTENTS

I am not a deaconess. I had never heard of deaconesses until I took a course on liberal Protestantism at Harvard Divinity School. There I discovered Methodist deaconesses acting out the Social Gospel at the turn of the twentieth century. These college-educated women forsook marriage to canvass tenements, Americanize immigrants, and attempt to solve the country's assorted social ills—all while dressed like Catholic nuns. My foremothers for generations were dyed-in-the-wool Methodists; how had I never encountered deaconesses, or even known that they existed? Their legacy should have been my birthright. Further study revealed additional deaconesses of a different sort. Instead of marching around the cities trying to fix people, these deaconesses lived together in tight-knit motherhouses, and the people they tried to fix in their work as hospital nurses were very similar to themselves, German-speaking farming folk with little education. I was inspired to figure out what it was about the deaconess vocation that spoke to such different women and compelled them to choose this unique life. I had to tell their story.

* * *

In the years that it has taken me to write this book, I have accumulated debts of gratitude that can never be repaid. David Hall, Ann Braude, and the late Bill Hutchison prepared me to meet the deaconesses in my studies at Harvard. At Princeton, Leigh Schmidt helped me to develop my idea, and Marie Griffith advised it to completion. The Religion Department's American Religions workshop was essential in helping me rework each chapter. May I never have to write a book without the benefit of careful reading and feedback from our graduate students and our powerhouse faculty Wallace Best, Jessica Delgado, and Seth Perry. Judith Weisenfeld, especially, offered continual, critical encouragement throughout the process, stepping in as my unofficial mentor at just the right time. Nicole Kirk provided crucial early inspiration, and she and

Kate Carté, Elesha Coffman, Rachel McBride Lindsey, Jessica Parr, Tisa Wenger, and Rachel Wheeler—my virtual village—have sustained me with camaraderie and grammatical advice. Colleagues and fellows at the Center for the Study of Religion have supported me both personally and professionally. Robert Wuthnow (may he never retire) has served as the ideal boss and wisest advisor. Anita Kline fixed my crown every day and never let the world know it was crooked. Meredith Butts proved a fearless research assistant. I thank the archivists who opened their doors to me, and the deaconesses who shared their stories with me. My editor at NYU Press, Jennifer Hammer, demonstrated faith in the project before it was warranted. My in-laws, Joan and Regis Legath, were always ready with care and babysitting. My father, Jeff Wiley, has always believed in me and never doubted I could write a book. May I do the same for my children, Jack, Will, and Cole, who remind me every day what is important. My husband, Jeff, read every word of this book and cheered me on when I needed it most. Having listened to me talk about deaconesses for most of our marriage, he is as happy as I am to see this book completed.

Introduction

At age ninety-two, Sister Ella Loew reminisced, "Across from where we lived there was a convent, and I used to admire those sisters, and I said to this old uncle, I said, 'You know, if I was a Catholic girl, I would want to be a sister.'" Loew's uncle surprised her with the news that their own Protestant church had sisters too, and in that moment, she knew she had found her calling. Ella Loew's mother objected to her new mission: "Oh my, my mother had a wooden ear. She would not listen to that. So, she would suggest, you go to business college, you do this, do that." Yet Loew persevered in declaring her intentions, and after three years, her mother finally relented. In 1910 Loew left her home in Leavenworth, Kansas, and traveled three hundred miles east to become a deaconess probationer at the hospital in St. Louis. After four years of classes and practical nursing training, Ella Loew became a non-Catholic sister when, at the age of twenty-five, she was consecrated as a deaconess in the Evangelical Synod, a small German American Reformed denomination that later became part of the United Church of Christ. Interviewed in 1981, she happily recounted her life's work as a nurse and her close relationship with her sisters, including the Mennonite sisters who had trained with her before going to work at their own hospital. Although Loew averred that women "are the making of the church," when asked if she would have gone to seminary had that option been available, she answered, "No, I never felt that was my life." She concluded, "I have never regretted it, never. It hasn't all been roses by any means. I've had many trials and tribulations, but we overcome them, too. I felt that it was a life worthwhile."[1] She was not alone in her calling. In the late nineteenth and twentieth centuries, thousands of Protestant women in the United States who sought a worthwhile life became deaconesses.

What these women pursued in the female diaconate, the order of deaconesses, was a total, encompassing life devoted to Christian service. Since her conversion as a young woman around the year 1900, Louise

1

Epkerrs had been teaching in her local Sunday School and engaged in mission work among the poor. Yet, she wrote to the German Methodist deaconess board, "I feel that I have fallen far too short in my sphere of doing & being what he would have me do & be."[2] Epkerrs had been doing plenty; it was the "being" part that was a problem. American women who became deaconesses were left unsatisfied with the piecemeal doing of acts of Christian mercy. They wanted to find a new way of being in which their very lives were a testament to God's grace. This is what made the deaconess movement unique in the history of American religion: it was an experiment in a new way of being a Protestant Christian woman. The work itself was not novel, but the holistic life in which it was embedded was. Deaconesses sought to consecrate every aspect of their lives to Christian service, from the way they dressed to where they lived to how they prayed and worshipped.

At the close of the nineteenth century, most young white Protestant women in the United States followed in their mothers' footsteps. Working-class women often labored to support their families before marriage, many of them leaving school early. Middle- and upper-class women usually completed high school and might go on to college. The average age of marriage was around twenty-two, and 75 percent of women had married before age twenty-six.[3] In the absence of reliable birth control, motherhood usually followed soon after. Before and after marriage, middle- and upper-class women might volunteer for any number of the mission or reform societies that were thriving in this time. They could—and did—raise money for missions, teach Sunday School, visit the poor, and nurse the sick, but few did so full-time. A Christian woman's vocation was generally assumed to be marriage and motherhood, even if she was active in her missionary society or took in laundry or boarders to supplement the family's income.

The life path of a deaconess diverged from that of her mother and sisters. She chose not to marry. She left her home to travel to a training school or hospital to prepare for her chosen vocation. The new candidate entered a community of women in a deaconess home or motherhouse and began wearing the garb, usually a dark, plain dress with a simple bonnet, cap, or veil. The community provided this uniform dress and the woman's room, board, and, in lieu of a salary, a small allowance sufficient for only the most basic needs. After a certain number of years of theological and practical training, the probationer was deemed ready, if she chose, to be consecrated as a deaconess. In a church service patterned after the ordination of ministers (but not called ordination), the candidate knelt and received the blessing of a minister or bishop and promised (but did not vow) to perform her ministry of service, whether it be nursing, teaching, childcare, missions, evangelism, or social-service work. This consecration service may well have been a deaconess's only official appearance in a worship service. Deaconesses did not have a liturgical role in the church, unlike many deacons. In most Protestant churches, the position of deacon was a traditional office of church leadership that was distinct from the office of pastor or priest and, until well into the twentieth century, was reserved for men. Although their scriptural mandate was to serve, by the turn of the twentieth century deacons had acquired additional business, managerial, and liturgical functions within their local congregations.[4]

Deaconesses did not think of themselves as female equivalents to male deacons. Instead, they claimed as their role model Phoebe, the woman in the New Testament whom the apostle Paul commends for her service to many. Although deaconesses clutched this biblical precedent tightly, the scriptures offered them precious few details about their foremother. In the late nineteenth century, Protestant women filled in the gaps in Phoebe's story with the resources available to them. In their missionary society journals, they read the reports of female foreign missionaries teaching and evangelizing abroad. In the cities they watched Salvation Army lasses singing and preaching on the streets and settlement workers reaching out to the urban poor. Some visited deaconess institutions in Germany and England and witnessed the thousands of women at work there. And they could not avoid noticing the Catholic nuns at work all around them across the United States.[5] Women used these models, European and American, Protestant and Catholic, quotidian and exotic, to limn the contours of a new life based on an old phrase: "Phoebe, our sister, a deaconess of the church."

This book tells the story of the deaconesses. It is a story with which most scholars of US religion have not engaged. Recent historians of women in American religion acknowledge the presence of deaconesses, but they do not seem to know how to interpret them.[6] Authors who have written on the diaconate have generally done so from within a particular denomination, or even a particular institution, and have defined the entire movement by the characteristics of that one group of women.[7] A reader today could not be blamed for concluding that all deaconesses were proto-feminist social workers, or, alternately, that all deaconesses were poorly educated nurses. These narrow treatments are misleading and obscure the larger picture and importance of the movement as a whole.

The deaconess story is a Protestant story; deaconesses strongly identified as Protestant.[8] But it is also a Catholic story: Catholic women religious were the most visible role models deaconesses had, and an imagined American Catholicism played an outsized role in deaconesses' understanding of their mission. The story of the deaconesses brings together Catholic and Protestant histories that are too often considered in isolation from each other. For example, recent scholarship describes a largely antagonistic relationship between nuns and Protestant reformers.[9] Yet deaconesses acted as a mediating group, complicating the neat dichotomy between celibate Catholic women in community and reforming Protestant mothers in nuclear families. The history of deaconesses offers a necessary corrective to telling the American religion story from an insular Protestant or Catholic point of view.

This is also a women's story. Deaconesses were committed to creating and maintaining a vocation that was for women only and especially suited to women. The founding generation was not interested in becoming gender-neutral deacons. Their benefactors, those who supported the deaconesses with money, supplies, and prayers, were primarily women as well, investing the larger female Christian community in the work of the diaconate. This work informs arguments about female institution builders mastering the arts of fundraising, publicity, and entrepreneurship.[10] Yet it is also the story of women's negotiations with men, particularly pastors, who often held competing understandings of what a deaconess should be. Into the twentieth century, men ruled church bureaucracies, controlling entry to seminary, ordination, and decision-making bodies. Deaconesses were forced to work creatively through these male power structures. As other scholars have argued, women often find a measure of power in patriarchal systems by using a gender-specific strategy.[11]

The deaconess story is not the story of women's ordination. In their search for a usable past, clergywomen and women's historians have looked to the deaconesses as early advocates for the ordination of women. When deaconesses are included in the American religious story, they are frequently shoe-horned neatly into a narrative of women's steady, inevitable march towards the pulpit. This search for the forebears of women clergy has driven some historians, particularly in the flurry of celebratory women's history from the 1980s and 1990s, to laud deaconesses as modern feminists, as in an early study of Methodist deaconesses subtitled "A Study in Religious Feminism."[12] In contrast, this book argues from the sources that the vast majority of women who became deaconesses were not terribly interested in ordination. Deaconesses—at least those consecrated between the 1880s and 1910s—did not consider ordination the brass ring and the deaconess vocation a mere consolation prize. Yet, although this is not a story of women's ordination, it provides an essential context for understanding it. Deaconesses claimed a role that was neither clerical nor strictly lay and in doing so challenged and sharpened the definitions of both. Comprehending the history of deaconesses helps us to understand women's complicated struggle for ecclesiastical equality as manifest in voting rights, access to theological education, equal pay, and, yes, ordination. It was not until Protestants transformed their ideas of women's unique, gendered contribution to the mission of the church that the idea of a gender-neutral ordained clergy could succeed.

The story of the deaconesses is a story about the United States of America. First- and second-generation immigrants play leading roles alongside native-born Americans. In key denominations, the women's diaconate was disproportionately composed of German and Scandinavian immigrants and the daughters of these immigrants. These immigrant-heavy churches constructed the deaconess vocation in such a way that it brought together ideas of the ideal woman and the ideal American. In promoting their deaconesses as ideal American women, these immigrant churches staked their claim to the whiteness that they saw as essential to their acceptance and success as Americans. These claims were buttressed by white deaconesses' treatment of the small number of black deaconesses who participated in the movement. Historians have produced illuminating accounts of the construction of race in the United States, but religion as a factor in this construction is often overlooked.[13] Religion played a crucial role in the racializing of these

German and Scandinavian Protestants. Other churches, already secure in their own white Americanness, attempted to use the diaconate to shape the Americanization of new immigrants. Regardless of their birthplace, deaconesses participated in the strengthening of the American racial dichotomy of black and white.

The deaconess movement offered Protestant women a new and distinct way of being in the world: deaconesses used the office to perform traditional works of Christian mercy embedded in an alternative lifestyle that bound them to God, each other, and other women. These women eschewed popular fashion for plain, dark uniform garb, lived together in communities with other single women, rejected a salary, and drenched their lives in prayer and worship. As deaconesses, these women alternately allied themselves with other white Protestant Americans, such as when they sought to Americanize new immigrants, and set themselves apart from American culture, such as when they rejected the wage economy.

In the wake of the Civil War, very few Americans had ever heard of deaconesses, whose numbers were already quickly multiplying in Germany and England. By the 1880s, Lutheran, Reformed, Methodist, and Episcopal Americans brought back stories of this European phenomenon and were attempting to plant the movement in American soil. They began in haste to consecrate women as deaconesses and to fund and erect the brick-and-mortar institutions in which deaconesses would train, work, and live. By the turn of the century, deaconess advocates were breathless with excitement and optimism about the movement's potential to transform the nation by harnessing the power of women to heal the sick, feed the hungry, and spread the good news of the gospel. In 1900, famed evangelist Dwight L. Moody remarked, "Deaconesses? Oh, I see them everywhere I go, and I believe in them heartily."[14] By the 1930s, deaconess institutions peppered the landscape of the United States, concentrated in the cities of the Midwest and Northeast but stretching out even to the Pacific Northwest and deep South. Thousands of trained consecrated deaconesses were hard at work in myriad avenues of service. However, just as the first generation succeeded in braiding together care-giving work and a consecrated lifestyle, younger women emerged intent on untangling these two strands. By the middle of the twentieth century, it was clear that Protestant women were saying "yes" to deaconess work but "no" to distinctive aspects of the deaconess life. The story of the deaconesses almost ended, as institutions closed one after another and the number of new consecrations dropped precipitously. Yet, as the century turned again, a new generation of deaconesses has emerged. These women have again taken up the threads and begun weaving together a new consecrated deaconess identity, one that reinterprets both diaconal work and the diaconal life in entirely twenty-first-century ways. Today the deaconess office continues to offer women an alternative way of being Christian in the world, and numbers are growing once again.

Back to the Bible (through Europe)

For deaconesses and their supporters, it all began with Phoebe. They read of her in the New Testament, in the sixteenth chapter of Paul's letter to the Romans: "I commend unto you Phoebe, our sister, which is a [deaconess] of the Church which is at Cenchrea. That ye receive her in the Lord, as becometh saints, and that ye assist her in whatsoever business she hath need of you: for she hath been a succorer of many, and of myself also." At the turn of the twentieth century, debates raged over women's voting rights (in and out of the church), women's preaching, and women's work. Christians on both sides searched their Bibles and found scriptures to support their views. But the founders of the deaconess movement found the words of Romans 16:1 beautifully clear; this verse was their proof-text that deaconesses were biblical and thus of unquestionable authenticity. The simplicity of that one Bible verse, however, belies a more complex history of interpretation.

English-speaking Protestants reading the King James version of the Bible would actually have read the words, "Phoebe, our sister, which is a servant of the Church which is at Cenchrea." Likewise, the German text of the Luther Bible translated Phoebe's role as "in the service of" the church at Cenchrea.[15] The word "deaconess" appeared nowhere in the keystone passage establishing the office of deaconess! Why then were deaconess advocates so confident in the office's biblical pedigree? During the 1870s, while Americans were endeavoring to garner support for a US deaconess movement, a group of English and American biblical scholars was laboring on the first major revision of the King James

Bible, aiming to promote unity among the Protestant churches.[16] The Revised Version of 1881 brought little apparent change to these verses of Paul, adding only a textual note to the word "servant" that read, "Or, deaconess." Methodist deaconess founder Lucy Rider Meyer disparaged the halfway measure, lamenting that "the revisers of the New Testament struggled with their conservatism in vain, and retained the word 'servant' in the text, but they have done Phoebe the half justice of calling her what Paul called her, 'Deaconess,' in the margin." Rider Meyer huffed, "Paul seems to have been less afraid that poor Phoebe would become puffed up if called by any other name than servant."[17] Yet, the power of that novel little footnote is not to be underestimated. The scholarly biblical revisers both drew on and promoted advances in textual criticism that sought to produce ever more accurate translations of scripture.

The Revised New Testament caused consumer frenzy when it was released in the United States in 1881. Even though readers would soon complain that it lacked the mellifluousness of the King James version, educators praised its close adherence to the original Greek. It represented the best scholarship of the textual or "lower" criticism, which was then championed by Christians of both conservative and liberal persuasions. So, even though it appeared only in a marginal note, the entry of this word "deaconess" into the printed Bible, a Bible that showcased the best textual criticism to date, must have carried great weight. For the first time English readers saw the word "deaconess" in print in their Bibles. Although most deaconesses could not read biblical Greek, key early deaconess leaders such as Methodist Lucy Rider Meyer, Episcopal deaconess Susan Trevor Knapp, and their clergy advocates could.[18] When they read their Greek New Testaments, they found Phoebe called a "διάκονος," which appeared to demand the cognate word "deaconess," on which Rider Meyer claimed that "nearly all the authorities" agreed.[19] When deaconesses quoted Romans 16 in their promotional literature, they were apt to substitute without comment the word "deaconess" for "servant."[20] It was no coincidence that the deaconess movement in the United States sprang to life in the same decade as the Revised Version of the New Testament. Nineteenth-century textual criticism and the Bible revision movement contributed to the emergence of the deaconess movement by dethroning King

James just enough to embolden these women to have confidence in their own translation of Romans 16.

Although deaconess advocates insistently pointed to the biblical warrant for the office, they could not help glancing over their shoulders at Europe for contemporary examples of the diaconate in practice. The primary European models were the Kaiserswerth motherhouse in Germany and the Mildmay institution in England. These early organizations emerged within their own particular contexts of nineteenth-century Europe. As industrializing countries where women were agitating for an increased public role, both countries were ripe for the movement. Between the Protestant Reformation and the nineteenth century, women were largely absent from public charitable work in Germany. The country's Lutheran heritage had eschewed celibacy, instead stressing woman's role within the family as educator of her children and supporter of her husband's vocation. The primacy of the preached Word, over against the performance of good works, privileged the male clerical position.[21]

Theological and devotional developments in Germany and England also fostered the emergence of the movement. In the 1830s a religious awakening swept through Protestant Germany. A development of this revival was the Lutheran Inner Mission, which coupled missionary zeal for personal redemption with an attempt to heal the wounds that industrialization had wrought on German society. The Inner Mission prompted church folk to bring the Gospel to people of their own country by first meeting the needs of the body. According to the Lutheran principle of the universal priesthood of believers, the human capital for the new charitable organizations of the Inner Mission was to come from "the living and active members of the Church." In 1833 Heinrich Wichern opened the Rauhe Haus in Germany for the training of deacons, or Brothers, to exercise this diaconal function.[22] German Lutheran pastor Theodore Fliedner took note of Wichern's deacons, and on a visit to Holland he observed Mennonites, whose unusual polity made use of deaconesses who performed works of charity in their local congregations. In England, Fliedner studied Quaker Elizabeth Fry's work among the poor and imprisoned. The pastor also could not help but notice the earnest work of the Catholic Sisters of Charity in his predominantly Catholic village of Kaiserswerth in the Rhineland.[23] Inspired by these disparate examples, Fliedner resolved to introduce the idea of deaconess work to Germany, and in 1836, Theodore and Frederike Münster Fliedner opened the first German deaconess institution.

The unmarried women who entered Kaiserswerth were usually of humble backgrounds and spent long, hard days training to be nurses. These were women strongly affected by the German Awakening and were supported spiritually by the frequent motherhouse worship services. More support came from the tight-knit surrogate family of the diaconate with Theodore as father and Frederike as mother.[24] Because in Germany the kind of work a deaconess did was not otherwise acceptable for a single woman, Fliedner had ensconced them safely in "families" and endowed them with the symbolic status of the married woman by prescribing the wearing of the married woman's headdress. The Kaiserswerth endeavor was stunningly successful. Within fifteen years, the deaconesses were running a flourishing enterprise that included a motherhouse, hospital, center for rehabilitation of female convicts, teacher training school, girls' high school and laboratory, kindergarten, orphanage, homes for female invalids and "lunatics," training school for deaconesses, and farm. At the turn of the century, there were almost fifteen thousand deaconesses affiliated with the Kaiserswerth motherhouse, and other deaconess motherhouses began to proliferate across Germany.[25] For the American deaconess movement, Kaiserswerth served as the primary institutional model and spiritual touchstone.

In England around the same time, a second epicenter of women's religious activity emerged in two related forms: sisterhoods and deaconesses. Members of the Oxford Movement, also known as Tractarians for their theological publications *Tracts for the Times*, urged a return to a catholic understanding of the historical church, the ministry, and the sacraments. The Oxford Movement, drawing from both catholic and evangelical impulses, emphasized the linkage of the modern church to the patristic and medieval church and enjoined a new attention to devotion. From this revival emerged Anglican sisterhoods, which took the form of a Romantic reimagining of medieval monasticism, replete with attendant aesthetic pleasures but also influenced by the practicality of modern active Roman Catholic religious orders such as the Daughters of Charity. In 1841 Marion Hughes became the first Anglican woman

Figure I.1. English deaconesses of Mildmay (Harriet J. Cooke. *Mildmay; or, The Story of the First Deaconess Institution*. London: E. Stock, 1893).

to take the three vows of poverty, chastity, and obedience (privately before Oxford Movement leader Edward Pusey), and in 1845 the first Anglican sisterhood was founded.[26] The sisterhoods gained a slow but steady following in England. As celebrated as the sisterhoods were by the Tractarians, other Low Church Anglicans adamantly opposed them as a Trojan horse for Roman Catholic ideas. Inspired by the German example, Low Church Anglicans instead encouraged the development of the deaconess office, asserting its biblical, rather than Roman Catholic, foundation.

In 1858, Englishwoman Elizabeth Ferard spent several months at Kaiserswerth and in 1862 was set apart by the bishop of London as the first episcopally ordained deaconess in the Church of England. In England and subsequently in America, there was slippage between Anglican sisterhoods and deaconesses, and women sometimes moved from one vocation to the other. The primary distinction was that, unlike deaconesses, Anglican sisters explicitly sought and were permitted to make vows.[27] Vows were seen as a defining feature of Roman Catholic nuns and as such marked a line that most Protestants refused to cross. Sisterhoods remained limited to the Anglican and Episcopal churches, never spreading to other churches or taking hold of the larger American imagination the way the deaconess movement did.

In England, the deaconess movement found an even better foothold outside the institutions of the Anglican Church in an ecumenical establishment named Mildmay. Anglican minister William Pennefather and his wife, Catherine King Pennefather, began recruiting young women to help the poor of his parish and in 1860 established a women's training center. This effort resulted in the establishment of Mildmay, a deaconess home and training school in North London.[28] Although the Pennefathers were Anglican, the deaconess superintendent and the treasurer were Presbyterians, and Mildmay was intentionally interdenominational. Catherine Pennefather explained, "We started with Kaiserswerth and its hallowed associations fresh in our minds, but the work was not intended, for many reasons, to be a copy of that valuable institution." She explained that the English institute would not adopt the domestic rules of another country—"We may learn, but not transplant"—and, interestingly, that "the name and dress (though our own sympathies might go with both) would enlist a host of opponents, whose only ideas of such distinctions were associated with nuns and sisterhoods of Romish reputation." Thus, Mildmay did not even call itself a deaconess institution until the end of the 1860s, and its members were not consecrated by any bishop.

Because the idea of single women working in public was less shocking in England than in Germany, English deaconesses did not require the pseudo-family structure of the motherhouse or the garb of the married woman. By the 1890s, Mildmay deaconesses did adopt the garb, giving recognizability and efficiency as their reasons. Also, because professional nursing was already established by lay women in England, nursing never became the primary mission of British deaconesses. Instead, motivated by the evangelical impulses of Low Church Anglicanism and other English Protestant churches, the deaconesses set out to "reach the unreached, and seemingly unreachable, masses of our large cities," primarily by means of house-to-house visitation. Mildmay was a success, boasting 220 deaconesses by 1893.[29] Although never the behemoth enterprise of the German Kaiserswerth, Mildmay was influential beyond its size as an accessible Anglophone example of the European diaconate for Americans.

American deaconess advocates were keenly aware of their European predecessors. In Protestant denominations with European deaconess roots, such as Lutherans and Episcopalians, deaconesses were imported directly from Europe to begin the American work. Other Protestants traveled abroad to study the European institutions.[30] Authors eager to promote the diaconate shared information about the deaconess movement in various Christian periodicals.[31] Early deaconesses were even profiled in the women's magazine *Harper's Bazar*, which, not surprisingly, focused on the novelty of the deaconesses' garb.[32] But Americans never saw themselves as importing a European invention; rather, they admired how the Europeans had revived the biblical institution of the diaconate and adapted it to their own needs. They understood their European cousins as gesturing them back to the Bible. Both European and American deaconess advocates saw themselves not as inventors but as restorers of the lost role of women in the great work of the church.

Chapter Outline

The first five chapters deal with the founding era of the deaconess movement in the United States, roughly from 1880 through the 1930s, spanning the Gilded Age and the Progressive Era, through the Great Depression.[33] The final chapter brings the deaconess story up to the second decade of the twenty-first century. Chapters 1 through 5 are organized thematically, each contributing to the argument that the deaconess office provided American women a creative way to live out a Christian calling that sometimes buttressed and sometimes stood apart from the larger Protestant American culture.

The book's opening chapter introduces the diversity of the deaconess movement. The unique histories and theologies of the many denominational groups produced different understandings of the deaconess lifestyle and mission. Yet the diaconates were linked by a shared belief in a practical theology that addressed the needs of the whole person, body and soul. This chapter uses demographic information to reveal the deaconess story's midwestern and urban center of gravity and its disproportionately immigrant character. It also examines the racialized arguments that deaconess advocates made. German and other Northern

European immigrant deaconesses argued that their very Germanness (or Swedishness, or Danishness) especially fitted them for deaconess work, and they saw their mission as ministering to their compatriots in America. Meanwhile, Anglophone deaconesses employed Social Gospel and Progressivist discourse about the (white) American's duty to help the less advantaged and especially to assimilate the new Catholic and Jewish immigrants.

Chapter 2 demonstrates how women used the deaconess office to participate in the construction of gender in the late nineteenth and early twentieth centuries. Deaconesses struggled to create a vocation that was an attractive, legitimate alternative to woman's "highest calling" of marriage, home, and motherhood. Deaconess advocates marketed the diaconate as the ideal vocation for woman, one that could utilize all of her natural inclinations towards self-sacrifice, moral influence, and maternal nurture. Deaconesses fashioned their vocation as sanctified spinsterhood and practiced diaconal maternalism.

Chapter 3 argues that Roman Catholicism, both as it actually existed and especially as deaconesses imaginatively constructed it, served crucial functions for the diaconate as catalyst, foil, and exemplar. Deaconess work was very much a reaction to the on-the-ground work of Catholic women religious, yet deaconesses preferred to contrast themselves with an image of corrupt cloistered nuns as they existed in some imagined past. Deaconesses argued that they were in no way like nuns, except of course in the *good* ways. How they parsed such distinctions is revelatory both of Protestant understandings of Catholicism at the time and of how those understandings could be changed, for deaconesses, by meaningful interactions with Catholic sisters and laity. We understand this time period, when Catholic immigration to the United States was reaching a new peak, as a time of heightened Catholic-Protestant tension and cultural clash. The deaconess movement complicates this picture; even though official deaconess literature disavowed any affinity for the Catholic Church, deaconesses on the ground admired and emulated their Catholic sister counterparts and promoted a common Christian faith among themselves and the Catholics among whom they worked. They used Catholicism to construct their own Protestant ideal of consecrated womanhood.

"The question always is not how much can you earn; but how little can you live upon?"[34] With those words, Methodist Lucy Rider Meyer troubles conventional stories of money in this era. Chapter 4 examines the deaconess allowance as a key component of deaconesses' consecrated lifestyle, as it sanctified their relationships with the rich, the poor, their families of origin and their new diaconal families, and the women who supported them. Although they considered it unique, the deaconess allowance was actually analogous to other women's relationships with money at the time, as it was based on women's presumed needs, rather than their earning power. Deaconesses crafted the allowance system in order to hold together particular ideas of Christian women's appropriate relationship to money and to others.

Chapter 5 probes the conflicted relationship between deaconesses and the ordained clergy. Historians have attempted to celebrate deaconesses as the forerunners of women's ordination in the Protestant churches. But the links between the diaconate and the ordained ministry are far more complex than a simple cause and effect. Deaconesses assumed much of the pastoral work of the clergy as ministers eagerly shed their responsibility for the less desirable "feminine" work onto the deaconesses. Deaconesses also took on clerical roles of preaching and leading worship but only by creatively reinterpreting their performance of those functions in ways that rendered them less objectionable. In the first several decades of the movement, very few deaconesses sought ordination because they interpreted their deaconess calling as the perfect womanly alternative to the ordained ministry. Instead, deaconesses bolstered the professionalization of the male pastorate by assuming certain tasks that were gendered female while also demanding respect as trained, professional women workers. When deaconesses began debating ordination for themselves in the 1920s and 1930s, it marked a new era for the diaconate.

Chapter 6 brings the deaconess story into the twenty-first century. In the mid-twentieth century, the deaconess movement faced a crisis. Recruits were at an all-time low, and deaconess institutions were merging or closing at an alarming rate. Some deaconess bodies did in fact die out. Other deaconesses became deacons, indistinguishable from their male colleagues in a newly gender-neutral diaconate. Yet other deaconesses sought to creatively reenvision their office in a way that made sense of new expectations by and of women yet remained true to the heart of the diaconate as a unique way of being and doing in the world. These women are leading the diaconate into a new period of growth and flour-ishing today.

The conclusion emphasizes the importance of the deaconess move-ment for understanding the role of women in American Protestantism at the turn of the twentieth century and still today. As the deaconess story intersects with stories of Catholic/Protestant relations, gender, money, professionalization, Americanization, and ordination, it neces-sarily alters the telling of those narratives.

1

A Tapestry of Diaconates

All schoolchildren know the story of Florence Nightingale, the "lady with the lamp" who nursed wounded soldiers during the Crimean War and is credited with founding the modern nursing profession. What schoolchildren are not taught is that Nightingale was trained for her vocation during a life-changing three months at the Protestant deaconess motherhouse in Kaiserswerth, Germany. In 1852, Nightingale railed against her own church for not providing women with opportunities to serve:

> The Church of England has for men bishoprics, archbishoprics, and a little work. . . . For women she has—what? I had no taste for theological discoveries. I would have given her my head, my hand, my heart. She would not have them. She did not know what to do with them. She told me to go back and do crochet in my mother's drawing room; or, if I were tired of that, to marry and look well at the head of my husband's table. You may go to the Sunday School if you like it, she said. But she gave me no training even for that. She gave me neither work to do for her, nor education for it.[1]

Nightingale argued that in Germany she had found in the deaconess office a way for women to give to the church their head, their hand, and their heart.

Influenced by Nightingale's 1851 *Institution of Kaiserswerth on the Rhine* and other reports of European deaconesses, the Episcopal and Lutheran churches began attempting to institute the office in the United States as early as the 1850s. These earliest efforts were fragile; it was another few decades before the movement gained traction on the US side of the Atlantic. Beginning in the 1880s, American Protestants increasingly became convinced that a female diaconate was essential to their gospel aims. Often women began deaconess work on their own or with the support of individual ministers, and the denomination came on board later, often reluctantly. But within a twenty-five-year span, more than a dozen denominations formally established the order of deaconesses in their church polities: Norwegian Lutherans, 1883; Methodist Episcopal Church, 1888; Protestant Episcopal Church, 1889; Evangelical Synod, 1889; Presbyterian Church (USA), 1892; German Reformed Church, 1892; German Methodist Episcopal Church, 1896; Church of the United Brethren in Christ, 1897; Evangelical Association, 1898; African Methodist Episcopal Church and General Conference Mennonites, both 1900; Methodist Episcopal Church, South, 1902; Danish Lutherans, 1903; United Evangelical Church, 1906; Methodist Protestant Church, 1908; and Lutheran Church–Missouri Synod, the outlying latecomers, 1919. As momentum built, Protestant denominations strove to stay abreast of each other in formally establishing the deaconess office. As early as 1880, Rev. Alexander McGill was appalled that the Lutherans had outpaced his own Presbyterians, who "ought to have been the first" to recognize that the deaconess office "is more at home and kindred in their system than anywhere else."[2] By the turn of the century, the deaconess movement was taking root in the United States, anchored by institutions such as training schools, hospitals, motherhouses, and deaconess homes.

American deaconesses looked to Europe and through Europe back to the Bible. But the result was a movement that looked very different from denomination to denomination, and even within denominations, from institution to institution. Each group felt free to interpret the biblical example in its own way by deciding what was indispensable and what was mutable. In an early, undated Evangelical Synod pamphlet entitled "How Can We Best Adapt the Biblical Deaconess Idea to Our American Conditions?" the authors "cheerfully" recognized "our great obligations to Theodore Fliedner for having revived and organized the diaconate of women" but asserted, "We must draw into consideration the prevailing conditions and requirements in the life of the American people that require methods different to those in Germany. In many very important matters we may be compelled to pursue a policy of our own, if the diaconate is to endure and become popular in America. The diaconate must be adjusted to conditions in America"—with the proviso that this "must be done in a manner so as not to impair the essential biblical ideals of the diaconate."[3] Of course, the decision as to what was essential and what was trivial was subjective. We will see that each group's culture, history, and theology sharply influenced the character of that group's diaconate.

The Warp: American Cultures, American Theologies

Because denomination was the key mechanism through which the deaconess office operated, understanding the denominational character of the deaconess movement is essential. I have identified by name more than five thousand deaconesses, a number that is certainly still understated.[4] These first five chapters will examine the almost thirty-five hundred women who were consecrated before 1940, the founding generations of the movement. During this formative time period, Methodists consecrated more than fifteen hundred deaconesses, while Lutherans followed at just under eight hundred. These two dominant groups were followed by the Episcopalians, with four hundred, the Evangelical Synod, with three hundred, and then the Presbyterian, Mennonite, German Reformed, Baptist, United Brethren, Congregational, and African Methodist Episcopal denominations, with less than a hundred deaconesses each. Differing church histories, cultural views of womanhood, and theologies shaped the diaconate within these different denominations.

In the 1840s, William Alfred Passavant, pastor of the First English Lutheran Church in Pittsburgh, visited Europe and was impressed by the groundswell of organized charitable activity by laymen and laywomen inspired by religious awakening. Deeply moved by this spirit of Inner Mission, Passavant spent time with Theodore Fliedner at Kaiserswerth and secured from Fliedner a promise to send him deaconesses to begin the American work. Passavant returned from Europe to found a hospital in Pittsburgh, "the oldest Protestant hospital in the U.S."[5] In 1849, Fliedner made good on his promise and accompanied four deaconesses to the United States, preaching his way from the coast to Pittsburgh, stirring up excitement for the deaconess cause. In 1850, the Institution of Protestant Deaconesses was founded in Pittsburgh with much fanfare and interdenominational support. Passavant was unsuccessful, however, in recruiting and maintaining an ongoing supply of deaconesses. Although one of the four original Kaiserswerth deaconesses, Elizabeth Hupperts, remained in Pittsburgh to serve faithfully for almost fifty years, the other three left between 1851 and 1853 and married. The first American deaconess was consecrated in 1850, and a trickle of deaconesses served for shorter or longer periods until the organization was effectively reorganized in 1893.

Midcentury Lutherans blamed anti-Catholic prejudice for the failure of the diaconate to take hold in this period.[6] By the mid-1880s, when seven more deaconesses arrived from Germany to revive the Lutheran diaconate in Philadelphia, conditions proved more favorable. The virulent anti-Catholicism of earlier decades had subsided somewhat. Western and Northern European immigration to the United States boomed, and many immigrants brought with them Inner Mission commitments and a familiarity with the female diaconate. With the backing of the wealthy Drexel/Lankenau family, the Philadelphia motherhouse thrived where the earlier Pittsburgh effort had faltered. The chief American expositor of the Inner Mission, J. F. Ohl, grandly concluded that at the Lutheran Philadelphia Motherhouse of Deaconesses, "one may learn as perhaps nowhere else how genuine Inner Mission links the Word and the Work together."[7]

The different Lutheran bodies in the United States were by no means theologically univocal, but they shared an Inner Mission commitment and respect for the Kaiserswerth model. Although they also each had unique theological traditions, Evangelical Synod, German Reformed, and German Methodist deaconesses shared this dedication, cultural history, and—not insignificantly—the German language. Together these groups created a diaconate that was quite faithful to the German motherhouse ideal. In the 1880s and '90s, German Americans from different confessions even worked together to found a handful of interdenominational motherhouses.[8] These German-derived diaconates were represented in two overlapping conferences. Beginning in 1894, representatives of German-speaking German Methodist, Evangelical, Reformed, Lutheran, and interdenominational motherhouses met annually in conference for the principal purpose of *gegenseitiger Ermunterung und Belehrung* (mutual encouragement and instruction). In 1896, a similar conference for German, Swedish, Danish, and Norwegian Lutheran deaconesses formed, representing the first intersynodical conference in the fractious history of American Lutheranism.[9]

As a result of their common commitment to salvation of the whole person, the German denominations focused almost exclusively on nursing as an evangelistic strategy.[10] An applicant to the German Methodist diaconate revealed her commitment to this understanding: "It has been my desire to help the sick and as this is a way in reaching the soul through the body, it is my ernest [sic] prayer that I may do it as my Lord would have me to do."[11] Instead of preaching the Word, these women were to embody it in their acts of service. Norwegian Lutheran deaconess Sister Elizabeth Fedde told her student nurses, "You sisters are the Bible the patients read."[12] German deaconesses' most lasting work was in the area of health care, centered on hospitals, with branch institutions of orphanages and homes for the elderly.

Beyond the theological virtues about being able to reach the sick through their suffering, there was another important reason why the German deaconesses focused on health care: they were meeting the immediate needs of their ethnic group. Germans constituted the largest group of foreign-born Americans in 1900 at 25.8 percent, with Scandinavians third (behind Irish) at 8.8 percent.[13] The German American deaconess sisters hailed from these poor, rural families with little education, and many did not read or speak English. Deaconesses from these immigrant communities felt compelled to minister first to their own people. As an example, once the German Methodists in Cincinnati had raised enough money for their own hospital, they pulled their deaconesses out of the English-speaking Methodist institutions in which they had trained in order to serve in the German hospital. United by their Inner Mission theology, motherhouse commitment, languages, and immigrant status, German and Scandinavian deaconesses created a distinctive diaconate in the United States.

The other denomination with mid-nineteenth-century diaconal roots was the Protestant Episcopal Church. Although influenced by the Oxford Movement, Episcopalians looked to Kaiserswerth and Mildmay as much as to Oxford and incorporated the theological rationale of the American Social Gospel. Under American Episcopal churchman William Augustus Muhlenberg's broad "Evangelical Catholic" influence, Anne Ayres broke with Episcopal tradition by taking traditional monastic vows in 1845. Eventually she and others would form the Sisterhood of the Holy Communion. Small numbers of American Episcopalian women followed, joining together in groups, some of them making vows, and variously known as sisters or deaconesses.[14] Episcopalians were highly suspicious of the Catholicity of these groups, and sisterhoods were unable to garner official church support in the United States. It was only after Mary Abbot Twing, the first general secretary of the Episcopal Church's Woman's Auxiliary, decided to drop the sisterhood idea entirely that the deaconess office received consideration by the church hierarchy. Finally, in 1889, the Deaconess Canon was produced, laying down in Episcopal Church law the official framework for deaconesses' work and defining their relationship to the church.[15] Meanwhile, dozens of deaconesses had already been consecrated and were hard at work in institutions such as the Church Home for Orphans in Alabama, which was founded in 1864 and still exists today.[16]

While the Methodist diaconate did not have the midcentury pedigree of the Lutherans and Episcopalians, in Methodism the deaconess movement flourished as nowhere else in the United States. One spark that ignited the Methodist Episcopal deaconess movement was the work of Lucy Rider Meyer. As a young woman, Rider Meyer, active in the Sunday School movement, visited Germany and met deaconesses there. Her friends included Hull House founder Jane Addams and evangelist Dwight L. Moody. She and her husband, Josiah Shelley Meyer, recognized the need for a religious training school for women and, in 1885, launched the Chicago Training School (and later the Chicago Deaconess Home) with no church funding, support, or authority.[17] The denominational hierarchy did not come on board until 1888, when Bishop J. M. Thoburn successfully argued, "I do not think that there is one man in this Conference who really knows what the term 'deaconess' means. I myself do not know clearly; however, my sister is in reality a deaconess, and I earnestly hope that the Church will regard this movement favorably, and that [the] General Conference will recognize the Deaconess Order as a Church office and introduce it."[18] As in the Episcopal story, women such as Methodist deaconess Isabella Thoburn, the bishop's sister, began using the title of deaconess and engaging in diaconal work years before the male denominational leaders granted them official recognition. Yet even within Methodism, the diaconate took different forms. Rider Meyer's Chicago Training School and Deaconess Home maintained a direct relationship to the

Rock River Annual Conference, establishing the "Church Plan" of deaconess organization. In 1888, the Woman's Home Missionary Society
(WHMS) organized a Deaconess Bureau and appointed to its head
Jane Bancroft Robinson, who had also crossed the Atlantic to study
deaconesses, publishing her book *Deaconesses in Europe and Their
Lessons for America* in 1889. Under Robinson's leadership, the WHMS
began deaconess organizations in dozens of cities. Instead of embracing the Church Plan, all of these institutions were administered directly by the WHMS, which was autonomous, led entirely by women,
and self-funded.[19]

The impetus behind the Methodist deaconess movement was in
large measure the Social Gospel theology that undergirded late-
nineteenth-century Methodism. The Social Gospel also provided support for the Presbyterian and Episcopal deaconess movements, and its
influence was felt in other denominations. As its name suggests, the
Social Gospel was an endeavor to redeem individuals by redeeming
society, and it gave special attention to the plight of the poor. Social
Gospel preacher Washington Gladden demanded that the Christian
churches address social and economic injustice in America.[20] Deaconesses were exposed to Social Gospel thought in their training school
curriculum, and their on-the-ground experience affirmed this theology. We can see this emerge in the development of the curriculum
at the New England Training School. Before 1900, the new training
school's curriculum focused primarily on Bible study, deaconess history, church history, and Methodist history and doctrine. But the arrival of the twentieth century brought to the Methodist curriculum
a formal emphasis on social questions. By 1905, thirty hours of sociology were required, and by 1914, the Department of Sociology and
Social Service was as central to the curriculum as was the Department of Old Testament.[21] The first course of training prescribed for
United Brethren (a branch of the future United Methodist Church)
deaconesses in 1901 included Social Gospeler Richard Ely's *Social Law
of Service* alongside works on the Bible and church history.[22] Methodist students read Walter Rauschenbusch and books such as *Jesus Christ
and the Social Question* and *Christianizing Community Life*.[23] Likewise,
the Presbyterians took courses on "The Social Settlement," "Causes of
Social Degeneration," and "Methods of Social Reform." An Episcopal

deaconess recalled "the social and industrial problems of the day" as a common topic of discussion among the residents of the Saint Margaret's House in the 1920s.[24]

A hallmark of the Social Gospel was the tendency to look beyond individual sin to systemic causes of poverty, intemperance, and other social ills and, for deaconesses working in cities, this rang true to their experiences. In 1905, deaconess Isabelle Horton articulated this key Social Gospel premise in a lecture to her fellow Methodists on "the great Western metropolis": "All around is squalor, ignorance, brutishness— sin, you will say; but I am not so sure about that. Evil there certainly is— sin there is somewhere, that is equally certain; but sin means a willful turning away from good, does it not? These people, it seems to me, have had little choice."[25] Horton and other Social Gospelers sought to solve the problems of squalor, ignorance, and brutishness with solutions such as municipal housekeeping, education, and reform. Deaconesses who worked among the poor became especially keen observers and critics of social problems. They learned about the plight of the poor and their economic vulnerability through their work in impoverished neighborhoods and with working women. As one Methodist deaconess advised, the deaconess ministering to working girls "should welcome the opportunity to acquaint herself with the industrial situation, for the time draws near when the church must set herself resolutely to the Christianizing of industry; and well it will be if many are able to speak out with authority on the intolerable wrongs of the present system."[26] Deaconesses who critiqued the depersonalization of the industrial system were especially observant of the plight of women within it. As a 1901 Methodist article entitled "Her Bleeding Hands" asked, "Do you ever give a thought to the poor woman, down on her knees, scrubbing the steps of the big store or office over which you pass on your way? Have you ever considered her, not as a scrubbing machine, but as a woman—a woman with a home, and, perhaps, children whom she loves and for whom she toils?"[27] Social Gospel deaconesses defended a just wage for women and the poor and also offered other ideas for remedying poverty and economic injustice.

As a result of their on-the-ground experience, deaconesses developed their own methods for dealing with social problems. Although they promoted the movement toward "scientific charity," they insisted on retaining their discretion to dole out small sums of aid as they saw fit.[28]

Deaconesses often mentioned instances when they encountered "genuine and worthy" cases. For instance, one Methodist deaconess insisted, "Now with due respect to the teachings of Christian sociologists—and I believe them, every one—I say to myself that this [Christian widow] is a proper case to which to take temporal relief. . . . I do not think there is the slightest danger that she or her children will be injured by what we give her, for the spirit of pauperism is as far as possible from her mind."[29] Deaconesses combined direct relief with small-scale efforts at structural change, such as setting up small grocery stores and employment offices.[30]

The Social Gospel commitment shaped what deaconess work looked like in several denominations. The Methodists, Presbyterians, and Episcopalians often took a social and structural approach in their work.[31] They concerned themselves especially with cities and new immigrants. They, too, found nursing an effective means of ministry, although like their English forebears in Mildmay, they spent more time in neighborhood visiting than in nursing.[32] Furthermore, they engaged in inventive partnerships with private and public entities. Individual deaconesses worked at YWCAs and settlement homes. They also could be found within government structures, serving as election judges, riding in police paddy wagons, assisting in the juvenile courts, or serving the immigrants detained on Ellis Island in New York and Angel Island in California.[33] Yet, the Social Gospel remained distinct from secular social service. These deaconesses always insisted that the Gospel was at the heart of the Social Gospel. A small yet significant number of the early Methodist deaconesses were influenced by the Wesleyan doctrine of Holiness. The Holiness movement encouraged believers to seek the "second blessing" of entire sanctification, the capacity to not sin. This idea of Christian perfection provided even more impetus for evangelism, and the Holiness movement proved amenable to women preaching. Holiness preaching affected Lucy Rider Meyer and even more so Iva Durham Vennard, founder of the Epworth Evangelistic Institute and Chicago Evangelistic Institute. These two women together influenced a large portion of the Methodist deaconesses. Some served as evangelists, seeking to remind their sisters and brothers that individual salvation was still necessary, even if it was not all that was necessary, in order to bring the kingdom of God to earth.[34]

Although the Methodist, Episcopal, and Lutheran churches varied theologically, they shared a church structure that was both hierarchical and connectional. The deaconess movement flourished in such churches and did not fare as well in congregational denominations. The relative absence of deaconesses in the Baptist Church, which rivaled the Methodist Episcopal Church as the largest evangelical Protestant denomination in the nineteenth century, especially begs explanation. The congregational polity and particular denominational history of the Baptists worked against the deaconess movement's success in that denomination. Baptists had an independent history of choosing women to serve as deaconesses within their home congregations, alongside male deacons. But in the nineteenth century, as male deacons assumed more administrative church functions, the role of the local deaconess declined. At the turn of the twentieth century, there did emerge a small number of "professional" Baptist deaconesses (as distinct from the congregationally based women). Unsurprisingly, these were concentrated in Baptist congregations with German roots, such as that of Walter Rauschenbusch.[35] Outside of Chicago and New York City, Baptist deaconesses did not make their presence felt beyond their local church. This failure of the idea of the professional deaconess to thrive in Baptist churches nationwide helps explain the underrepresentation of women of color in the deaconess movement. As for black Methodists, they shared white Methodists' hierarchical polity but not their enthusiasm for the deaconess movement. The African Methodist Episcopal Church did establish a deaconess position, but it never gained much of a following. In the absence of supporting institutions of training schools or motherhouses, or any super-congregational associations, it appears that the deaconess role did not offer AME women anything new other than a new name for work they were already doing within their congregations.[36] Other denominations' attempts to establish deaconess orders never got off the ground. For example, the Pentecostal denomination the Church of God established an ordained deaconess order in 1908 but abolished it the following year, presumably without ever having ordained a deaconess.[37]

Denominations that were successful in instituting the deaconess office shared similar structures and an ideological commitment to holistic theologies. Yet, there remained concrete distinctions among the many diaconal groups that prompted them to employ varying strategies and kept them from forming closer alliances in their work. A published dialogue between Lucy Rider Meyer and a Lutheran minister of the Philadelphia Motherhouse of Deaconesses highlights how deaconess proponents of heterogeneous theological persuasions could utterly fail to understand each other's aims. In 1890, Rev. Adolph Spaeth opined in the Lutheran periodical the *Messenger*, "Of course, this [Chicago Methodist] Training School with its faculty and students and the elaborate plan of study it presents, looks very different to us from what we are accustomed to recognize as a model Motherhouse of Deaconesses. The principal object in Chicago is to train *female ministers of the word*, to engage in evangelistic work. The other ministrations of Deaconesses, such as nursing etc., have only a secondary and far subordinate place."[38] Spaeth believed that the diaconate's purpose was the ministry of the work (acts of mercy), not the Word (the scriptures preached), so to paint Methodist deaconesses chiefly as evangelists was to accuse them of misconstruing and misrepresenting the entire diaconal enterprise.

Upon reading this assessment—and it is significant that she was apparently a subscriber to the Lutheran publication—Lucy Rider Meyer responded that she feared that the Methodist work was being misunderstood. Spaeth duly reprinted Rider Meyer's explanation in the next issue:

> We have never had in our school or Home more than two or three "Evangelists" in the modern use of the word, and among our visiting Deaconesses at present we have none. Their work is far less ostentatious,—that of going from house to house, looking up Sunday School scholars, finding sick ones, whom the nurse afterwards cares for etc. These "visiting" Deaconesses are sometimes called "Evangelistic" Deaconesses, but by the term we do not mean preaching Deaconesses as I think perhaps you understood.—This is true not only in the Chicago Home, but also in the other homes in our denomination.[39]

Rider Meyer assured Spaeth that Methodist nurse deaconesses were well trained and equally valued. But Spaeth remained unconvinced, judging by another article in the same issue in which he argued that the Lutheran "Deaconess is neither an 'Evangelist' in the methodistic nor a 'Sister' in the ritualistic sense of the term. [The diaconate] originally and essentially is not an office of the Word, but instituted in distinction from and for the assistance of the ministry of the Word."[40] These two ardent advocates of the deaconess cause were unable to agree on what a deaconess was.

Another Lutheran pastor in the 1930s roundly condemned the Social Gospel emphasis of Methodists and other groups and sought to define the Lutheran deaconess office against it: "The Social Gospel teaches salvation by good works without spiritual regeneration and the redeeming blood of Jesus Christ. The Christian Diaconate holds that good works is the inevitable and essential result of a soul touched by God. The Social Gospel relies on man's alleged inherent goodness to bring about the desired reformation of Society. The Diaconate holds that God alone can bring healing to a wounded world."[41] According to Rev. Pederson, the theology of the Social Gospel was flawed, leading to a flawed methodology. Although sources are lacking to tell us whether Lutheran deaconesses themselves shared this ministerial antipathy to the Social Gospel, they did read the core Inner Mission writings in German as part of their deaconess training.[42]

Although Rider Meyer claimed that this was just a misunderstanding, these two Lutheran pastors were actually identifying strands in the Methodist diaconate that were distinct from the Lutheran diaconate. As noted above, Holiness (with its openness to women preaching) and the Social Gospel both influenced the Methodist Church and its deaconess office in this time period. These two ministers sought to distinguish the Lutheran deaconess from those influences and, notably, also from their Catholic and Anglican counterparts, as indicated in Spaeth's indictment of the "'Sister' in the ritualistic sense of the term."

In the United States, deaconesses in the Lutheran and the Methodist churches represented the two ends of the spectrum of the female diaconate. Other denominations generally lined up with one or the other of these models, although each with its own variations. The German and other European Lutherans, along with Evangelical Synod, German Reformed, Mennonite, and German Methodist deaconesses, strove for the motherhouse ideal, focused on health care, and generally ministered to their own immigrant and ethnic enclaves. Especially in the years before World War I, their training and work were primarily conducted in German (or Norwegian, Swedish, or Danish).[43] The Methodists, Presbyterians, Episcopalians, and others could be found either in deaconess homes (as they preferred to call motherhouses) or working independently in a variety of ministries, often serving those outside their own church and socioeconomic group. While they emphasized, and even sentimental-ized, the importance of deaconess homes, deaconess founders in these denominations lacked the fierce commitment to the motherhouse ideal. Possibly in an effort to distinguish themselves from the more contro-versial sisterhoods, Episcopal deaconesses were more likely to live inde-pendently, or in twosomes, than they were to live together in a group, developing "self-reliant lifestyles that enabled them to continue their ministries with very little outside support."[44]

This independence allowed Social Gospel deaconesses more freedom to innovate, although deaconesses in German denominations would argue that this freedom came at the cost of the weakening of the deacon-ess's loyalty to her sisters. Deaconesses in these Social Gospel denomina-tions in fact were more likely to disappear from the deaconess rolls and take up "secular" professions. Despite the many deaconess nurses and deaconess hospitals in these denominations, "deaconess" was not synon-ymous with "nurse" the way it was in the German denominations. One Episcopal deaconess, writing in 1931, had to contest the assumption that nursing was old-fashioned work for a deaconess: "Perhaps one wonders why a Deaconess would go back to nursing, but we often wish there were more Deaconesses, who were Registered Nurses, for there is a wonder-ful opportunity for spiritual work in the medical field."[45] In creating the Social Gospel diaconate, denominations with few European ties, such as the Methodists, felt they were instituting an equally authentic diaconate by following the biblical principles and leaving the cultural flotsam of nineteenth-century Germany behind.

American deaconesses across denominational, regional, and language boundaries recognized each other as modern-day Phoebes, succoring the world. Yet, the cultural, historical, and theological distinctiveness of each denomination and ethnic group, even filtered through the same biblical hermeneutic, produced a vivid tapestry of diaconates: a move-ment to be sure, but never a unified one. Reading the same Bible verse, denominations produced diaconates so different that they sometimes failed to understand each other completely. Taken together, the Ameri-can deaconess movement tells the story of turn-of-the-century women who co-opted and contested the contemporary understandings of gender, Catholicism, economics, and the professional ministry, but how they did so depended upon both shared assumptions and distinct theologies and cultures.

The Weft: Geography, Language, and Race

Deaconesses negotiated boundaries of geography, ethnicity, language, and race. Demographic research reveals a diaconate that was almost exclusively white, ethnically rooted in Northern and Western Europe, and based primarily in cities of the Midwest. Of the known American-born deaconesses, more than half hailed from the Midwest, compared to one-third of the general population.[46] These influences produced a diaconate that was attuned to the needs of immigrants and the problems of the city yet failed to include fully deaconesses of color.

Deaconess homes, motherhouses, and all their related institutions were the visible diaconal presence on the American landscape. During the formative period of 1880–1930, more than two hundred deaconess institutions were founded in cities across the United States. Methodists were the great institution builders, and Lutherans, the Evangelical Synod, Episcopalians, and German Methodists followed behind. Slightly more than half of deaconess institutions were in the Midwest, while deaconesses and deaconess institutions were underrepresented in the South and West. Midwestern deaconesses and institutions were concentrated in the "German Triangle," an area of dense German settlement bounded by Cincinnati, St. Louis, and Milwaukee.[47] German immigrants there were familiar with both the Protestant diaconate and Catholic women religious from the fatherland.[48] Before the German Triangle became the epicenter of the deaconess movement, it boasted a robust panoply of Catholic institutions staffed by Catholic sisters. The importance of this Catholic presence cannot be overstated. Would Ella Loew ever have become a deaconess if she had not lived across the street from a convent? In most denominations, the deaconess movement in a certain location began with a single institution, usually a hospital for the German denominations or a training school for the Social Gospel denominations. If the primary establishment thrived, then deaconesses could establish and staff satellite institutions nearby: orphanages; day nurseries; settlement houses; kindergartens; and homes for working women, prostitutes, the elderly, and unwed mothers. In large cities, there were multiple deaconess communities from different denominations, all staffing their own various institutions.

The fact that some cities laid claim to multiple deaconess institutions while many others were completely bereft of their presence suggests the role of denominational competition or "peer pressure" in the founding of institutions. As one Lutheran minister argued, advocating the founding of a Lutheran deaconess hospital, "How often it is among our Lutheran families with serious infectious diseases that an Evangelical or Protestant Deaconess or Catholic sister is called because they cannot afford a Lutheran nurse," further cautioning his fellow clergymen, "What temptations and dangers lay ahead for [those] believing Lutheran families becomes very clear."[49] Although Protestants were most worried about competition from Catholic sisters, the quotation above makes clear that partisans were also concerned that their Protestant rivals not outstrip them in institution building. Chicago was the shining example; in the heart of the Midwest, it boasted Lutheran, Methodist Episcopal, German Methodist, Evangelical Synod, Congregational, Presbyterian, Episcopal, Evangelical Association, Baptist, and interdenominational deaconess institutions.[50] Deaconess associations commissioned postcards to commemorate the completion of these institutions, demonstrating their pride in their brick-and-mortar accomplishments. Most are drawings or photographs of the exteriors of the hospitals, orphanages, and motherhouses. These postcards are easily found in private collections today, a hundred years or so later. Many of them are blank, suggesting that they were kept as souvenirs, but some were inscribed and mailed, sent from hospital patients to family, exchanged with friends interested in the deaconess work, or dispatched from deaconesses themselves to their supporters.

The deaconesses who inhabited these picture-perfect institutions shared other key features. More than a quarter of all deaconesses whose birthplace is known were immigrants, compared to 13 percent of the general US population in 1920.[51] By a wide margin, the largest number of these immigrants came from Germany, followed by Scandinavian countries, Canada, and England, countries where deaconess institutions were already firmly established by the Anglican, Lutheran, or other German church.[52] The importance of this direct importation of deaconesses, and future deaconesses, from Europe cannot be overestimated.

Figure 1.1. *Clockwise from top left*: Mennonite Deaconess Home and Hospital, Beatrice, Nebraska; Methodist Deaconess Hospital for Tuberculosis Patients, Albuquerque, New Mexico; interior of a patient's room at the Evangelical Synod Deaconess Hospital, St. Louis, Missouri, printed in Germany and postmarked 1908; and Bethlehem Children's Home, Immanuel Deaconess Institute, Omaha, Nebraska. All author's collection.

Perhaps just as important is the large percentage of deaconesses who were the daughters of immigrants. Taken together, immigrants and second-generation immigrants comprised more than half of the deaconess population.[53] Both the first- and second-generation immigrant populations were instrumental in establishing the American diaconate's European-American flavor.

The ethnic picture that emerges from this research is of a diaconate that was highly Anglo-American and European, especially Northern European.[54] Yet, the relative numbers and countries of origin of immigrant deaconesses differed greatly from denomination to denomination. Forty percent of Lutheran deaconesses were immigrants, whereas (if we exclude the German Conference) only 9 percent of Methodist deaconesses were born outside the United States. Again, we see the diaconates fall along a continuum, with a high density of immigrants on one end and a high concentration of US–born daughters of US–born parents on the other. Methodists (including the Methodist Episcopal Church and the Methodist Episcopal Church, South, but excluding the German Methodist Church), Presbyterians, and Episcopalians mirrored the national average, with 12 percent immigrants. Another 15 percent were the children of immigrants. But significantly, the vast majority of their countries of origin were Anglophone (England and English-speaking Canada). On the other end of the spectrum, the German/Scandinavian denominations (German Methodists, Evangelical Synod, German Reformed, Lutheran, and Mennonite) boasted a diaconate that was more than one-third immigrants, and a large majority of the deaconesses who were US born had foreign-born parents. These women's countries of origin were much less likely to be Anglophone. Immigrant density was a key feature in distinguishing the characters of the female diaconate in different denominations. All deaconesses considered immigrants one of their special concerns for care. The difference was that one group perceived that mission as helping other people, while the other group saw it as helping their own people.

As deaconesses understood it, language was a key differentiator between the approaches of the different denominations. Although Lutherans from Denmark, Norway, and Sweden also built and staffed their own institutions with their own deaconesses in their own languages, German was the main rival to the English language. German- and English-speaking Methodists together built the Elizabeth Gamble Deaconess Home and Hospital in Cincinnati in 1888, but within just a few years, German Methodists began raising funds for a motherhouse of their own. As one advocate wrote, "Our mission is fully as significant in every respect as that of our English-speaking brethren. There is but one difference, and it is that we must accomplish it through the medium of the German language, and have regard for the education, views, and approval of the [German] Church."[55] The Anglophone Methodist Hospital amicably released seven German deaconesses to staff the new enterprise. German women found in the US diaconate a way to learn English and train for a career. Many immigrant deaconesses tell the same story: deaconess training allowed them to learn the new language and adjust to American customs while living and working among others who shared their background and mother tongue.

For young women born in the United States to immigrant parents, the situation was more complex. Many second-generation women sheepishly confessed their inadequacy in the German language in their applications, expressing their eagerness to improve it (one woman took German grammar lessons with the pastor's wife in preparation for deaconess training) and revealing that they expected the work to require a command of German.[56] In her 1897 application, German Methodist Clara Bay revealed the conflict she felt. She could understand German but could not speak it or read it and confessed her fears to the Cincinnati superintendent: "Sometimes I think it would be better for me to enter the English Deaconess Home. I am so English myself that I am afraid it will be awfully hard for me at the German."[57] Yet, in her next letter to the *Oberin* (directing sister) she declared her identity: "Since I wrote to you last week, I have fully decided to enter the German Home. I think it will be better for me to be with the Germans for that is where I belong."[58] Despite their perceived shortcomings, these second-generation deaconesses felt that they belonged among the people who spoke their parents' language.

World War I, and later World War II, played a large role in reducing the amount of German used by deaconesses, at least in public. In 1919, the handbook of the Philadelphia Lutheran motherhouse reported that the "language of the land" was now used in classes and conversation, "so that candidates who understand no other tongue feel perfectly at home."[59] Clara Bay would have been relieved! German, however, did not disappear from the Philadelphia motherhouse. Deaconess candidates were expected to learn some German for study and for their practical work. Other deaconesses agreed that hospital patients appreciated their German-speaking nurses. As German-born deaconess Bertha Grollmus reminisced, the St. Louis deaconess choir would "go from ward to ward, even inside into the ward, and they enjoyed that so much too, especially the older people, you know there was a lot of German at that time, [laughs] we used to sing a lot of German songs, and yeah, most of those old ladies they were all German, we had German literature to give to the patients, too."[60] Sister Bertha recalled that the probationary period before her 1923 consecration was difficult because the doctors spoke in English. The motherhouse's pastor, however, "was good to me"; he taught her the religion courses in German.[61]

For deaconesses in these denominations, religion and the German language were woven together so tightly that it took two world wars to untangle them. Anna Benz reported that she learned most of the German she knew "in catechism class."[62] Mary Elaine Kluge Preuter reported that her mother always prayed in German, but her father refused to pray in German after World War II.[63] Significantly, it was the elimination of German in worship services that caused deaconesses the most consternation. When the deaconesses from the Philadelphia Lutheran motherhouse reported in 1919 that they had eliminated the German language from their worship, they credited "the older Sisters for their spirit of self-denial."[64] Yet, these same sisters, weighing in on the matter of a new assistant pastor for the motherhouse in 1925, advised, "One from Germany is preferable."[65] The close association of the diaconate with the German (or Swedish, Danish, or Norwegian) language in the Lutheran, Evangelical Synod, German Reformed, Mennonite, and German Methodist churches was difficult to break.

With its roots firmly planted in Northern Europe, the deaconess movement boasted very few women of color. As noted, the idea failed to thrive in either black Baptist or Methodist groups, the early loci of the black church. The African Methodist Episcopal Church instituted the office in 1900, produced a deaconess manual, and purchased a Deaconess Home in Roanoke, Virginia, but evidence survives of only one consecrated AME deaconess, Sarah J. Slater Stewart.[66] Florence Spearing Randolph was consecrated a deaconess by the African Methodist Episcopal Zion Church in 1901, but it seems that this was only as an intermediary step towards ordination, as she subsequently was licensed to preach and ordained an elder.[67] Individual deaconesses of color were more likely to be found in the predominantly white denominations, with occasional mentions in the Episcopal, Lutheran, and Methodist records.[68] In 1900, the Methodist Episcopal Church founded the Deaconess Home for Colored People in Cincinnati, which graduated at least four consecrated deaconesses, but black deaconesses also trained with white deaconesses in training schools and hospitals. Lutheran sisters Edith Prince and Emma Francis from the US Virgin Islands were trained at the Philadelphia motherhouse in the 1920s. The Lutheran motherhouse in Baltimore struggled mightily with the decision to admit African American students as late as the 1940s, with a flurry of letters documenting the controversy. Despite "knowing that Maryland does not look with favor upon having both white and colored students in the same school," the Baltimore motherhouse determined to integrate, with a promise from

Figure 1.2. Sister Edith Prince. Courtesy of the Archives
of the Evangelical Lutheran Church in America.

the Lutheran Ministers' Association to "use its influence to help avoid
any opposition on the part of the laity."[69]

When African American deaconesses entered training, it was expected that they would exercise their ministry among other African
Americans, and the limited evidence demonstrates that they did. Black
Episcopal deaconess Anna Alexander, daughter of formerly enslaved
parents, was consecrated in 1906 to work "among the Negroes in Pen-
nick, [Georgia]." Deaconess Alexander founded and sustained the Good
Shepherd Mission there, offering the only education available for local
black children, until her death in 1947.[70] One "colored" Methodist deaconess was celebrated by her white coreligionists for "giving the Gospel to her own race in Africa."[71] The two Philadelphia-trained Lutheran
deaconesses from the Virgin Islands worked in New York for a time but
were eventually sent back home by the motherhouse to resume their
work there.[72]

Although immigrant and black deaconesses both worked among their own people, an important difference is evident. When black deaconesses were trained and consecrated by white denominations, there was never the expectation that they would work side by side with white deaconesses in hospitals or schools. When Rev. Gold recommended a deaconess candidate, he wrote that, although born in Denmark, "Miss Hansen uses the English language well and . . . has just a slight brogue, but it is not displeasing and when she gets away from the family with which she is now living, who speak Danish considerably, I am sure she will soon lose all trace of the foreign."[73] Miss Hansen and other immigrant deaconesses could with effort "lose all trace of the foreign," but black deaconesses would always be black. By being dispatched back to their hometowns instead of incorporated into the existing deaconess homes, black deaconesses were kept at the margins of the movement. The paradigm that the deaconesses had established of white women as

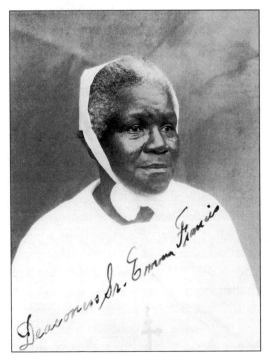

Figure 1.3. Sister Emma Francis. Courtesy of the Archives of the Evangelical Lutheran Church in America.

maternalistic caregivers of infantilized disadvantaged populations could not accommodate the presence of black deaconesses working alongside white deaconesses.

Deaconesses also reflected and contributed to a demographic shift in the United States. The founding years of the deaconess movement coincided with the United States transforming from a rural to an urban nation. The year 1920 marked the first census in which a majority of the population lived in urban areas.[74] Of the native-born deaconesses in this period, two-thirds were born in rural places.[75] However, almost 75 percent of all deaconess institutions, and all but two of the institutions that trained deaconesses, were in cities.[76] Thus, in the process of becoming deaconesses, a vast majority of these women moved from rural areas to urban areas.

Recognition of the deaconesses' simultaneous training and urbanization is essential to understanding the deaconesses' fear and suspicion of the city. One deaconess periodical urged its young women readers away from the dangerous city, with its temptations of opportunity: "Don't come alone to the city, girls, to seek your fortunes. Better wear calico dresses and stick to the farm."[77] Yet, coming alone to the city was exactly what deaconess candidates did. One of the very first students of the Chicago Training School, a Missouri-bred woman, told how her parents were afraid that the school "was a snare set for her destruction in the wicked city." In case she was confined against her will, her parents told her to throw a stamped addressed letter to them out the window and they would rescue her.[78] One Lutheran deaconess articulated the trepidation many candidates felt about the city: "And I was sure it was going to be absolutely miserable. Because it would be dirty, and it would be smelly, and there wouldn't be any trees; and—after all, I was a country girl! And Frankfort Avenue was *all* of those things! But after five days—why the staff was fine, and the work so satisfying that I forgot all about the dirt and smells."[79] Deaconesses' urban fears undergirded their interaction with the city and its poor inhabitants.

Although there were certainly a few deaconesses of means who consecrated both themselves and their fortunes to the work, the vast majority of deaconesses were from the middling and working classes. Writers in the German denominations praised working-class values in their deaconesses. A Lutheran minister warned that "ladies brought up in luxury, not used to hard work and with all kinds of opportunities before them, are not, as a rule, likely to become deaconesses." He thought that successful deaconess candidates would be "mostly brought up in poor, but good Christian homes. From childhood they are used to hard work and sacrifice."[80] Methodists, on the other hand, attempted to recruit wealthier women to the diaconate. One historian in the 1920s explained, "It was confidently expected by those influential in establishing the [deaconess] work in Methodism that women of independent means would be attracted to it, and to some extent this expectation has been realized."[81] Yet the qualified nature of this statement suggests that Methodist deaconesses were more likely to hail from the middle class than the upper class. Understanding the socioeconomic background of the deaconesses is crucial to understanding their relationship with the destitute people they served and their commitment to respectability.

What emerges from this exploration of the deaconess movement in the nineteenth and first half of the twentieth century is indeed a tapestry of diaconates. Motivated by a biblical call to service and united by holistic theology, Northern and Western European heritage, midwestern rural origin, and working- to middle-class economic status, the different deaconess groups were nonetheless differentiated by language, immigrant status, race, and theological and confessional differences. Yet all of these thousands of women sought to create an office that would allow them to live out their shared call to service. The fact that they were called into service *as women* is perhaps what was most distinctive and unifying about the deaconess movement. We now turn to the idea of the deaconess office as created specifically for women.

2

Negotiating Gender

In 1899, Mrs. Annie Fellows Johnston, a lay supporter of the deaconess movement, wrote a novel entitled *What the Deaconess Does; or, Where the White Ties Lead*, "white ties" being a reference to the distinctive white bows with which Methodist deaconesses secured their bonnets. Although it was a work of fiction, the author insisted in her preface that the novel depicted "real scenes, real people, real work." By 1910, the publishing arm of the Chicago Methodist deaconesses had printed and distributed twenty-four thousand copies of this slim novel to explain and promote the movement.[1] As the book opens, young Marion Warden is restless upon returning to her family after college graduation. Her mother assures her that there is plenty to do at home. "Oh, I know," Marion responds, "but what does it amount to? Who is any better for it? I may make myself useful here at home, but I am not really needed. Martha and Sue and Grace could easily do all there is to be done, without my help. I want to be where I am needed—where I'd be a force that would count for something—out in the thick of the world's fight."[2] Marion seeks to define a new role for herself as a Christian woman. Instead of being a helpmate to a husband, she wants to be a helper to the world. Instead of being a mother to biological children, she wants to mother others. Instead of creating a nuclear family, she wants to join a family of like-minded women. By the end of the book Marion finds her calling as a Methodist deaconess. Deaconesses, like the fictional Marion, adopted and adapted various roles available to them in order to create their singular vocation, and in so doing, created a new way of being a Protestant woman.

Gender Rhetoric: The Messages Women Heard

As they lived and worshipped together, Protestant churchgoers in the late-nineteenth-century United States were also participating in the

historical process of creating gender. Mothers, fathers, preachers, journalists, authors, clubwomen, missionaries, and politicians all contributed
to the creation of womanhood and manhood in this time period by
speaking and writing about what women and men should be, weaving
new ideas in with the old ones. As deaconesses constructed their vocation, they braided these strands together anew, creating a novel ideal of
womanhood.

Presbyterian minister William Auld began his letter of support for
the Philadelphia Deaconess Training School by praising women's efforts
during World War I, but he concluded with the reminder, "There is,
however, and ever will be, as by divine ordination, a fundamental and
unmistakeable [sic] distinction and difference between man and woman,
which this war will not and cannot obliterate. . . . Man is the complement of woman and woman the complement of man in all phases of
life."[3] As spiritual authorities over their flocks, Protestant ministers were
powerful voices in the creation of gender. Rev. Auld's letter contains two
themes foundational to deaconesses' understanding of gender during
this formative late-nineteenth- and early-twentieth-century period: first,
that women and men were essentially different but complementary, and
second, that this difference was ordained by God and thus good. When
these men told women what they should be, they bolstered a binary conception of gender by focusing on the divine complementarity of male
and female. Furthermore, they were very specific about the content of
woman's essential nature: women's divine gift was their capacity to *feel*
and their ability to *influence*.[4]

A Southern Presbyterian minister writing about home missions in
1904 argued, "It may be that God has not endowed woman with the wisdom of man, nor has He created her with the strength of man, and she is,
therefore, designated 'the weaker vessel.' But He has given her that which
is better, He has enriched her with *more heart and irresistible influence.*
Her heart is a match for his wisdom, and her influence can cope with his
strength."[5] A minister writing in 1891 to promote the Lutheran deaconess movement echoed this assertion and revealed an anxiety that women
were not focusing on their *God-given* gifts: "The active women of our
era are too exclusively active with the brain. Much is said in our day
of strong-minded women; but God has given in rich measure to every
true woman a gift which is as much more precious than mind, as love is

greater than knowledge." The gift that was greater than knowledge was, of course, "that great heart which makes her the image of His love and tenderness, as man is the image of his law and sovereignty—a possession which makes woman's profoundest sorrows a richer treasure than man's brightest joys."[6] At the 1903 dedication of the Homer Toberman Deaconess Home in Los Angeles, a Southern Methodist bishop gave an address, reprinted in the Southern Methodist journal *Our Homes*. The bishop argued that woman's chief role in the church was "influence, the noiseless movement of an element that accomplishes a mighty work." He asserted that through influence, "womanhood at large determines the manners and morals of our country, and their work in the homes is so far-reaching as to be immeasurable. Out of the home the Church comes, the State develops, and civilization arises."[7]

These three ministers, from Lutheran, Presbyterian, and Methodist churches, are representative of the messages that Protestant women heard from the pulpit during the time of the founding of the deaconess movement. Women were told that they reflected different aspects of God's person than did men. Men were to demonstrate God's wisdom, law, sovereignty, and strength. Women were to embody God's mercy. It was women's role to use their hearts to feel, especially to feel sorrow, and to use their actions to influence not only the church but the home, the country, and the world. In the decades of the 1880s through the 1920s, ministers perceived that their traditional understandings of gender roles were being challenged. This time period became known as the "Woman's Era," when Americans were preoccupied with the "Woman Question," which encompassed not just political suffrage but also ecclesiastical suffrage and legal rights of property and in marriage.[8] Protestant ministers responded by speaking even more forcefully about women's roles when they felt these roles were being contested.

One of the threats the ministers perceived was women's higher education, long the exclusive province of men. The Lutheran minister Rev. Krauth revealed this anxiety when he complained about the women of his era being "too active with the brain." While first- and second-generation immigrant women often had very limited opportunities for education, young women in the Social Gospel denominations were graduating from high schools, normal schools, and colleges in greater and greater numbers, and ministers from these denominations were even more worried. In 1918, Dr. W. H. Roberts, speaking on behalf of the Philadelphia training school of the Presbyterian and Reformed churches, observed, "The spread of education which has been very great during the past two generations, has given knowledge into the possession of women as well as of men, and 'Knowledge is power,' either for good or evil. Women, because they are educated, are now doing much thinking, and their thinking needs to be in the right direction."[9]

The first volume of the *Presbyterian Review*, founded in 1880 by prominent Presbyterian theologians Charles Hodge and Charles Briggs, featured an article promoting the deaconess movement. In this genre we can listen to ministers speaking not to women but to each other. And here we hear perhaps the most strident example of ministers' anxieties about women's role. This author, theologian Alexander McGill, worried about the combination of women's increased education and her extra time:

> [Woman's] beautiful energy is more and more tempted to pass the boundary of her sphere, for something to do, unless we hasten to fill with Church work the vacuities made in that sphere by the applied arts which have brought leisure to her home. The professions of law and medicine, the pulpit also, and even the political arena, invite her enterprise and win her ambition. We know already the embarrassments we have had to stop her from preaching in Presbyterian churches. And we cannot but see that all she needs to level the barriers of Bible forbidding is the suffrage of her own sex. . . . Now, let us consider in time what we may give her to do in the service of Christ and the Church.[10]

Dr. McGill and many of his ministerial colleagues believed that the deaconess office was the solution to the problem of bored, ambitious, overeducated women. German Methodist minister Christian Golder agreed. Around the year 1900 he reflected, "The woman's movement, which, in the past decade, has seized upon the public mind more than in the entire preceding century, finds an outlet in the Deaconess Movement, and it is possible that the female diaconate will contribute more to the solution of the woman question than any other factor."[11]

Ministers were worried, in effect, about the real-life versions of the fictional character of Marion Warden, the college-educated woman who was restless at home. Protestant women were also concerned about Marion, and they too had the answer. Women heard the messages that they were supposed to use their hearts, their influence, their leisure time, and, if necessary, their education for the betterment of the other people in their lives. To these strands of heart and influence, they braided in their own ideas of meaningful, significant work for Christ.

Female deaconess proponents could be just as forceful in urging their sisters to embrace self-sacrifice as their greatest virtue and influence as their greatest strength. Women shared with their ministers a concern that the need was urgent and the stakes were high. An early article promoting the deaconess movement in a Christian women's magazine emphasized the power, and responsibility, women had to influence men: "If women do not lift men to heaven they drag them to hell. So long as many sell themselves to fashion and folly, bartering their souls for less than a mess of pottage, even a few flaunting gewgaws to hang upon their person; so long as there are those whose 'feet go down to death, and whose steps take hold on hell'; so long as yellow-backed literature, wine, and women drag men to perdition, there is work for true-hearted Christian women to do."[12]

Although these women authors' words sound like harsh indictments of their sisters, they can also be read as contesting certain cultural constructions of womanhood. These women were urging their sisters to prove that women were not weak-willed, vain, or shallow. One Presbyterian woman asked of potential deaconess candidates, "Are they frittering away their precious years with fancy work, social dissipation, frivolous calls and amusements?" and challenged her readers to "rise up, then, ye women that are at ease, ye careless daughters! Give ear to the voice of Him that would call you from a life of self-seeking that leads to death, to a life of self-renunciation which alone is true living."[13] The fictional Marion hears this same biblical admonition, drawn from the thirty-second chapter of the book of Isaiah. While sitting in the church listening to a call for women to consecrate themselves to the deaconess office, Marion "seemed to see Isaiah's bony finger of prophetic warning as he pointed to her through the centuries, crying with a voice that was like a trumpet call."[14] Another woman extolled the deaconess office thus: "What a big thing for young women who want to ring the bell with their lives, instead of fiddling around preparing excuses—which will not be accepted when we carry our cases to the Supreme Judge for final sentence."[15] Like their ministers, women could also marshal threats of divine displeasure should their sisters fail to embrace a self-sacrificial role.

These ministers and women, all writing during the founding years of the American deaconess movement, sought to build up the deaconess as the exemplar of white womanhood. Inextricably bound up in these attempts to create womanhood were constructions of race and class. When the Presbyterian woman urged the "women of ease" to rise up and embrace the deaconess vocation, she was not speaking to African Americans. When the minister argued that the women of his day were overeducated, he was not talking about immigrant women. Though rarely articulated explicitly, deaconess advocates' concerns for women's roles and opportunities were imbricated with their concerns for the future of the Anglo-Saxon race. At the turn of the twentieth century, white Protestant Americans concerned about immigration were growing increasingly anxious about "race suicide," a term coined by sociologist Edward A. Ross.[16] The usual strategy of eugenically minded reformers and preachers was to encourage privileged white women to have more children. No less than President Theodore Roosevelt pleaded time and again that unless the married woman had an average of four children, the Anglo-Saxon race would die out.[17] From this point of view, only the prolific mother was a dutiful white woman. Thus deaconess advocates walked a fine line in defending deaconesses' decision not to marry and bear children while also claiming that they were supporting efforts to bolster the white race.

The German/Scandinavian denominations deployed slightly different strategies. In these churches, ministers also argued that the deaconess was the exemplar of true white womanhood, but they argued specifically that their women were the best candidates for the job. Rev. Golder reported that the deaconess office "appeals, in the first place, with particular force to the German mind and German sentiment in contrast with the prevalent ideas of woman's emancipation, which in these times have obtruded themselves upon us in so marked a manner." If they could not point to their educational advantages, German writers often emphasized the work ethic and strength of German women. Golder rejoiced that "there are in our German Methodist Churches, in city and country, hundreds and hundreds of strong, healthy, and consecrated young women who have the necessary physical, intellectual, and religious endowment to choose this vocation."[18] In 1908 Lutheran Rev. E. F. Bachman argued that the deaconess movement flourished better in Germany than in the United States because American women were not accustomed to hard labor, as European women were.[19] Another Lutheran pastor argued that the second-generation immigrant daughters would combine the best of European and American qualities to form the perfect deaconesses: "I am thoroughly convinced, that from among the descendants of the immigrants from northern Europe, particularly among our *Scandinavians in America*, we shall find the best material for workers of this kind. . . . They are very industrious and intelligent. *They Americanize faster, they assimilate themselves to true American ideas and institutions more easily, and they are more loyal than any other foreigners.*"[20]

By equating the deaconess with the epitome of white womanhood and specifically arguing that German or Scandinavian women were the best deaconesses, these ministers effectively argued that their women were the ideal white women. This was a powerful claim to make as these largely poor, uneducated, non-English-speaking immigrants strove to claim the mantle of whiteness with its attendant privileges. Yet it makes sense in the context of the late nineteenth century's ongoing construction of race. As more and different immigrant groups arrived on American shores, Americans sought more nuanced and complicated racial taxonomies to sort and make sense of them.[21] And if German women failed to embrace the diaconate in sufficient numbers, the racialized risks for their immigrant group were especially great. The stridency of the German Methodist Conference's lament that "our young womanhood is entirely lacking a spirit of service that would urge them to enter" the deaconess order is more understandable when the stakes are clear.[22] If German American women did not become deaconesses, what did that say about the German race? Maybe they were not as white as they claimed to be.

On the Ground

Sanctified Spinsters

Potential deaconesses heard both their ministers and their sisters exhort them to embrace their God-given mission of love and beneficent influence. Amidst an undercurrent of anxieties about race and woman's nature, the deaconess office was constructed to epitomize the ideal Christian woman in her performance of sacrificial service for others. But on the ground, a deaconess enacted her womanhood in nontraditional ways. Instead of exerting her womanly influence and self-sacrifice in relation to her husband and (at least four) children, and perhaps in her local church or community, a deaconess performed her womanhood outside the boundaries of a traditional family. For their adaptation of ideal womanhood, deaconesses fashioned their vocation as sanctified spinsterhood and embraced the practice of diaconal maternalism.

Young Protestant women at the turn of the twentieth century were given specific messages about their sexuality. They were told that it was good to marry, with the implication that a heterosexual relationship with a husband was a good choice, indeed the only choice. Deaconesses diverged from the American norm by remaining unmarried. Certainly, deaconesses were not the only single Protestant women at the turn of the twentieth century. There were unmarried teachers, stenographers, servants, and factory workers, but these women were presumed to be at least marriageable. What set deaconesses apart was their understanding of the diaconate as the only alternative to marriage that had a specific biblical warrant and a divine sanction. Deaconesses argued that they were called to be sanctified spinsters.

With some creative biblical exegesis, deaconess writers suggested that the biblical Phoebe set the precedent by remaining unmarried, and throughout the formative years of the deaconess movement, it was assumed that the female diaconate and marriage were mutually exclusive.[23] Women who decided *for* the diaconate were deciding *against* marriage. As one deaconess candidate wrote in her application, "I am single with no hopes of getting married for I have the intention of devoting my life to this work."[24] Sophie Damme, an elderly deaconess interviewed in 1989, recalled that for her, the office was an alternative to the default option of marriage:

> So I remember in my teen-age . . . and, I guess it would have been the early twenties, my mother being rather concerned: why didn't I . . . why did I put off this fellow, or why did I put off that fellow? He was really pretty nice; and yet there was nobody that really . . . *hit*—that was—that

I was really interested in. They were all . . . we had good times together. But this matter of . . . getting married just to *be* married—*just* was not a part of my life.[25]

Sister Sophie heard the message: the fact that she was eschewing heterosexual marriage was a cause for concern. And she struggled for years to reconcile her family's expectation of marriage with her lack of desire for it. Instead, she found her calling as a Lutheran deaconess.

Since marriage was presumed to be a full-time occupation for women into the first decades of the twentieth century, married women were able to perform charitable work only in a piecemeal fashion. Deaconesses contrasted their full-time work to the haphazard benevolent work of married women. Marriage was seen as impeding women's church work, and church work was seen as problematic for married women. A writer for a Southern Methodist women's magazine made the comparison: "We all know how many men complain if their wives do 'too much Church work.' We also know that many times the binding duties of children and home render such service impossible to mothers. . . . A deaconess has none of these difficulties to overcome."[26] This author suggested that the existence of full-time deaconesses would allow wives and mothers to be more devoted to their husbands and children.

Among Catholics there was an established tradition of women remaining single, either to help their families or to become sisters or nuns. In the absence of such a tradition in Protestantism, deaconesses had to work hard to convince their fellow Protestants of the validity of a woman's choice to remain single. Sister Sophie's mother was not the only one concerned that her daughter would not settle down and marry. The fact that writers were continually insisting that the deaconess office was not subversive of the institution of marriage tells us that many people suspected it was. As an Evangelical Synod pamphleteer explained, "The service a woman can render as the helpmeet for her husband and as the nurturer of her children is the highest position to which a really pious woman may aspire. . . . But conditions often prevail that render this exalted position impossible or undesirable for many." So what was a reluctantly single Christian woman to do? "To such, Kingdom needs and Kingdom tasks, and especially the deaconess calling, present themselves as desirable objects to which they may aspire with the assurance that they are engaged in a service in accord with the high calling of Christ, our Lord."[27]

Deaconesses relied on both demographic and theological arguments to explain why certain women were divinely appointed to remain single. The deaths of so many men in the Civil War, followed by the migration of men to the cities, gave rise to a perception of "surplus women" in this era, particularly in rural areas. When Lucy Rider Meyer asked in 1888, "Can not many a prairie town spare a *woman* for this work?" her readers presumed that the answer was yes.[28] Historically, the period between 1880 and 1930 did mark a rise in the number of unmarried women. The percentage of Americans who had never married by age forty-five reached double digits for men *and* women for the first time in 1910, peaked in 1920, and then began to fall again, reaching single digits again by 1940 for women.[29] So the formative period of the deaconess movement did map onto a time in which more women and men were choosing to remain unmarried, although deaconess rhetoric emphasized only the unmarried women.

Beyond demographics, deaconesses made theological arguments on behalf of deaconesses remaining unmarried. Some claimed that the fallen state of the world demanded the help of unmarried women. In an 1893 Methodist deaconess novel, the young protagonist explains, "Cousin Emma, I'm not so foolish as not to know that it is the right and proper thing for most girls to marry. And if there were no sorrow and sin and trouble in the world, perhaps God would put the desire to marry in the hearts of all of us. But think of the orphans, and those who need special care from some one, which they would never get if all women were absorbed by family cares. It seems as if God wanted some of us to be the mothers of humanity's orphans."[30] Here voluntary spinsterhood is linked to the deaconesses' spiritualized motherhood, all for the sake of God's work. Others, treading carefully around anti-Catholic prejudices, marshaled biblical evidence for deaconesses' celibacy. The superintending pastor of the largest Evangelical Synod deaconess motherhouse, Frederick Jens, wrote a textbook for deaconess candidates in which he constructed a biblically based argument for the celibacy of the deaconess. Jens invoked the first letter to the Corinthians, in which Paul encourages believers to remain unmarried for the sake of serving the Lord, and Jesus' teaching about eunuchs in Matthew 19:11–12, claiming that continence was a valuable divine gift but not to be expected of everyone.[31]

If answering "yes" to the diaconate meant answering "no" to marriage, women at least took time to consider the question. They waited to enter deaconess training and delayed consecration until after the average age of marriage for women. During the period of 1880 to 1930, the mean age of marriage for native-born white women in the United States was between twenty-one and twenty-two.[32] Among the deaconesses in my study, the mean age of entrance was approximately twenty-seven years old.[33] Consecration followed later, at a mean age of thirty-two years.[34] Perhaps these women waited until they thought their marriage prospects had dwindled, or perhaps the marriage age was seen as the age of adulthood when parents acknowledged daughters' right to choose for themselves a vocation. As one deaconess described her decision for the diaconate (at a younger age than most), "Well, I was over, a little over eighteen years old, and I had to decide on something."[35] This pattern suggests that deaconesses took time to consider marriage and took the step of consecration only after they had rejected that possibility.

Yet, even for deaconesses who had shunned marriage, circumstances could change. Deaconesses and their supporters insisted that the deaconess was free to leave to marry at any time, and a significant number took advantage of this possibility. Of deaconesses for whom we know the reason why they left the diaconate, more than half resigned in order to marry.[36] This number may still be understated. The records do not often record the reason for departures, and deaconesses may have been reluctant to report that they were planning marriage, fearing disapproval from their sisters. Others did not marry immediately upon leaving the diaconate but waited some time after returning to their homes. This news occasionally filtered back to the motherhouse, appearing in the records in entries such as, "It was reported that she had become married."[37] For a substantial number of deaconesses, the "no" to marriage eventually turned into an "I do."

The attitude toward deaconesses who left the office for marriage varied according to each denomination's understanding of the diaconate. Deaconess proponents in some denominations considered a wedding a perfectly natural conclusion to a period of service as a deaconess and felt that marriage did not invalidate the years of deaconess service that preceded it. The annual report for one Methodist deaconess home declared, with tongue firmly in cheek, "Emilie S. Freeman and Mary L. Andros have changed their names, and are now engaged in more distinctly home missionary work."[38] Some claimed outright that the deaconess office could serve as a temporary vocation, specifically to fill women's time, as a Presbyterian theologian put it, "from the close of attendance at school, to the entrance of married life."[39] As the fictional deaconess-turned-wife in a Methodist novel opined, "'I think every girl would do well to give a few years of her life to such work, . . . even if she did marry sometime. I think those years were the very happiest of my life, or among the happiest, rather,'" giving "a bright glance at her husband."[40]

Other deaconess administrations, specifically Lutheran and Episcopal, were significantly less enthusiastic about their deaconesses leaving for marriage. Instead of characterizing marriage as an acceptable next step for deaconesses, they distinguished marriage and the diaconate as two mutually exclusive life callings; one could never be called to one and then to the other. An Episcopal bishop voiced this interpretation of the diaconate as a permanent estate: "If a Deaconess is to be solemnly ordained and commissioned, it should be felt that it is for a life-long service, not for a work which can be laid aside whether for a time or altogether."[41] The housemother of an Episcopal deaconess home advised candidates to refrain from consecration until their calling was unmistakable. In this way a woman would avoid making the "mistake" of becoming a deaconess if her true calling was marriage.[42] A Lutheran deaconess advocate, Emil Wacker, spoke the harshest words against deaconesses who married, insisting that God would not call a woman to the diaconate and then to marriage: "If it was His will, that a young woman should become a deaconess; if after careful trial and examination, the inward and outward vocation, as in the sight of the Lord, received his confirmation by her consecration, it is not likely, that He will soon afterwards desire something different for her. It is more probable, that in devoting herself to the calling, the Sister now desirous of leaving did not go carefully to work, and that she did not take her vow before the Lord's altar as seriously as she should have done." Wacker implied that a deaconess who left for marriage was probably never a true deaconess. And he hinted that the consequences of marrying could be grim. If a deaconess failed to truly seek the will of God, "It will be her own fault, if there rests upon her forsaking her calling and upon her marriage, the stain of fickleness or unfaithfulness. . . . The experience of the Motherhouses shows that the chapter of deaconess-marriages, besides a few bright pages, contains many dark ones."[43] This interpretation did not recognize the validity of temporary deaconess service.

By analyzing the numbers on the denominational level, we discover that the marriage practices of deaconesses in the different denominations reflected their denomination's rhetoric. One Episcopal deaconess, looking back over fifty years of service, informed a newspaper reporter that, although not bound by vows, few deaconesses left the order for marriage. "We have given our lives to the Lord," explained Deaconess Dellema King in 1973, "and we shouldn't ask for it back."[44] While Deaconess King did not speak for all deaconesses, we can envision her Episcopal sisters nodding their heads in agreement. Three-quarters of Episcopal deaconesses were "lifers."[45] Episcopalians, with their particular history of coeval diaconates and sisterhoods, led the movement in retaining women in the diaconate for their lifetimes. It is notable that Episcopalians had the oldest average consecration age: thirty-seven compared to the pan-denominational average of thirty-two. Maybe Episcopal women really did refrain from taking the step of consecration until they were confirmed in their singleness, or the older deaconesses were simply less likely to find a marriage partner. Probably, it was a combination of both factors.

Lutherans, despite their dire warnings, were in the middle of the pack: 39 percent of Lutherans were confirmed lifers, and 26 percent were confirmed "leavers." The Methodists left the leanest records as to duration of service: only 6 percent were confirmed lifers, but only 5 percent were confirmed leavers.[46] It appears that peripatetic Methodist deaconesses were especially prone to fading away and out of the records. The Methodists (and Presbyterians, for whom there are only enough records to hazard a guess) seem to have been more focused on consecrating women and sending them out into the world, wherever they may have ended up, while the Episcopalians and the German denominations insisted more strongly on lifetime consecration.

Anecdotally, deaconesses were often warding off marriage proposals by the ministers and doctors in whose close proximity they worked. The records reflect some success on the part of the ministers. Almost a quarter of those who left the diaconate for marriage married ministers.[47] A Norwegian Lutheran, Sister Superior Elizabeth Fedde, recorded her irritation when the new pastor proposed marriage to her best probationer, implying that this was not her first protégé lost to matrimony: "I was so upset both that we had to part and that we had to have the same story happen all over again."[48] Deaconesses who left to marry ministers or missionaries spoke of their diaconal experience as formative and beneficial to their new station in life; as Methodist deaconess Hazel Blanchard explained in 1926, "I assure you I shall forever be a Deaconess in spirit. I shall be a better minister's wife for having been a consecrated deaconess."[49] Another Methodist woman considered herself now called by God to the mission field, as a missionary spouse, just as clearly as she had previously been called to the diaconate: "I shall still find the experience which I gained in Deaconess work very valuable, I am sure in the new field to which God calls us, which will be, we expect, either home or foreign missionary work."[50] These women and many others considered their new lives as ministers' wives an extension of their consecrated lives as deaconesses.

Deaconesses' relationship with marriage was complicated. For all their praise of the married state, deaconesses challenged the norm of marriage simply by choosing to remain outside it. They argued that their spinsterhood, far from being a forlorn and failed female state, was sanctified by the devotion of their lives to the deaconess office. Some deaconesses forsook marriage permanently, others temporarily. Deaconesses who left their office for marriage sometimes perplexed their supervisors but interpreted their new roles for themselves as the logical conclusion to their deaconess service. When certain deaconesses began advocating for the right to marry and retain their deaconess office, it signaled a significant change of mindset about the incompatibility of women's consecrated work and marriage.

Motherhood and Maternalism

Most young women in the pews of the Protestant churches in the late nineteenth century would become not just wives but mothers as well. Deaconesses did not challenge the value of the institution of motherhood, but they appropriated it for their own ends. As defined by historians of the Progressive Era, maternalism was a concept used by women in the late-nineteenth- and early-twentieth-century United States to extend their traditional roles as wives and mothers to an ethical mandate to care for all children.[51] This maternalism led women to become involved in reform efforts directed toward children and families. Recent scholarly work has sought to clarify different justifications women made for their work using the language of motherhood: distinguishing the "sentimental maternalism" of the National Congress of Mothers from the "progressive maternalism" of Hull House workers, and separating "traditional maternalists," usually married clubwomen, from the secular, college-educated single women of the settlement house movement, labeled "professional maternalists."[52] Deaconesses complicate these scholarly efforts by braiding together different maternalist strands in a unique way. They were unmarried and professional, but they had various levels of education and came from varying socioeconomic classes. While the more educated deaconesses did invoke social science, the sentimental language of motherhood deeply rooted in Protestant Christian ideals of gendered self-sacrifice came easily to all deaconesses. They fashioned their own kind of maternalism of Christian service—diaconal maternalism.

Deaconesses used maternalism both as a rhetorical device in their propaganda and as a relational strategy in their practice. They drew on the prevailing assumption that women naturally possessed the attributes of motherhood and that motherhood was the divinely ordained vocation of all women. Deaconesses, however, argued that motherhood could be expressed in ways other than biological motherhood. Some aligned themselves with other Progressive women and extended their argument that scientific training could equip deaconesses to be even better at motherhood than biological mothers. Deaconesses and their allies argued that all women had "a mother side" to their natures that rendered them especially fond and protective of children.[53] An admirer of Episcopal deaconess Virginia Young revealed this assumption when she recounted, "Virginia had that instinctive love of children that all childless women who are born mothers have."[54] A Lutheran minister's manual for deaconess candidates explained the essential qualification for a Nursery Sister as "a large measure of innate *love* for children, sanctified by the Spirit of Christ. One who lacks this love is not fitted for service in the Nursery." A footnote to this sentence, presumably added by his female translator, reads, "Should not every woman love children?" as if to clarify the heretical implication that there might be some women who did not.[55] This remark hints at an important tension.

In their apologetic rhetoric, deaconesses agreed that motherhood, similar to marriage, was the norm for women, but they always linked this agreement with the contention that not all women could marry and bear children. As one deaconess ally wrote, "No womanly woman would ever grant that the first responsibility of woman is not in the realm of motherhood, provided the proper opportunity presented itself, but there are many women today, and in every age, who have not, and are not likely to find that opportunity for many and legitimate reasons."[56] Deaconesses and their advocates agreed with the idea that all women should be mothers, but they expanded the definition of "mother." As deaconess Belle Harris Bennett reminisced, "I never married, never had children of the flesh, but God has given me many spiritual children."[57] Deaconesses took for granted that self-denial was a womanly virtue, manifest in both motherhood and the diaconate. As a Mennonite deaconess explained, every woman possesses the God-given desire to sacrifice herself for others, and most women fulfill this desire in motherhood. "But," she continued, "a woman can also mother the children of another, she can mother the sick and aged, the poor, and helpless."[58] Thus, because both deaconesses and mothers were denying themselves and working for others, deaconesses could link their work with ideal motherhood and describe their mission as "mothering the world."[59]

In publications promoting the deaconess office (of which the Methodists were the most prolific producers), deaconesses were often visually represented as mothers by being photographed with children. Figure 2.1 shows two versions of a postcard published by the Chicago Methodists. The postcard on the left is postmarked 1910, and the one on the right is postmarked 1912. While the earlier card shows the deaconess and child presumably in their natural environment of the city street, the later card erases the background, forcing the viewer to focus solely on the relationship between the two. Lest anyone miss the point, the caption makes this relationship explicit, "Orphan Child and Deaconess Mother."

The white dress of the child, while common for the time, also served to symbolically reinforce the view of children as morally pure, or at least

Orphan Child
And Deaconess Mother

Figure 2.1. Two versions of a postcard published by the *Deaconess Advocate*, Chicago, postmarked 1910 (*left*) and 1912 (*right*). Author's collection.

morally neutral. The children whom deaconesses were called to mother were the disadvantaged ones: orphans, children of immigrants, and children of the streets. This view of the child as a moral *tabula rasa* made her the deaconesses' best hope for the improvement of the slums. As the deaconess teaching the "kitchen-garden" class explains to the fictional Marion, "We could not go into their homes and say to their slovenly mothers, 'You must air your beds and sweep the corners of your rooms and keep your cooking vessels clean'; but these children can; and they practice at home what we teach them here, with an energy that often produces an amazing revolution."[60] The caption accompanying figure 2.2 in its original publication reinforces this idea that children were morally malleable: "Our little ones shake off their past as one drops off a cloak, and are as sweet and pure as snowdrops." This deaconess and girl were photographed together for Lucy Rider Meyer's 1900 collection *Deaconess Stories*. The child's hold on the deaconess and the deaconess's embrace of the child emphasize both the deaconess's mother-like stance and childhood's dependence on the woman.

This use of motherhood could be turned into a sharp injunction to single women to employ themselves in the maternal act of helping others. One ministerial deaconess advocate noted how "pathetic" it was that so few women were answering the deaconess call. He implored single women to devote themselves to the diaconate, noting, "There is no beauty like that shown in the sweet faces of consecrated women. The happiness of their service is reflected in the radiancy of their expression.

Our little ones shake off their past as one drops off a cloak, and are as sweet and pure as snowdrops.

Figure 2.2. Illustration in Lucy Rider Meyer's *Deaconess Stories*. Author's collection.

Figure 2.3. Postcard from the Deaconess Baby Fold, Normal, Illinois, undated. Author's collection.

There is no happiness like that acquired in making others happy."[61] Maternal work in the diaconate allowed unmarried women to fulfill their destiny of nurturing. In awkwardly gender-neutral language, another Lutheran minister wrote, "It is in accordance with the divine order of things that they who have outgrown childhood have the duty to lead and direct others. This fact is very important for the development of true unselfishness and love. Those persons who have not the duty to provide and care for others mostly become coldhearted, selfish, one-sided people." He proceeded to emphasize the maternal responsibility of a deaconess engaged in nursing or other caring work: "Unintentionally she exercises a motherlike, comforting, guiding influence over him, frequently unknown to himself."[62] Here we see invoked the power of women's influence, especially on men. This identification of womanhood and motherhood could flatten into biological determinism; not only could childless women be mothers, but they must: "Woman's intimate relation to childhood lays upon her a duty and a responsibility which she can never wholly escape. Woman is childhood's appointed teacher; to this, public school and Sunday School and home eloquently testify."[63] Motherhood was woman's destiny; even if she forsook biological motherhood, she still could not escape her inner motherhood.

Just as deaconesses argued that their unmarried state equipped them specially to be helpmates to the world, they also contended that their childlessness made them especially good spiritual mothers to the world's children. For one thing, these Progressive Era writers could not resist lauding the economies of scale, and deaconesses' sheer efficiency at helping many children was hailed. A postcard (figure 2.3) promoting the Deaconess Baby Fold (orphanage) of Normal, Illinois, showed one deaconess serenely holding two babies and surrounded by a dozen more. A Methodist deaconess recruiting pamphlet simultaneously complimented biological mothers and deaconess mothers, linking their work together: "Hats off to mothers who have brought up their children in the right way! But hats off as well to Deaconess Mothers who have reared not one child only but many. In fact, one deaconess has helped rear over two thousand children and as far as statistics show they became citizens of whom the country can be proud."[64] What biological mother could claim credit for raising two thousand good citizens? Lutheran L. M. Zimmerman, in his panegyric, "Glory of Consecrated Womanhood," explained:

> Often unmarried, godly women can grace and glorify womanhood by becoming in their lives of consecration, "mothers" unto the motherless. The consecrated Deaconess is often a real mother, yea, more than are many mothers themselves, a mother to the suffering and the dying. Some mothers mean well, but are not qualified in many respects to be a good mother. The consecrated Deaconess steps forth into the homes of many such and there performs the part of a loving and intelligent mother. Her very presence in many homes is as if an angel had alighted and shook his wings.[65]

Zimmerman argued that deaconesses were better mothers than some biological mothers because of both their consecration to the cause and their "qualifications," which could be interpreted as ability, scientific training, and experience. The term could also be interpreted as whiteness, a certain socioeconomic class, and Protestantness. The flip side to this valuation of deaconesses' skills was a critique of the skills of working-class mothers: their "bad cooking, extravagant expenditures, and unsanitary housekeeping."[66] This was the rationale for organizing children's "kitchen-gardens": mothers were unable to teach their children the scientifically proper way to keep house because they did not know themselves; therefore, trained deaconesses were required to step in as surrogate mothers.[67]

This maternalistic rhetoric was itself problematic. The fact that these childless deaconesses were needed to "mother" implied that there were other women (supposedly "natural mothers" as well) whose mothering was insufficient. In fact, deaconess literature was full of stories of bad mothers, like one prostitute deemed "as unworthy of the sacred name of mother as any woman that ever lived," or the poor woman whose children died of diphtheria who confessed, "I never thought of teaching them anything good. I never cared, myself. Oh, what a mistake my life has been!"[68] Usually these mothers were portrayed as victims themselves, of poverty, immigration, or religious ignorance, but they were bad mothers nonetheless. The existence of bad mothering in the world belied the assumption that all women were "born mothers" but provided further rationale for the maternal work of deaconesses.

To the outside world, deaconesses described their vocation as "mothering," and they also enacted this relationship with the people with whom they worked. In 1903 Methodist deaconess Josephine Fisk reported on the impoverished children taken to the country for fresh air. Of "Little Annie, a wee, winsome maiden of four years," Fisk wrote, "Poor little waif! She will be mothered to her heart's content for two weeks, at least."[69] This motherhood language came easily for those working among children, yet deaconesses referred to their charges indiscriminately as "children." They exercised their maternal authority not only over the young but also over those who were disadvantaged and those whose morals they deemed compromised. Working girls of fragile economic means were of special concern. In her deaconess manual, Sister Julie Mergner advised deaconesses to be mothers to servants and factory girls: "Let them talk to you about their childhood. . . . Give them kindly instruction how they may help themselves here and there and how to improve their condition. Show an affectionate interest in their joys and sorrows. . . . Try to replace what is doubtful by something higher and better, and so get rid of it; in short, endeavor in every way, by word and example, to bring your charges nearer the ideal of noble womanhood."[70] For Social Gospel deaconesses, immigrants were also special objects of maternal care. A Presbyterian deaconess working among immigrants at the ports made this clear: "All work done among immigrants is work among immigrant children, for what are the grown-ups, but children when they arrive in this country."[71] Deaconesses certainly related to "fallen" women as mothers to disobedient children. Sister Julie Mergner reminded her deaconess readers that prostitutes "have the same inclination to good or evil" that children have.[72] The maternalistic strategy enabled deaconesses to assume an authority not just over children but also over immigrants, Catholics, the impoverished, the nonwhite, the disabled, the imprisoned, and the "fallen." It also contributed to white deaconesses' inability to integrate fully deaconesses of color into their sisterhoods.

The maternalism the deaconesses deployed was composed of both traditional and newer social scientific ideas.[73] Deaconesses could harness the ambiguity of both approaches for their own purposes. Deaconess Virginia Young made this appeal to a mothers' club in a settlement house: "You can do so much more than I can, I am just one person doing one thing, but you are mothers and homemakers, the wives of citizens. If only you will all stand for decency and safety for every woman and give a helping hand to the girl that's down, then my work would not be needed any more." This plea clearly articulates the "woman's work for woman" ideology and makes an appeal to the power of motherhood to change the world. But when Deaconess Young spoke to the Society of Medical Jurisprudence, according to her biographer, "She made no sentimental appeal, it was all clear common sense, statistics and data gathered in her work."[74] Thus deaconesses could consciously choose which posture they would assume with different audiences. Their own interpretation of maternalism thus proved a useful and flexible tool for deaconesses. By arguing that all women were born mothers, they could wield maternal authority by virtue of their sex, notwithstanding their own childlessness. But by pointing out the insufficient mothering of others, especially the lower classes, they argued that the world needed trained, consecrated deaconess mothers to stand in the gap. Bringing together strands of both traditional/sentimental and professional/progressive maternalism, deaconesses fashioned a diaconal maternalism that empowered their work.

Home and Family

Deaconesses' relation to marriage and motherhood was crucial because of women's prescribed role in the family. One chagrined deaconess quoted the Methodist preacher Anna Howard Shaw's warning, "Men cannot see us as individuals. They see us only as relatives."[75] In joining a deaconess community, a woman created a new female home and family of her own. Mothers to those among whom they worked, they were sisters to each other and daughters of the motherhouse. Yet they remained daughters of their families of origin as well, leading to occasional conflicts. In relation to home and family, deaconesses continued the process of creating a new model of womanhood. They agreed that a woman's place was in the home, but they completely redefined that home. And it was from within these deaconess homes and families that women cultivated their identities as sanctified spinsters and diaconal mothers.

Deaconess communities strove to be families of women. Deaconess candidates were "little sisters," and younger deaconesses would speak of older ones as "big sisters," with all the awe and resentment that little sisters will have.[76] They were exhorted to relate to the head deaconess with childlike obedience, love, and trust, and she was instructed to earn her mother-like position with love.[77] In this way, the motherhouse was linked not just with the family home but also with other female-centered spaces like boarding schools, women's colleges, settlement houses, and convents, all of which used these sororal and maternal appellations to create a nurturing environment.[78] Deaconesses sought to create for themselves a sanctified fictive family home. It was patterned after the ideal Protestant Christian home, but the residents were tied together not by kinship but by a sisterhood of their shared consecration to the work of the Lord.

As we saw earlier, the German denominations, in an attempt to replicate the diaconate of Germany, especially insisted on the centrality of the motherhouse. Lutheran, Evangelical Synod, German Reformed, German Methodist, and Mennonite deaconesses usually lived together in motherhouses, and in smaller groups in outstations such as orphanages or homes for the elderly. But even among the German groups, and especially among the Anglophone denominations, deaconesses could find themselves in all sorts of living situations. As institutions were continually being built and outgrown, deaconesses were shuffled around and lodged by twos and threes in rented rooms nearby. Methodist and Presbyterian deaconesses were more likely to be found outside a deaconess home than inside. Women serving as parish deaconesses sometimes boarded with the minister's family. Some deaconesses lived in rooming houses, such as Methodist deaconess Helen B. Reeves, found in the 1930 census in a boarding house with a few dozen other single women, all employed in "secular" professions such as clerk and stenographer.[79] Rarely, a deaconess would live with her family of origin, or an elderly parent or a sibling would live with her. Episcopal deaconesses were especially likely to live either by themselves or with one sister deaconess.[80] Episcopal deaconess pairs often became devoted life companions, such as Mary Louise Kneeves and Eva Hammitt Crump, who "began a life long friendship" as students at the New York Training School, named each other sole heir in their wills, and after forty years were buried in adjoining graves.[81] Although the public records do not disclose the nature of these relationships, and intense friendships between women did not raise suspicions in the nineteenth century as they would in later years, this arrangement could have provided an accommodating space for discreet same-sex couples.

Despite deaconesses' disparate living arrangements in practice, they were univocal in their praise for the home setting for the diaconate, a setting that would imitate the family home. As discussed above, women were considered good for the home, and the home was considered good for women. "It is the Mother House that obviates all dangers of emancipation which women in public life so easily encounter," German Methodist pastor Christian Golder reassured his readers. And the motherhouse, Golder continued, would care for "those natures whose feminine qualities are exceptionally fine and delicate, and who, on that very account, are particularly well qualified for the ministration of love, but who also need the influence of a firm hold and connection and secure guidance to find the way to a consecrated public usefulness."[82] Golder affirmed that these women especially needed the protection of a secure home, headed by a firm ministerial patriarch (Golder himself, in the Cincinnati motherhouse). The motherhouse served a dual purpose: as protection of delicate women and as protection from "emancipated" women. Others characterized homes as havens for deaconesses wearied

Figure 2.4. The Lutheran Deaconess motherhouse, Baltimore, Maryland, postmarked 1915. Author's collection.

Figure 2.5. Lutheran Deaconess Home and School, Ruxton, Maryland, postmark date illegible. Author's collection.

by their work. As Marion's fictional deaconess host explained, "We need a bright, cheerful spot to come back to after the severe strain our nerves and sympathies undergo all day. We must relax sometimes or else we would break down."[83]

The physical plant of the deaconess home or motherhouse was an essential component of creating this family atmosphere. Deaconess homes could be modest, as in figure 2.6, or grand, as in figure 2.4, and the architectural styles varied greatly. Postcards were printed and distributed by dozens of different deaconess homes and motherhouses, demonstrating the pride that deaconess communities and their supporters felt in the very brick and mortar of the home.[84] Correspondents who used these postcards frequently annotated the images as they wrote. One Lutheran deaconess claimed her space on the image of her home, writing across the top of figure 2.7, "This is where I live," and drawing an arrow in the lower left corner to indicate "my room on the first floor."

Although the postcards most often pictured the exterior of the buildings, the deaconess families were created in the communal spaces inside, especially in the dining hall, parlor, and chapel. Leisure time was spent in the parlor. Some deaconess homes observed "family evening," when, as a Lutheran deaconess described, "the family gathers for recreation rather than for study. Knitting, embroidery, sewing and mending occupy the hands of the Sisters, leaving their minds free to absorb the stories, biographies or travel tales read to them by the Directing Sister or 'mother' of the family." Sometimes the family evening entertainment was a slide show, lecture, or music program.[85] In 1916, a Baltimore deaconess sent her friend a picture postcard of their Lutheran motherhouse's comfortable but not lavish parlor (figure 2.8), enthusing, "Don't you think it's pretty?" The parlor in the Baltimore motherhouse bears a strong resemblance to the one in the Evangelical Synod motherhouse in St. Louis, pictured in the 1909 postcard shown in figure 2.9 and the Norwegian Lutheran motherhouse in figure 2.10. All three feature an abundance of chairs, pictures on the wall, potted plants (especially ferns), and a piano. Turn-of-the-century domestic reformers certainly would have noted the decorative flair of the more recent immigrants in St. Louis and especially Chicago, featuring more pictures, more lace, and overstuffed furniture, in contrast to the very restrained décor of the Baltimore motherhouse, populated almost exclusively by American-born deaconesses.[86]

NEW ENGLAND DEACONESS HOME
691-693 MASSACHUSETTS AVE., BOSTON

Figure 2.6. New England Deaconess Home, Boston, Massachusetts, post-marked 1908. Author's collection.

Figure 2.7. The Mary J. Drexel Home and Philadelphia Motherhouse of Deaconesses, Philadelphia, Pennsylvania, undated. Author's collection.

Figure 2.8. Interior of the Lutheran Deaconess motherhouse, Baltimore, Maryland, postmarked 1916. Author's collection.

Figure 2.9. Sister's [sic] Parlor, Evangelical Deaconess Home, St. Louis, Missouri, postmarked 1909. Author's collection.

Figure 2.10. Sisters' Parlor, Norwegian Lutheran Deaconess Home, Chicago, Illinois, image from US Library of Medicine Exhibit, "Pictures of Nursing: Nursing and Respectability," available at http://www.nlm.nih.gov, uploaded August 18, 2014.

However, the difference is one of degree. All three conformed to images of middle-class Protestant domesticity, with interior design intended to honor and elevate the communal spaces of the family.[87]

These homes sought to replicate the interactions of an ideal Christian family, most importantly at mealtime and prayer time. Interviews of the Evangelical Synod deaconesses in St. Louis point to two recurring themes that were often combined in deaconess memory: communal meals and communal prayer and worship. Sister Elizabeth Lotz recounted to her interviewer (a sister deaconess) that because she had no family in America, her deaconess sisters were her family, and that "mealtime meant relationship time. Sister Magdalene sometimes used to make us sit next to her, to urge us to eat more, to drink more milk and cream. Of course we giggled about that. Mealtime was a wonderful time for us, a time for relaxation. . . . And we all put on a lot of weight, didn't we, Velma? I think it was thirty pounds you put on during that first year and you were so mad about it; I know I did too." Here the audio records Sister Elizabeth laughing. Sister Velma is silent, perhaps not finding her own weight gain so humorous. Sister Elizabeth's reminiscences of family time and supportive relationships then moved from the dining hall to the chapel:

> We forgot all about the favorite meals we had at home. These meals became our favorite meals. There was relationship, there was affection for each other, and that caused us all to draw closer to each other. We told each other's troubles, we shared each other's joys, and in the evening at seven o'clock, and I remember this especially in the old hospital but it was continued for a while in the new hospital on Oakland Avenue in the evening at seven o'clock Dr. Jens would conduct a short service and we could not make any excuses not to attend. And it was good; it was inspirational. Whatever he said was meaningful, and it lasted, oh about twenty minutes, don't you think? . . . I actually walked away strengthened in the spirit.[88]

For the more than a decade during which he was the superintendent of the motherhouse, Rev. Frederick Jens would arrive at the hospital each morning at 6:30 a.m. to pray with the deaconesses before they began their work and would return each evening to lead the 7:00 p.m. evening devotions in the chapel.[89] In Sister Velma Kampschmidt's own

Figure 2.11. Chicago Training School for City, Home, and Foreign Mission, 4949 Indiana Avenue, Chicago, postmarked 1910. Author's collection.

Figure 2.12. Interior view of the Evangelical Deaconess Home, St. Louis, Missouri, undated but before 1930. Author's collection.

reminiscences, she asserted that these communal services, probably held in the chapel pictured in figure 2.12, provided essential spiritual support for a deaconess's work: "Evening chapel services and eating together with prayer before and after meals fills a spiritual need. . . . As far as I am concerned, being in prayer with others gives a spiritual lift that one does not find in the devotions and prayers by one's self."[90] For these Evangelical Synod women, the heart of deaconess family life was entwined around meals and worship: food for the body and the soul.

Although the St. Louis sisters had the most to say about food, deaconesses of every stripe pointed to prayer and worship as the heart of their home life together. Daily worship could vary from a short but formal service held in a chapel led by a minister in the German motherhouses and Episcopal training schools to a fireside prayer meeting in some of the smaller Methodist homes.[91] Deaconesses valued these times of corporate worship and found strength in prayer together. A Chicago Training School student marked up a postcard to her friend, indicating the locations of the two foci of her education: the "main building" and the "chapel" (figure 2.11). Episcopal deaconesses at the New York Training School for Deaconesses began each day with corporate worship, and their influential early dean, Deaconess Susan Trevor Knapp, insisted on a rigorous prayer life at the school.[92]

Likewise, Johnston writes her story of the ideal Methodist deaconess home in a way that links together prayer, worship, and meals with a beneficial home life. When protagonist Marion joins the deaconesses for dinner, "she was prepared to meet a dignified row of black-gowned, meek-faced women, for she could not rid herself entirely of the idea that a deaconess is a sort of nun." Yet Marion is surprised to discover "it is as jolly as a boarding school," with bright faces and laughing conversation. Marion finds the source of their joy in the evening prayer service, held in the parlor, "a cheerful place, made home-like by many books and softly shaded lamps, by potted plants and a blazing fire in the open grate." With the addition of the fireplace and books, Marion could have been describing the Lutheran or Evangelical parlors pictured above, or, significantly, the ideal Protestant middle-class home. After the singing of hymns accompanied by piano, Marion is further struck by the authenticity of the outpouring of prayers, so different from "the set phrases of her father's daily petitions," in which he asked the Lord's blessings "in a general sort of way." By contrast, the prayer of the deaconesses "called people by their names. It asked for 'work for Jan Ericson' and 'a home for the orphaned sisters'; 'peace for a penitent girl in jail' and 'hope for a grief-stricken woman whose baby had died by the hand of a drunken father.'"[93] Whether in the chapel or the parlor, deaconess worship shared a key trait of the ideal Protestant family worship described by historian Colleen McDannell: it was oriented around women and their assumed religious strengths and sensibilities. McDannell argues that over the nineteenth century, Protestants "slowly moved the father out of his position as the household priest while moving mother into her role as family minister and redeemer." Music was an important part of worship in both the family home and the deaconess home, and playing hymns on the piano was a feminine activity that linked together woman's talents with her religious sensibilities. "Like a mother's loving reassurance, prayers at home were personal, individual, and founded on affection," just like the deaconess prayers that awed the fictional Marion and made her father's general prayers seem impotent and inauthentic. Yet, without children in the home to nurture and instruct, deaconess worship diverged from Protestant domestic piety by remaining focused on prayer, hymn singing, and Bible reading.[94]

Prayer and worship were crucial to linking the deaconess home to the model Protestant family home. Sometimes this idealized home was under the spiritual authority of a clerical "father," such as the Evangelical Synod deaconesses' Rev. Jens. Outside of the German denominations, the success of a deaconess home was more often linked to the presence of a deaconess "mother." Deaconess housemothers (also known as Oberin, or dean, or any number of names) were praised for cultivating a homey atmosphere. One tribute to Methodist deaconess Anna Neiderheiser, head of Fisk Bible and Training School, extolled, "She always had the knack of making a place seem home-like and comfortable. That was why she managed to keep the Training School a home instead of an institution." Another complimented Miss Neiderheiser on her affection for her deaconess daughters, even if they later chose the more traditional path to motherhood: "She has a real mother interest in the marriage of any of her girls, and is quick to express her joy when a little one comes to bless the home."[95] This intentional cultivation of feelings of home and family extended outwards to the orphanages, schools, and

retirement homes that deaconesses administered. One Episcopal deaconess related how these too could be good for women's home-loving
nature: "My experience leads me to think that it is a very happy thing
for a deaconess over forty to take an institution, for it satisfies the natural woman's longing for a home and home life, and the effort to make
a real home of an institution is what is most desired in these days."[96]
Again and again this symbiotic relationship between women and the
home was emphasized.

Deaconesses linked the deaconess home to the family home, and the
diaconal community to the family. But in order to join a deaconess family, a woman had to negotiate first with her family of origin. Deaconess
literature affirmed again and again that only women "free from direct obligations to their families" were sought for the deaconess office.[97] Young
women considering the diaconate were advised to first ask themselves,
"Have I other duties—not only imaginary ones?"[98] A woman needed
her family's permission to become a deaconess candidate. A Lutheran
pamphlet explained, "The parents' written consent is necessary. Were
we to disregard this rule, we would have more Sisters, but less blessing,
for 'obedience is better than sacrifice.'"[99] Women whose parents would
not grant them permission were advised by the deaconess homes "to
ask the Lord in prayer to direct the mind of the parents so that they will
give their permission, if it be His will."[100] Parents were also reminded
not to selfishly hinder their daughter's fulfillment of her vocation and
warned of the consequences of so doing. "We have learned of instances
where parental objection has prevented young women from entering
this calling and has made them unhappy for the remainder of their life,"
the authorities of the Philadelphia Lutheran motherhouse intoned.[101]

While some deaconesses were supported and encouraged by their
families, many deaconesses spoke of having to overcome parental resistance in order to fulfill their chosen vocation. Sometimes it was only
after a parent's death or a younger sister's assumption of family responsibilities that a woman was free to enter deaconess training. Sister Ella
Loew, whose story opened this book, recalled that it took three years
and some divine intervention to convince her mother to accept her decision for the diaconate: "I said, 'You know what I want, and I will never
be satisfied until you say yes.' Well, then, we went over to a mission feast.
It was on a Sunday evening, and Rev. Fred Click, he was a pastor's son,

and his topic was 'Stand by your convictions,' and that rang a bell. And the next day I said to my mother, I said, 'Momma, you heard what this pastor said, and that's what I'm gonna do.' 'Very well,' she said. After three years, she finally said yes."[102] Wage-earning women faced the possibility of even more family resistance. When working women entered the diaconate, they no longer contributed their earnings to the family coffers. Young women workers living at home were expected to surrender their entire paycheck to the family, whereas young men handed over only a portion. In the early twentieth century, a daughter's six dollars a week added to a father's twelve could make the difference between want and getting by.[103] A Lutheran pastor recognized this as a strong force inhibiting deaconess recruitment: when a working girl entered the diaconate, "the income of the family is decreased, and though perhaps not indispensable, lends weight to parental objections."[104] When women reported their families' hesitancy in their application letters, much of it was explicitly or implicitly financial, like the German Methodist woman who asked "to have Mother to see the House and hear more about the Deaconess work she does not think about it as I do she thinks one ought to earn money and thinks I am too careless about the matter but I always think the Lord will provide and the money does not bother me any at all."[105] For these women to join the diaconate meant leaving the wage economy behind.

After entering the deaconess home or motherhouse, a deaconess still remained a part of her family, and the family's needs retained a competing claim on her services. The deaconess favorably compared her continuing relationship with her family to the Catholic nun's perceived rejection of her family of origin, such as the Methodist pamphlet that assured prospective deaconesses, "She is initiated into no order which annuls or ignores the sanctities of the family."[106] Figure 2.13 illustrates the ideal relationship of a deaconess with her two mothers: biological and diaconal. Deaconess proponents emphasized that the deaconess home was an analogue to the traditional family home, not a heretical alternative. Deaconess daughters could and did leave their work to care for family members, either permanently or temporarily on a leave of absence. Nonetheless, deaconesses and their parents were warned against abusing this opportunity. One Evangelical Synod pamphlet explained that "if the parents need their help or assistance they get a furlough, and

Figure 2.13. A scrapbook photograph of Lutheran deaconess
Louise Stitzer (*center*). Courtesy of the Archives of the
Evangelical Lutheran Church in America.

if the parents wish them to return home permanently, they are gladly
dismissed with the best wishes of the motherhouse authorities."[107] But
Rev. Jens proceeded to caution deaconesses with the words of Matthew
10:37: "He that loveth father or mother more than me is not worthy of
me."[108] In other pamphlets, the warning is directed toward the family:
"If the parents gladly gave their consent to the daughter's entering this
work, then they will not expect her to come back to them without good
reasons; other members of the family very seldom have a right to expect
it of her."[109] The author had reason to be concerned: according to the
records of the Evangelical Synod, as many deaconesses left the order

between 1889 and 1930 for "family responsibility" as left for marriage. Far fewer Methodist deaconesses departed the diaconate permanently for family reasons than for marriage, perhaps because the Methodists seemed especially willing to grant temporary leaves of absence to deaconesses needed at home.[110] For Methodists, caring for family members was second only to pursuing continued education at college or a training school as a reason for a leave of absence. Rarely, deaconesses arranged to live at home and take care of family members while still continuing their deaconess work.[111]

Certain deaconesses chafed at feeling beholden to the needs of their families of origin. One Methodist deaconess, Sarah Church, described her obligation to her family in her autobiography: "I loved this [deaconess] work . . . and was very grieved when I was called home to care for my parents, I hated to give up my work. . . . While at home those ten years I was busy in . . . some ways probably the most effective work I have done in Deaconess work."[112] While Church was irked at her parents' demands, she interpreted even this service as an extension of her role as a deaconess. An Episcopal deaconess, Bertha Conde, betrayed more indignation in a 1921 letter to a colleague:

> As to your mother you may not be able to go far afield in your outside work because of her, but here again I think you should be sure that your family is not taking it for granted that because you are unmarried you should be chiefly responsible for her. . . . I confess my soul gets stirred up when people take it for granted that only a married woman has any vocation of her own. Personally I believe that I was called to be a spinster, and that my work is just as important as if I were a mother of a family.[113]

Conde's passionate words aptly express the deaconess position: while still connected to her family, she felt "called to be a spinster," to perform a role in every way as significant and meaningful as motherhood.

Deaconesses felt called to a vocation that demanded of them consecration and self-sacrifice, not for a husband and children but for the world at large. In their creation of this vocation, they helped craft a new way to be a Protestant Christian woman. These women engaged in a complicated relationship with late-nineteenth- and early-twentieth-century views of womanhood. Deaconesses argued that they used women's divine gifts of heart and influence to serve others, the way ideal white women should. They challenged the norm of marriage by remaining single but then sometimes challenged the permanence of the diaconate by leaving it for marriage in the end. Deaconesses used the valorization of motherhood as a tool in their work, but only by denigrating some mothers. In creating female families of their own, deaconesses found a degree of freedom from their biological families. At the turn of the twentieth century, deaconesses and their supporters were able to take prevailing cultural assumptions about womanhood, marriage, motherhood, and family and weave them anew to create the deaconess vocation.

3

Uses of Catholicism

Sister Ella Loew might never have become a deaconess if she had not grown up admiring the Catholic nuns in the convent across the street from her house.[1] Deaconesses interacted with two versions of Catholicism: (1) the imagined construction of Catholicism in Protestant American culture that they amplified and on which they capitalized; and (2) their on-the-ground experience with the Catholics around them. Deaconess views of Catholicism, encapsulated in their views of the nun, were an ambivalent mix of antagonism and envy, solidarity and suspicion. This complex view of Catholicism catalyzed the deaconess movement and helped give it its shape, as deaconesses sought to provide a ministry as expansive as that of nuns, while ever remaining on the defensive against charges of Romanism. Deaconesses imaginatively used Roman Catholicism to construct themselves as *Protestant* women religious.

The antebellum era witnessed the nadir of US Protestant and Catholic relations, with the emergence of the nativist Know-Nothing Party in American politics and the burning of the Charlestown convent in 1834. In the second half of the century, as Poles and Italians joined the earlier streams of Irish and German Catholic immigrants, the Catholic Church became the largest religious group in the United States. By century's end, native-born Protestants feared the enormous influx of poor, largely Catholic immigrants into the cities. Although some Protestants were attracted to the ritual and aesthetics of Roman Catholicism, as exemplified by the rise in High Church Anglicanism, most Protestants viewed Catholicism, with its supposed secrecy and hierarchy, as incompatible with their ideas of American liberty and democracy.[2] In 1885, Josiah Strong's immediate and enduring bestseller *Our Country* decried Catholicism as among the greatest threats facing the United States, declaring the "irreconcilable difference between papal principles and the fundamental principles of our free institutions."[3] Protestants feared that the Roman papacy was ever seeking to gain political control over the United States.

Fear of the papacy was fear of the priest writ large. Since the Enlightenment, Protestants had repudiated "priestcraft," linking ancient pagan and modern Catholic priests together as wily individuals bent on deluding the ignorant masses.[4] In fictional works of the nineteenth century, priests were the sadistic and sexually deviant perpetrators and nuns their innocent victims.[5] Nuns were constructed as sad, pale, sick prisoners, dissolute aristocratic daughters, or tyrants.[6] These images drew from antebellum convent exposés, which purported to expose the nunnery as antithetical to the American values of liberty, freedom, and morality.[7] If priests were feared because of their power as demagogues, nuns were to be feared even more as they wielded the female power of influence. Methodist deaconess Isabelle Horton warned, "The Romish Church has won its victories in America far more through its white-capped sisters than its black-cassocked brethren."[8] The German Methodists agreed: it was the ministrations of the "merciful Sisters of the sick and poor," rather than Catholic priests, that impressed the masses.[9]

Deaconesses could write of nuns abstractly as a well-intentioned but corrupt cadre whom they were to supersede, but they could not escape the fact that Catholic sisters were all around them, not just praying behind cloister walls but teaching, care giving, and nursing—especially nursing. Catholic sisters rose to the challenge of meeting the immediate needs of the immigrants who flocked to the United States; even congregations dedicated to teaching were summoned to the cause of ministering to the sick.[10] The Civil War brought many Protestants in contact with Catholic nuns for the first time, as one in five wartime nurses was a nun.[11] By contrast, Florence Nightingale's secular nursing reform had just begun with the publication of her *Notes on Nursing* in 1860. One Catholic sister historian contends that as a result of the Civil War, "It became evident to all, that [nuns] were not mournful prisoners doomed by unhappy love affairs to lives of sinful indolence, but happy, holy, efficient women whose lives were dominated by the spiritual values of the Gospel."[12] This overly optimistic assessment is belied by deaconesses' continuing distancing of themselves from their Roman Catholic counterparts, but nursing nuns did earn admiration from their patients and observers.

As we saw earlier, the theological rationales of the Inner Mission and Social Gospel prompted deaconesses to meet the physical needs of the body in the service of the soul. Protestant deaconesses recognized the influential position of the nurse over the patient and sought to wrest this influence away from their Catholic counterparts. An early deaconess proponent pointed to the evangelical power of the nurse in times of sickness: "It is then she stands by the 'well of water,' and can watch for the propitious moment when spiritual medicine may be administered."[13] Another echoed this testament to the nurse's gospel efficacy: "Because always present she has a better opportunity than the physician to win a hearing for the divine message, and though health return, and cares and everyday temptations reassert themselves, her influence remains, and is always more potent than that of the occasional visitor."[14]

The need for deaconess nurses was linked to the need for Protestant hospitals. As Isabelle Horton recounted in 1910, "Hospital accommodations were far more limited in those days than now, and truth to tell, were largely in the hands of the Catholic Church."[15] Origin tales of deaconess institutions often attribute their founding to a threatening Catholic precedence. In Omaha, Nebraska, the Lutheran Rev. Fogelstrom wrote of going to visit a sick parishioner at the Catholic hospital and being denied entrance: "Moved with compassion for his own people, he exclaimed when he came home, 'Mama, we *must* have a hospital!'"[16] A Southern Methodist writer exclaimed, "What city of any size but has a Catholic hospital, and who can get so much money out of our Protestant business men as these costumed silent solicitors?" She fumed, "How deplorable the fact that twenty-five would cover the number of hospitals in all Methodism over against five hundred Catholic hospitals!"[17]

Ministers and other deaconess advocates baldly held up the success of the Catholic Church, driven by its nuns, both to shame and to catalyze their fellow Protestants. Even the small Evangelical Synod denomination could cry out, "But, should the Evangelical Biblical Church be less zealous than the Roman Catholic Church in this service of love and mercy?"[18] A Lutheran pamphleteer returned to the suspicion of Catholicism as a foreign power, praising the Catholic sisters for "systematically doing a great work among the masses" while concluding, "We fear, *if they are left to do this work alone,* there is nothing that can prevent this great Republic from eventually coming more and more under the influence of Rome!"[19] Protestants admired the Catholic Church because it was so effective, but they feared it for the same reason. The only answer to the powerful nun was an equally powerful deaconess. A Methodist minister contended that "a concerted effort is being made in the lower quarters of our city to convert all the Protestants to Romanism. . . . The gracious ministry of the 'Sisters' is everywhere in evidence." The minister concluded momentously, "Our one hope of holding the few Protestants who now dwell in the tenement regions in that quarter lies in the deaconess."[20] Deaconesses promised another means of winning souls in the American marketplace of religions.

Defending against Charges of "Romanism"

When deaconesses recounted the history of the deaconess office, it always followed a familiar pattern of creation, fall, and redemption. The female diaconate, with Phoebe as its archetype, had been created and thrived in the early Christian church, as affirmed by the New Testament writer Paul. The disappearance of the primitive deaconess was linked with the emergence of the Roman Catholic nun, or, as the partisans put it, "The valuation of cloister life increased to such a degree as . . . to suppress, the true evangelical life."[21] Deaconess historians reported that just as the pure apostolic church became the tainted Catholic Church (apparently sometime around the fifth century), deaconesses became nuns.[22] It was up to Protestants at the turn of the twentieth century to redeem the deaconess office and restore it to its original purity, as "the best of the old Church ideal not spoiled as by the convent, not spoiled as by a life vow; it is the real thing, the ancient deaconess idea adapted to modern times."[23] Deaconesses and their supporters enacted this targeted Protestant Reformation with aplomb.

But how much of the pure biblical deaconess survived in the modern nun? This was a question deaconesses answered with every decision about how they would act, dress, and live. Deaconesses then had to defend their decisions to the fellow Protestants who shared their assumptions about the corrupt nature of the Catholic Church. They struggled to distinguish themselves from nuns and define themselves against what they saw as the mistakes of Catholicism. The emblems of Catholic religious life that drew the most Protestant fire were the habit, the cloister and the contemplative life, and vows, especially the vow of chastity. As deaconesses created their own garb, lifestyle, and consecration, they touched live wires of anti-Catholic prejudice. The way deaconesses negotiated each of these contexts revealed the extent of their fraught relationship with their Catholic counterparts.

Garb versus Habit

The first charge that deaconesses had to face was that they looked like nuns in their habits. In the United States, many Catholic women religious wore secular clothing on the street until an 1889 papal decree made wearing the habit obligatory.[24] For Americans unused to seeing habited Catholic sisters, in the 1890s it must have seemed as if suddenly nuns were everywhere. Whether impressive or appalling, the habit made a strong impression on the Protestant mind. Deaconesses too chose to wear a garb that set them apart visually. The same year as the papal decree, *Harper's Bazar* published an article on the Lutheran Deaconess motherhouse in Philadelphia. This article, which may have been the first introduction to the deaconess movement for women who did not read church-related publications, analyzed the garb in great detail:

> Her garb is somewhat peculiar, but not startling. Dress is of blue cotton, although it looks like wool. "Frau Oberin," the Superior, afterward states that it is manufactured in Germany, and has the double merit of durability and washing well. The cap is the distinctive feature of the uniform, which otherwise differs little from that of the mechanic's wife or daughter. . . . This particular cap resembles the English widow's in that it fits closely to the head in front. Behind, it flares off like a discontented havelock, while under the chin the bows are remarkable for fullness. It is, however, a sweet, pure, religious, womanly face that looks out from this non-Parisian setting.[25]

The *Harper's* article alludes to the Europeanness of the garb, and American deaconesses did loosely pattern their dress after their Protestant sisters across the ocean. They wore dresses of a dark color (usually black, sometimes gray or blue) with long sleeves, fitted waists, high necks, and long, full skirts. Various denominations and institutions differed mainly in the headgear. Methodist deaconesses wore small black hats tied with perky full white bows, shown in the portrait of Deaconess

Figure 3.1. Portrait card of Methodist deaconess May Spencer,
undated. Author's collection.

May Spencer in figure 3.1. Most Episcopalians wore short veils or nurses'
caps (figures 3.2 and 3.3). Lutherans wore caps or veils with those aforementioned bows "remarkable for fullness." Deaconesses in the Evangelical Synod wore bows that were equally striking: "Sr. Anna Lenger, our
oldest living Deaconess . . . says that when she first came here to Deaconess Hospital for an interview as a possible probationer this cap was still
being worn. She was invited to have lunch with the Sisters and she says
that she did not hear one word that was said about Deaconess work. All
she could think about was that she would never make it as a Deaconess
because she was sure that she could never eat without spilling something

Figure 3.2. Episcopal deaconess Mary Amanda Bechtler, pictured alternately in veil and nurse's cap. Courtesy of the Archives of the Episcopal Diocese of New York.

Figure 3.3. Clara Mueller and other Lutheran deaconesses from the Milwaukee motherhouse. Author's collection.

Figure 3.4. Lutheran probationers from the Milwaukee motherhouse.
Author's collection.

on her bow."[26] Sometimes the street uniform was modified by adding
an apron for work, as shown by a group of probationers in figure 3.4.
In the early days of the movement, a garbed deaconess walking down
the street looked like a curious cross between an ordinary woman and a
nun. While the cut of the garb resembled women's fashion of the day, the
garb's plainness and simplicity of style set it apart.[27] Compare a portrait
of a Methodist laywoman from the 1880s (figure 3.5) and a Methodist
deaconess wearing the garb instituted in that decade (figure 3.6).

The deaconess's garb was the visible manifestation of her sanctified
life. Deaconesses had to convince their fellow Protestants that the wearing of a distinctive outfit was necessary to their mission. In their efforts
to defend their garb, deaconesses constructed a sartorial ideal for Protestant Christian womanhood. Rejecting the particularities of the nun's
habit, they argued that a uniform religious dress was still desirable because it was feminine yet simple, recognizable yet economical, tasteful
yet not trendy. The garb was among the most contentious issues facing
deaconess proponents; even some supporters of the movement opposed
it. A Lutheran minister lamented, "It is doubtful if any people as a class
object more to the garb than the typical Pennsylvania Germans. To them
it smacks of Romanism, and they want no suggestion of that."[28] One
young homesick deaconess concurred, lamenting to her minister, "The

Figure 3.5. Methodist laywoman, 1880s. Author's collection.

Figure 3.6. Methodist deaconess. From Lucy Rider Meyer, *Deaconess Stories* (Chicago: Hope Publishing, 1900).

garb seems so Catholic; black clothes and white cap. Apron, collar, cap, that is all."[29]

While there was great variety in the habits of contemporary American Catholic sisters, deaconesses contrasted their garb with a stock image of a black, flowing habit and veil. In covering the hair and concealing the figure, the habit seemed to deaconesses to have crossed the line between modest and desexualized. Because so much of the rationale for their office depended on the argument that theirs was a uniquely female role, it was important to deaconesses that the garb be womanly. In contrast to nuns' "coarse and shapeless garments," deaconess garb, still fitted around the waist and bust, did not hide the curves of the female form. Lucy Rider Meyer recalled choosing the first Methodist garb: "One thing we were very decided about: it should be Protestant, not Romish in character. There should be no enshrouding veils, and the hair should not be cut, nor covered with white bands." Hair was considered woman's crowning glory, so it was important to deaconesses that the hair not be hidden.[30] Deaconesses argued that, unlike the Catholic habit, their garb was the appropriate garment for a consecrated *woman*.

While deaconesses generally differentiated the garb from the habit, there was one similarity they appreciated: a protection seemingly supernatural in nature. As a contemporaneous Catholic author reported, nuns were "protected marvellously by their religious garb."[31] One deaconess promoter frankly admitted this influence of the Catholic Church, asking, "Need we reject [the distinctive dress] simply because it has been used in the Romish Church? It has been a good thing for them. Their sisters of mercy go everywhere, and their dress protects them."[32] "Even drunkards and ruffians respect" the garb, it was said.[33] Deaconess promoters stressed that the recognizable uniform gave its wearers protection, even in "the lowest slums," which was to say, among the Catholic poor who already recognized the sanctity of the nun's habit.[34] Tales of the protection afforded by the garb approached mythic status, as if its inviolability were divinely sanctioned. "Nobody will hurt us deaconesses," confidently opined a Methodist deaconess, and another asserted, "They would as soon think of assaulting an angel."[35] A Presbyterian journal reported, "It is said that never an indecent attack has been made upon a deaconess, wearing her dress," and a Southern Methodist journal explained, "Deaconesses must often go alone at night into dark alleys and dangerous streets to minister to the sick or dying, and one has never yet been known to be molested, but she dare not go uncostumed."[36] For young women from farms and small towns encountering city slums for the first time, and their worried friends and families, the fantasy of the protection of the garb surely provided a welcome assurance.

In adopting a standardized dress, deaconesses plainly drew on the model of the Catholic habit, but they invoked other contemporaneous examples. As Diane Winston in her insightful analysis of the Salvation Army uniform explains, at the turn of the century the uniform was identified with service, donned by members of special professions dedicated to helping others.[37] Clergymen, both Protestant and Catholic, along with soldiers, postmen, nurses, train conductors, and police officers, all wore uniforms, and the deaconess invited comparisons with all these, affirming that she "wears her garb as a soldier wears his uniform."[38]

Southern Methodist Ida Dickey linked the dress with the uniform of
these professionals, beginning with the railroad conductor. Dickey explained that the conductor's uniform not only provides recognizability
but also permits the bypass of social protocols: you do not present him
with your card, you can ask him questions, and "you feel that he be-
longs to you." Dickey further compared the uniformed deaconess to the
policeman and the clergyman, pointing out that the garb is "known in
all large cities as a badge of love and mercy and good will to men" and
enables the deaconess to "travel as the clergyman, on one-half fare."[39]
Deaconesses especially coveted the respect and recognition that ministers demanded, not just their savings on transportation. A Presbyterian
reported, "The people soon learned that 'the lady in blue with the little
blue cap' was able to help them, and frequently now I am asked on the
street for food and money."[40] In equating their garb to other professional
uniforms, deaconesses argued that their uniform's recognizability served
the goals of their mission.

A more oblique anti-Catholic critique of the garb was that deaconesses were "restricted" to wearing it, and thus deprived of the "freedom"
of choosing their attire. Deaconesses turned this critique on its head
and argued that the garb represented real freedom: freedom "from the
tyranny of changing styles and fashions."[41] The key to this freedom was
the garb's simplicity. Deaconesses directly linked this to Jesus' injunction in the twelfth chapter of Luke to consider the lilies of the field and
not be anxious about clothing. A Lutheran deaconess paraphrased verse
22 when she explained that because of her garb, "I do not have to 'take
thought for raiment.'"[42] The simplicity of the garb saved money on trim-
mings and embellishments. The standardization of the garb saved time
spent on the selection and design of clothing because, as one writer
complained (with no apparent irony), "It is not always easy to get a
simple dress made without study and care."[43] The garb effectively saved
deaconesses from the oppression of fashion.

In touting the simplicity, economy, and convenience of the garb, deaconesses inveighed against the frivolity and expense of ordinary women's
clothing of the time. At the end of the Gilded Age, glittering department stores beckoned women into their temples of fashion to consume
ready-made style, and rapidly changing trends encouraged women to
discard clothing because it was out of date rather than worn out. It took

an ongoing commitment of time, money, and effort to be a well-dressed woman of the day. Deaconesses argued that these resources would be better expended on Christian endeavors such as nursing the sick, helping the poor, teaching the young—in other words, deaconess work. A Methodist deaconess journal lampooned the immobilized fashionable woman: "Her dress now occupies pretty much all the floor beneath her; her sleeves all the room beside her; her fan all there is in front of her; her hat all the space above her." Since such a woman was unable to advance or really accomplish anything at all, the article suggested that "the only thing for her to do seems to be to back gracefully out."[44]

Deaconesses contrasted the constraints of popular fashion with the freedom of the garb. German Methodist Rev. Golder recommended the prescribed garb because "feminine nature is easily beguiled on this subject" of fashion.[45] Yet deaconesses also expressed sympathy for the real fashion victims, women who felt compelled to go to great lengths to keep up with the trends in order to be considered respectable Christian women. In the words of an Evangelical Synod pamphlet, "The garb . . . *saves much money, time* and *thought* which women think they must spend in order to keep their clothing in the current fashion."[46] In a curious little story written by Methodist Lucy Rider Meyer, a talking deaconess bonnet recounts the good works it has seen atop its deaconess's head. The bonnet wishes that the money women spent on "all the feathers and flowers and jewels" for their bonnets could be given to the deaconess for her works of charity. Yet the bonnet acknowledges, "I know it isn't wrong for folks to want to look pretty."[47] Deaconesses criticized women for their attention to fashion but acknowledged their legitimate right, as women, to seek beauty. They did not urge laywomen to adopt the garb, but by wearing the uniform themselves, they modeled an alternative way to overcome societal pressure and direct their energy to Christian ends.

While the garb could be described as simplified dress or plain dress, it was not reform dress. Deaconesses joined with other nineteenth-century religious groups who, concerned about women's fashion, were more likely to encourage some kind of simplified dress than the "bloomer costume" or short skirt and pants ensemble proposed by certain reformers.[48] Invoking other religious forms of plain dress, one pamphlet asked and answered rhetorically, "But the Deaconesses will be mistaken for the Nuns? O no, they won't. They'll be much more likely to be mistaken for Quakers." Then, as if to clarify the Methodist bona fides of the garb, it added, "Their dress is almost a copy of that seen in Susannah Wesley's pictures."[49] Other radical departures from conventional dress, such as the Salvation Army uniform, were condemned by deaconess supporters as strongly as was the nun's habit: the garb was equally far removed "from the conventual garb of the Roman Catholic nuns" as "from the somewhat bizarre and discordant garb" of the "devoted and well-meaning 'hallelujah lasses.'"[50] Deaconesses appreciated the bold evangelism of the Salvation Army, especially those involved in the Holiness movement, such as Iva Durham Vennard, who once "worked the altar with General Booth and Mrs. Booth-Tucker of the Salvation Army."[51] Like Salvationists, deaconesses rejected fashion and its demands in favor of a uniform that broadcast their identity as Christian workers.[52] However, particularly in the last decades of the nineteenth century—the founding years of both the Army and the deaconess movement—the Salvation Army costume was seen as so distasteful that deaconesses sought to distance themselves from it.

Here deaconesses sought to walk a fine line: rejecting fashion but embracing "taste." They were at pains to argue that their garb, while not subject to the latest fashion, was never unfashionable. It was, on the contrary, "the very essence of good taste."[53] Deaconesses insisted that the garb was "becoming," that is, attractively suitable.[54] The standardized dress was also intended to keep sartorially challenged deaconesses from committing any fashion faux pas: "It prevents bad taste in dressing. Every good or cultured woman has not good taste or a sense of appropriateness that will make her appearance desirable in many places the deaconess must go."[55]

A desirable appearance was deemed an asset to a deaconess's Christian mission, which spanned social worlds. Deaconesses considered themselves "a bridge between the rich and the poor" and pointed out that the garb was appropriate to any situation in which they found themselves: "It is elegant enough to gain admission to the 'brown-stone front,' and not too contrasting when it finds itself in a tenement or hovel, and the wearer of it forms a link between the two."[56] The photograph in figure 3.7 was captioned "Twas the day before Christmas," and we can imagine the deaconess pictured receiving donations from a wealthy home and then distributing these many parcels to the poor,

Figure 3.7. Methodist deaconess. Caption reads "Twas the day before Christmas." From Lucy Rider Meyer, *Deaconess Stories* (Chicago: Hope Publishing, 1900).

thus acting out her role as bridge between rich and poor, all in her practical street garb. As the liaisons between givers and recipients of help, deaconesses implied that high fashion and luxury were especially inappropriate in places of poverty and suffering. As Rider Meyer cautioned, "One cannot sit down by the side of a woman dressed in calico and sympathize with her poverty and sorrow, if she herself wear a sealskin sacque or even a plush cloak. The rustle of a silk dress is worse than the rattle of musketry for driving poor people out from the reach of helpful Christian influences."[57]

But neither did deaconesses adopt the rags of the poor as a mark of solidarity. As opposed to the Salvation Army's "slum sisters," who dressed in ragged clothing to blend in with their impoverished surroundings, the distinctive deaconess uniform ensured that they would never be mistaken for inhabitants of the tenements. It had taken most of the eighteenth century for the middle class to achieve gentility of dress, marked by deep, clear color, smooth, high-quality fabric, and clean white linen "where skin met suit or dress."[58] The garb's construction from "good black" material with the requisite "snowy collar and cuffs" testified to the importance deaconesses placed on the respectability of their dress.[59] Even the fitted waist of the garb evoked eighteenth- and nineteenth-century notions of gentility, as the waistcoats and bone stays of respectable men and women's clothing held the torso erect in the desirable posture.[60] By contrast, describing the nun's habit as "coarse," "shapeless," and "filthy" pointed out distinct ways in which the habit did *not* conform to classed notions of gentility. The Social Gospel deaconesses and the German deaconesses, many of whom were marginally middle class at best, insisted that the deaconess garb, on the contrary, maintained this mark of respectability. Rather than embrace the dress of the tenements, deaconesses sought by example to raise the poor up to their own standards of cleanliness and good taste, both in dress and in adornment. This could be accomplished by persuasion or craftiness, if necessary. For example, after sending a poor woman and her paralyzed daughter on an outing for the day, a Methodist deaconess sought to put their tenement home to order, beginning with the wardrobe. She announced to her helper, "We'll sort over this pile of—not goods but—bads, and burn up the worst of it—purify it by fire; it's the only way. . . . Think how long these things have lain around gathering dirt and vermin!"[61]

The garb was also intended to bridge the distance between rich and poor within the deaconess ranks. An Evangelical Synod pamphlet explained that the uniform "makes the sisters outwardly alike, however much they may differ in origin, culture, talents, etc., and in this way becomes a symbol of the spiritual relation of the sisterhood into which the sisters have entered with one another."[62] It was the Methodists, however, who evidenced the most concern about wealthy and poor women joining together in the diaconate. Chief among the reasons for the garb given by Rider Meyer was to "prevent hurts and grievances in the [deaconess] homes": "The woman who can only give herself and who must be clothed with such simple garb as the Home may provide, will be sitting side by side with the woman of wealth, who supports herself in the Home, and whose common every-day dress—were she allowed to do as she had been accustomed—would be such a striking contrast to her humbler sister that that sister would hardly be human if grieved and envious thoughts did not flit through her mind."[63] At first glance it would appear that Rider Meyer was as concerned as Rev. Golder about the foibles of "feminine nature," but I believe this preoccupation with overcoming class distinctions was also indicative of anxiety about the ongoing gentrification of Methodism itself.[64]

By the 1920s, however, waists had dropped and hemlines had risen, and attitudes toward the traditional garb began to shift. As an example of what Beverly Gordon has termed "fossilized fashion," the deaconess garb became increasingly difficult to understand as the years lengthened.[65] When it was instituted in the last decades of the nineteenth century, the garb was described as "not so very different from other women's clothes" and, as we have noted, "becoming."[66] By the 1910s, even a committed deaconess could admit that the garb "at first seemed unbecoming."[67] Here, deaconesses shifted their argument, emphasizing that wearing the garb was a beneficial exercise in true consecration and selflessness. In 1923, Lutheran Sister Anna gently counseled potential deaconesses worried about feeling conspicuous in the dress, "Self-consciousness alone causes one to feel conspicuous [in the garb] and this is soon overcome by your interest in something besides self."[68] Nevertheless, most deaconess communities in the 1920s began making serious modifications to the dress, exemplified in the modified Episcopal uniform in figure 3.8. Over the next couple of decades, some groups made the wearing of the garb optional, and most deaconess nurses exchanged the garb for the secular nurse's white uniform. The United Church of Christ deaconesses, who by then had abandoned the garb, staged a nostalgic pageant in 1971 modeling all the different iterations of the Evangelical Synod/UCC garb (figure 3.9).

These deaconesses, their ministers, and their female and male supporters struggled to define exactly how the consecrated Christian woman (and, by implication, the Christian woman in the world) should appear. They firmly agreed that she should not look like a nun. Her dress should bear enough resemblance to ordinary women's clothing for her

Figure 3.8. Episcopal deaconesses from the New York Training School for Deaconesses, ca. 1920s. Courtesy of the Archives of the Episcopal Diocese of New York.

Figure 3.9. Deaconesses modeling different versions of the Evangelical Synod/United Church of Christ garb. Courtesy of the Deaconess Foundation, St. Louis, Missouri.

to look womanly, but modest. Her simple, economical clothing should show her to be a good steward—thrifty, and not frivolous. She should be attractive, in the sense of attracting people to her. She should be genteel enough to mingle with the rich but approachable enough to work effectively among the poor. Episcopal sister Virginia Young, as described by a friend, epitomized this image: "In the open doorway she stood to welcome me, a figure in black with golden hair waving back from her forehead, a cross on her breast, and crowned with the white wings of her chosen profession."[69] This deaconess in her traditional garb was a model of Christian femininity: hospitable, attractive, even angelic.

Garbed deaconesses walked a fine line: women's elaborate dress of the time seemed to reveal a specifically feminine weakness for frivolous fashion, but other styles of dress such as the Salvation Army uniform or slum sisters' rags defied respectability. And the nun's habit was seen as both unrefined and desexualized in a way that was out of line with the deaconess's understanding of her vocation as womanly. Thus, deaconesses were happy to benefit from the perceived protection afforded by the garb, based on its resemblance to the habit, but otherwise shunned any association of the deaconess costume with that of the Roman Catholic nun. Deaconesses' discussions of the garb crystallized their conflicted views of Catholicism, as they sought to code the garb as womanly and attractive and the habit as unwomanly and unrespectable. Deaconesses did not want to be mistaken for nuns, unless, of course, they were on the city streets late at night!

A Healthy, Active Life versus Cloister and Consumption

Although the garb was the most visible symbol of the deaconesses' conflicted relationship with Catholicism, the idea of cloister was another flashpoint for Catholic anxieties. The vast majority of Catholic sisters in the United States belonged to active orders rather than contemplative ones. Even orders that were constitutionally strictly contemplative obtained dispensations to nurse or teach in America. Furthermore, almost none of the nineteenth-century communities were cloistered. Proper papal enclosure was almost impossible under American conditions, and sisters and their superiors found it inadvisable to seek strict enclosure when their services were needed beyond the convent in schools, hospitals, and other institutions. Yet, when deaconesses contrasted themselves against nuns, they turned a blind eye to the true living and working situation of the Catholic sisters around them. Instead, they harked back to antebellum convent tales and invoked a default image of the cloistered, consumptive, "pale and sad" nun.[70] In deaconesses' rendering of history, the cloistering of women religious marked the end of the primitive New Testament deaconess office: "The high walls of the nunneries of the Roman Catholic Church shut in all that was left of the office of deaconess."[71] The convent had snuffed out the original deaconess spirit, just as it had cut off the nuns' freedom and created a secretive and unhealthy atmosphere. In contrast, deaconesses sought to define their own sanctified lifestyle as active and healthy and emphasized the openness of deaconess homes and motherhouses. In choosing the cloister as a defining quality of Catholic women religious, deaconesses demonstrated that it was easier to define themselves against imagined nuns from the past, preferably the Middle Ages, than to engage with the active Catholic sisters of their own time.

Convents had aroused the suspicion and ire of US Protestants throughout the nineteenth century. Protestants justified their harassment of convents in the 1830s with the excuse that the cloistral walls, grilles, and bars could be imprisoning women against their wills.[72] Antebellum images of convents as "priests' prisons for women" (the title of a popular 1854 convent exposé) lingered into the twentieth century. A group of Lutheran ministers acknowledged this longstanding fear in their pitch for deaconess candidates: "Do you share any of the old-fashioned prejudices against the Deaconess Motherhouse? Are you disturbed by the talk of those that suspect nunnery and Romanism in the Motherhouse?"[73] The ministers invited young women to visit—to "come and see" just how Protestant the motherhouse was. The *Harper's Bazar* piece referenced above contained not only a drawing of a garbed deaconess but also a full-page spread of images of the motherhouse. It is not surprising that *Harper's*, a fashion magazine, depicted the deaconess's dress; what is surprising is how much more space is given to illustrating the motherhouse, with no less than six different drawings of interior views. Was this not a visual invitation to inspect, to "come and see"? When placed in the context of traditional suspicions about Catholic convents, the *Harper's* montage is best understood as an effort to contrast Protestant transparency with Catholic convent secrecy.

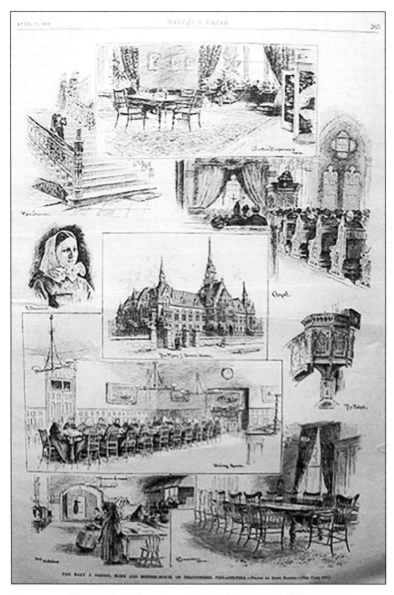

Figure 3.10. Alice Barber, illustration for "The Mary J. Drexel Home and Philadelphia Mother-House of Deaconesses," *Harper's Bazar*, 13 April 1889, 265.

In addition to promoting the openness and availability of their homes, deaconesses sought to portray their residences as sites of engagement with the world, rather than retreats from it. A German Methodist pamphlet made this distinction: "Convents are ostensible houses for the sheltering of those who think that they can serve God better by retiring from the world for the purpose of meditation and prayer. Deaconess institutions are for those women who desire . . . to be set apart for active work in the Church of God. . . . The Order of Nuns sought sanctity by withdrawing from all contact with the world. Of course, this was not the spirit of Him who came 'to minister.'"[74] Contrasting deaconesses' active service with the presumed inactivity of cloistered nuns, the pamphleteer concluded, "The whole cloister system is built up on false principles, and is, therefore, unscriptural and thoroughly unevangelical."[75] One author even rhetorically warned away young women who were seeking in the motherhouse a Protestant convent: "That young woman would feel very much disappointed who had imagined the deaconess home to be a kind of Evangelical convent where divine worship, prayer and song are occasionally interspersed with some work. On the contrary, a deaconess home is a place where there is much strenuous work to be done."[76] As previously noted, deaconess homes and motherhouses were linked instead with the traditional family home and touted as especially suited to women's sensitive nature. Deaconess authors sought to solidify the association of nuns, cloistered convents, and misguided withdrawal, on the one hand, and deaconesses, motherhouses, and Christ-like service on the other.

Deaconesses described cloistered nuns with the language of sickness and death. This was evident in portrayals of nuns' "enshrouding veils" and habits "like the cerements of the grave."[77] Their decayed, moribund state was linked to a tradition of self-renunciation that Protestants interpreted as unhealthy and unbiblical. As deaconesses interpreted church history, as early as the fifth century, "Ascetic self-righteousness had entered in, and now [nuns] ruined their health by austerities and brought loathsome diseases upon themselves."[78] American Harriet Cooke contrasted the English deaconess institute Mildmay with "the asceticism of the mediaeval sisterhoods which have fastened upon the Roman Catholic Church, clinging to it like moss upon old walls," remarking, "There is such a healthful, vigorous Christian life at Mildmay—nothing morbid."[79] A Canadian minister concurred, remarking, "There is nothing of mediaeval asceticism or sacerdotalism about this movement. The deaconesses are eminently practical."[80] An Episcopal deaconess who vacationed at a convent in Naples enjoyed her visit with the Catholic sisters but confided to her friend, "I don't believe they do so much."[81] To counter the image of the consumptive nun, deaconesses argued that if cloister and inactivity led to disease, an active life of service was indeed very hearty.[82] In their own stories, deaconesses took pains to portray themselves as healthy, normal women, "not . . . ascetic in any sense of the word."[83] The deaconess nurse inevitably had a "strong constitution."[84] Deaconess applications routinely required candidates to provide a doctor's certification of their good health, but a 1906 Southern Methodist article entitled "The Ideal Deaconess" commented further on the deaconess as the embodiment of healthy American womanhood:

> It is a matter of congratulation that American women are now aspiring to be strong. The willowy, fragile, dainty, clinging type of woman is passing away. It is no longer fashionable to be delicate. The deaconess should possess a strong physical constitution. . . . She should cultivate an appetite for plain, wholesome food, and gratify nature's demands for eight hours' sleep. She should possess that strong and perfect self-control which springs from the realized presence of God. Hence she should not be afraid of heat or cold, hard work or diseases when duty calls on her to pursue her calling amid untoward conditions. One article of her creed should be that perfect health of body is second only to health of soul.[85]

By 1921, the yearbook of the Kansas City National Training School documented the numerous opportunities for exercise for student deaconesses. They went on hikes, practiced calisthenics, and played intramural volleyball and tennis games with neighboring Southern Methodist rivals at the Scarritt Bible Training School. A story in the yearbook explained that "the best part of all their athletics is that they can study better, recite better and be glad all the time, because they take care of their bodies as God wants them to do."[86] A full-page spread documented the uniformed women engaging in some of these healthful activities.

These authors made explicit the connection between good physical and spiritual health. Other writers emphasized that healthy deaconesses

Figure 3.11. Students of the Kansas City National Training School for Deaconesses and Missionaries, *The Shield*, 1921, 63.

were happy deaconesses. As was discussed earlier, deaconess writers sought to link the ideal deaconess with the ideal American Protestant woman, so by describing the deaconess as strong rather than fragile, they were contributing to the ongoing definition of the proper white woman. This was even more true for the German denominations, who often pointed to their "strong, healthy, and consecrated" German women; these immigrants had even more of an interest in reframing the model of true womanhood according to what they saw as their own ethnic contribution.[87] In all cases, deaconess promoters coded the ideal woman as *Protestant.* In their promotional literature, vitality, happiness, beauty—and often a good appetite—all characterized the deaconess. The typical deaconess "had been the most popular girl in her class on account of her fun-loving disposition, and now her bright face had lost none of its dimpled prettiness by being framed in the black bonnet of a deaconess."[88] Deaconesses were "jolly" and had "laughing conversation."[89] For Christmas they were "a merry group—why shouldn't deaconesses be merry?" They ate turkey, too, for "why shouldn't deaconesses have turkey?"[90] Although deaconesses were economical, they argued that they did not seek to ruin their health by austerities, as nuns did. Deaconesses went out of their way to emphasize their robust good health and happiness, juxtaposing themselves with the image of pale, sad, listless nuns.

Despite the fact that almost all orders of American Catholic sisters in this period were uncloistered and maintained active rather than contemplative lives, it was the imagined construction of the medieval convent as a refuge from the world that still prevailed among Protestants. It was this image that deaconesses used as a foil against which to contrast their own lifestyle, which was always promoted as vigorous and joyful.

Voluntary Service versus Vows

A final motif deaconesses employed to differentiate themselves from nuns was to claim a superior motive for their service. Invoking the traditional Protestant identification with "faith, not works," they depicted their vocation as an act of faith, freely rendered, and described the Catholic equivalent as merely a good work, enforced by vows. In this, they both echoed and redefined the gendered understanding of Protestant freedom. Deaconesses denied that their vocation was a "higher calling," but they asserted that nuns claimed such a distinction: "The Deaconess differs from the Roman Catholic Sister of Charity in this, that she does not claim a peculiar holiness, or a special heavenly reward by reason of her service and vocation. She knows very well that her work is not in itself more holy and pleasing to God than any other in which true Christian faith and love are exhibited."[91] As we have seen, deaconesses sought to equate deaconess service with uxorial and maternal responsibility and claimed that the diaconate bolstered rather than subverted the institution of marriage. According to a promotional brochure of the Evangelical Synod, "Deaconesses want to serve in gratitude and love for the grace and salvation granted them by faith in Christ, but according to Roman Catholic teaching the Sisters of Mercy serve to gain honor and a reward in heaven."[92] When threatened by the Catholic comparison, deaconesses marshaled the familiar Protestant accusation that Catholics attempted to earn their salvation through good works rather than accepting the free gift of grace.

Deaconesses argued that while they served freely, nuns' service was compelled by selfish motivations and constrained by vows. A Catholic sister usually joined an order with temporary vows that culminated in a lifelong vow of poverty, chastity, and obedience. Although canon law differentiates between simple and solemn vows, deaconesses and their supporters neither knew nor cared about such a distinction. They were suspicious that vows interfered with a Christian's freedom and viewed them as a hindrance to the free exercise of mercy. Harking back to Martin Luther's interpretation of evangelical liberty, deaconesses reiterated *The Freedom of a Christian*'s cardinal assertion: "A Christian is a perfectly free Lord of all, subject to none. A Christian is a perfectly dutiful servant of all, subject to all."[93] According to this understanding, monastic vows interfered with perfect freedom and perfect obedience. An early deaconess proponent argued for unvowed, unmediated reliance on Jesus as the key distinction between the diaconate and Catholicism: "delivered 'from the snare and sin of perpetual vows,'" deaconesses "depend not upon penance or good works, but upon Christ."[94] Melding this Christocentric understanding with the language of evangelical freedom, a German Methodist pamphleteer argued that "the deaconess is free to act under the impulses of the Spirit of Christ, who reigns in the heart." The Catholic nun, on the other hand, was bound by vows that "deprive the soul of the highest and purest motives that lead to works of piety and benevolence, which is obedience to the commands of Christ for the love we bear to Him as our Redeemer and Saviour." Thus the works freely performed by the deaconess took on a different character as "the gracious out-flow of a consecrated, holy heart, not a hard task performed in the fulfillment of a self-imposed vow."[95]

A nun's vow of poverty might seem curious, a vow of obedience suspiciously un-American, but it was the vow of chastity that really aroused the ire of the average Protestant. Suspicion of nuns' celibacy is evident throughout nineteenth-century anti-Catholicism. Celibacy gave them, in the words of antebellum historian Jenny Franchot, "a suspicious autonomy from marriage and motherhood."[96] Although deaconesses stressed their commitment to a life of singleness, they avoided even using the words "celibacy" or "chastity," terms so associated with nuns. Deaconesses strongly opposed lifelong vows of chastity, arguing that they had no biblical warrant. As an Evangelical Synod deaconess manual stated, "All laws forbidding marriage are doctrines of demons as plainly taught by the Apostle Paul."[97] According to the standard declension narrative of the primitive diaconate, "By incorporating the vows of celibacy, rejecting marriage as unclean, and looking on virginity, in every kind of monachism, as the flower of Christian perfection," the biblical deaconess order withered and died, and in its place emerged the corrupt nun.[98] Also, because this celibacy was seen as an unnatural repression, Protestants imagined that it could sicken the body, resulting in the aforementioned image of the consumptive nun. Supporters implied that if the celibacy became too much of a burden, deaconesses had a safety valve that nuns did not. They could always leave and marry, and many of them did.

Deaconesses' rejection of vows, however, was not quite unanimous. A very few authors, primarily Episcopal, argued that a vow of celibacy would set deaconesses apart as definitively unmarriageable and protect them from the advances of the ministers and doctors with whom they worked. As one exasperated Episcopal bishop pleaded, "Some authorities expect a Deaconess to remain unmarried but earnestly protest against any vow or rule of celibacy, which would serve as a protection."[99] Several years later, Bishop Hall continued to argue that a deaconess should at least be "regarded from the first as an unmarriageable person. This for her own protection, and in fairness to those, including young clergymen and young doctors, with whom she is brought into close contact."[100] A few Episcopalians did in fact take vows; Deaconess Margaret Booz's 1958 obituary claimed that she "was one of about fifteen in this country who had taken complete vows, including that of celibacy, it is believed."[101] (Note that the vow of celibacy is specifically called out.) Episcopal women also had another option: sisterhoods. Those who were drawn to lifelong vows were more likely to choose one of the Episcopal sisterhoods, where vows were integral to the order, than to become deaconesses. Slippage between the sisterhoods and deaconess orders may explain why some Episcopalians were less opposed to vows than other Protestants.

Deaconesses used their defenses against Catholicism to contribute to their ongoing construction of gender. According to Catholic historian Maureen Fitzgerald's analysis, in anti-nun discourse we see "anti-Catholicism's most explicit discussion of the superiority of the Protestant gender system, with 'liberation' to be found within the home as wives and mothers." Deaconesses and their allies both echoed and redefined this Protestant understanding. They agreed that convent life was the "negative referent in constructing a normative Protestant womanhood," but the normative Protestant womanhood they constructed was of a different character. Fitzgerald argues that American Protestantism as constructed in the late nineteenth century, with its distinctive gender system, was "inseparable from a new emphasis on the household as the primary institution through which a gendered distribution of civic and moral authority was ordered."[102] As demonstrated above, deaconesses used maternalist rhetoric to claim moral authority for their ministry, but they universalized the maternalist claim to apply to all women. They launched their mission to save the world not as wives and biological mothers, but as women, especially as trained and consecrated women. Thus, in defending their office and defining it against the convent system, they expanded the notion of the freedom of Protestant women. Liberation was not to be found only, as Fitzgerald asserts, "within the home as wives and mothers" but also in the deaconess order. The convent still represented a prison, but freedom could now also consist in living together in consecrated but *unvowed* association with other single women.

Deaconesses employed a variety of strategies to differentiate themselves from their Catholic counterparts. They argued that their garb was completely different from the habit, but that if it was similar in some ways, it was only in the good ways. In this rhetoric they engaged ideas of the diaconate as appropriate for Christian womanhood, as opposed to a desexualized (or potentially sexually deviant) Catholicism. They contrasted their healthy, active, womanly lives of service with the familiar image of the corrupt, contemplative, and consumptive nun. In so doing, they invoked an image from fiction of imagined Catholicism, as it may have existed in the past, and blithely ignored the living evidence to the contrary around them. Finally, deaconesses argued that only their voluntary, unvowed Christian service flowed from the properly pure motives of faith. In this regard, they retreated to the common Protestant trope of evangelical liberty while opening up the possibility for Protestant liberty for women outside the home.

"All the Same in Christ"

What deaconesses disparaged was the negative image of nuns rather than nuns themselves. When deaconesses dealt with Catholic women religious in real life, they demonstrated not antipathy, but admiration and solidarity—tempered with jealousy. Although they posed a threat to be feared and countered, nuns simultaneously presented a model to be imitated. In 1947, a deaconess pointed to the power and success of the Catholic nuns who operated so many schools, hospitals, and institutions, asking, "Who can estimate the helpful service which is thus rendered to all classes of people? Who can estimate the respect and honor which they bring to their church?"[103] Historian Fitzgerald has argued that the charitable work of Catholic sisters has been sorely overlooked, and that the male hierarchy has been given the credit. Undoubtedly this has been true in both Catholic communal memory and academic literature. Although perhaps motivated primarily by the desire to shame and catalyze their fellow Protestants, deaconesses were more willing to give recognition to Catholic sisters for the work they were doing.

Deaconesses believed that they shared a mission with nuns as consecrated women workers transcending confessionalism. A Mennonite deaconess argued, "The fact remains that though formalism, spiritual degeneracy, and other evils may be present in some orders [of nuns], true consecration and devotion to the Lord Jesus Christ and His church can only produce the fruits which are evident to the world at large."[104] In this statement, Sister Frieda began with a familiar anti-Catholic stance and ended by recognizing in nuns a kindred consecrated spirit. Evangelical Synod Sister Velma Kampschmidt reminisced about relying on her Catholic counterpart when she was called on to begin a new nursing school: "I didn't know a thing about starting a school . . . so I called St. Mary's where there was a school and talked to the nun who headed it, Sister Alcaque, whom I knew. She told me, 'Don't worry; I'll bring you all my books.' She really, really helped me."[105] It is significant that Sister Velma already knew Sister Alcaque and turned to her in a time of need. Unfortunately, but not surprisingly, deaconesses did not widely advertise their personal friendships with Catholic sisters, so we cannot know how representative Sister Velma's experience was.

Deaconesses emphasized their shared Christianity with the Catholics they encountered in their work. Lutheran Sister Jennie Christ was impressed with the devotion of two Catholic women patients she nursed, noting in her diary that they were "very devout in the worship."[106] In Methodist Lucy Rider Meyer's stories, deaconesses and other women often downplayed dogma and emphasized the transcendent nature of Christianity. Of the presumably Catholic O'Hara family, one of Rider Meyer's deaconess characters opined, "I think they're Christians up to the light they have."[107] Elsewhere Rider Meyer related a story of deaconess work in Chicago: "It was a comfort to find in another dying Roman Catholic, a trusting Christian. 'Are you a sister?' she asked of the Deaconess who went to spend the night with her. 'Yes, a Protestant sister,' was the reply. 'It is all the same in Christ,' said the dying woman, and through a night of pain she was comforted by the words of promise that are the joy of all the saints in the dark valley."[108] Rider Meyer implied agreement with the sentiment that the work of deaconesses and nuns was "all the same in Christ." In another of Rider Meyer's accounts, an Irish Catholic woman related her own view that Protestants and Catholics would share an eternal reward: "'Shure! An' it's all one place we're going to, I belave!'"[109]

Instructions for Evangelical Synod deaconess nurses included compassionate directives for treating Catholic patients and efforts to treat confessional differences with gentleness:

> If [Catholics] desire to have their priest call on them, the sister will notify him. If they want the sister to read to them from the Bible or hymn-book, she is to do so gladly. If she is asked to read to them from their prayer-book, she must look it over before reading aloud, and if the prayer contains nothing contrary to the word of God or to Evangelical faith, she complies with such request. There are Catholic prayer-books that contain pure biblical prayers. Should their conversation touch upon the doctrinal differences then the deaconess is to confess her most holy faith simply but firmly and to prove it by love.[110]

Although the theological distinctions remained and were not to be minimized, the author emphasized how Protestants and Catholics could read the Bible together, sing together, and even pray together.

When speaking in the abstract, it was easy for deaconesses to fall back on common Protestant, anti-Catholic tropes: nuns were ascetics, old-fashioned, unwomanly, idle, and trapped by vows and works-righteousness. But when they were relating personal stories, or were speaking of individuals, they were more inclined to recognize devout Catholics as kindred spirits. For deaconesses, Christian faith could trump confessional divides, both Catholic and Protestant. This points to what women's historians have identified as the "pragmatism" of American Protestant women. Excluded from Protestant church hierarchies and seminaries, women tended to ignore doctrinal controversies and to work cooperatively and ecumenically.[111] We noted earlier the cultural and theological limits on the deaconesses' ecumenical cooperation. German-speaking deaconesses and Social Gospel deaconesses sometimes failed to connect because of different interpretations of the diaconal principle. But the records also reveal incipient ecumenism. Often pastors from other local churches would speak at the occasion of the dedication of a deaconess home or hospital, demonstrating Protestant Christian solidarity.[112] Editors of deaconess journals routinely reprinted articles from other denominations' journals, indicating that they both subscribed to and read each other's writings. Deaconesses quite regularly trained with other denominations. The Presbyterian Training School in 1930 boasted that "the Presbyterian, United Presbyterian, Reformed (US), Magyar Reformed, Methodist Episcopal, and Lutheran Churches are represented in the enrollment this fall."[113] In turn, Presbyterian deaconess candidates at that Philadelphia school received their practical training in cooperation with the Baptist and Episcopal Training Schools.[114] Individual deaconesses gave short-term help to churches of other denominations, for instance with Vacation Bible Schools or Sunday School curriculums.[115]

Deaconesses reproduced and subverted anti-Catholic rhetoric at the same time. They were impressed by the Catholic Church they vilified, and they admired the nuns they disparaged. Catholic sisters' work provided direction for deaconesses, as they sought to match the success of the nuns, especially in nursing. When deaconesses sought to distinguish themselves from their Catholic counterparts, they put new spins on familiar Protestant arguments. In their discussions of garb, deaconesses constructed a model of Christian dress that was Protestant, womanly, and respectable, juxtaposing it with a Catholic habit that was asexual and disreputable. As deaconesses denigrated convent life as unhealthy, they created an alternative communal opportunity for themselves that epitomized robust Protestant womanhood. And while they characterized Catholic vows as impinging on evangelical freedom, they redefined Protestant liberty for women in a way that did not necessitate occupying the traditional position of wife and mother in the home. Lucy Rider Meyer's characterization of nuns and deaconesses, and by implication Protestants and Catholics, as "all the same in Christ" could be seen as nothing more than literary wishful thinking. But the fact that deaconesses were wishing for such ecumenism provides crucial nuance to our understanding of Protestant views of Catholicism. Deaconesses emphasized the shared Christian faith of Protestants and Catholics even while defining Catholics, often in gendered ways, as the other. The nun was a necessary part of the construction of the deaconess as a new consecrated Protestant woman.

4

Deaconesses and the Allowance

I would like to have Mother to see the House and hear more about the
Deaconess work she does not think about it as I do she thinks one ought
to earn money and thinks I am to careless about the matter but I always
think the Lord will provide and the money does not bother me any at all
but nevertheless she says if I wish I may go as far as I am concerned am
anxious to work I feel I must go ahead and do something.[1]

Anna D. Schmidt's 1896 letter to the superintendent of the Cincinnati
German Methodist deaconess home revealed her intertwined feelings
about money and becoming a deaconess. Schmidt epitomized the early
deaconesses' approach to money: the compulsion to "go ahead" and
work outweighed their concern over money. Although others, particularly family members, might have wanted them to take advantage of
newer opportunities for women to earn money, deaconesses chose to
believe that "the Lord will provide." Deaconesses' monetary provision
came in the form of an allowance.

Neither a salary nor an entitlement, the allowance represented deaconesses' complicated relationship with money as consecrated women.
Until the 1930s, the vast majority of deaconesses did not receive a salary
for their work.[2] Instead, they received a small monthly allowance, room,
board, and the promise of support in old age. From the inception of the
movement, deaconesses and their supporters promoted the allowance
as a key feature of the diaconate. One Methodist defending the allowance system emphasized that the monetary allowance itself was only the
smallest part of a larger system of support. A deaconess received, "first
of all, her home," which included room, board, and laundry. "This would
be worth at least $25.00 a month," Iva Durham Vennard insisted in 1908,
"but it is furnished as freely by the church as if she were living at home
with her parents."[3] Deaconesses were cared for in the motherhouse or

deaconess home in sickness and old age. In time, cottages were established where deaconesses could spend their retirement years and vacations if not staying with family. Beyond that, a deaconess received her garb and an allowance for "private incidentals."[4]

The actual amount of the allowance varied greatly among denominations and among institutions within denominations. In the nineteenth century, the monthly allowance was often whatever could be scraped up after the institution's expenses had been paid. At the low end, before 1910, Evangelical Synod deaconesses in St. Louis received $3 a month, probationers $2.50.[5] Around 1910, allowances averaged $10 a month, with a supplement of that amount or more for deaconesses' yearly vacations.[6] By 1920, the average had risen to $20 a month and was rising further. As a Methodist author reported, "At the opening of the General Conference of 1920 the allowance was from $20.00, down; at the close it was from $20.00, up."[7] By 1927 the German Methodist deaconesses in Cincinnati were being rewarded for long-term service: after three years of consecrated work, they received $30 a month, after five years, $35 a month.[8] In 1925, a Methodist Episcopal group recognized the validity of an allowance on a scale from $25 to $75 a month. Although the principle of the allowance dictated that all deaconesses received the same amount, variations among institutions of the same denomination and larger allowances for veteran deaconesses indicate that this ideal of equality was difficult to maintain from the beginning. The same 1925 Methodist Commission on Deaconess Work that authorized the large range of allowances resolved, momentously, "We also recognize groups of deaconesses who may prefer to work on a salary basis and recommend that those receiving more than $75.00 per month be considered in the salaried group. We agree that the determination of the group in which she shall work shall be left to the personal choice of the deaconess."[9] By the 1930s, many if not most deaconesses worked for a salary. Both allowanced and salaried deaconesses were affected by the vicissitudes of the US economy. As a Lutheran minister lamented during the Great Depression, "The meagre quarterly allowances for the deaconesses for personal expenses, ranging from $8.00 to $20.00 per Sister, have not been paid promptly and it will likely be impossible this year to give to each Sister the small vacation allowance of $25.00."[10] When World War II necessitated a Victory Tax on salaries, the Philadelphia Lutheran sisterhood secured a legal opinion that their allowances were not to be considered salaries and were thus exempt from the tax.[11]

There was more to the term "allowance" than simple tax avoidance or semantics. In theorizing the social and cultural uses of money, sociologist Viviana Zelizer uses the category of special money to call attention to the ways in which certain currency is marked off from others in qualitative ways, ways that negotiate relationships between people.[12] Deaconesses consciously marked their funds as separate from the regular money of the market. By insisting that the money that they received was an allowance, deaconesses created a category of special money. This created category did important relational work for deaconesses: it gendered their relationship to money in a specifically female way; it enabled their efforts to interact with both the poor and rich from a position outside the economy; it reinforced their relationship with their deaconess and nondeaconess sisters; and it was intended to sanctify their lives.

Women's Money

By giving their money a special name, deaconesses set it apart in distinct ways. Today the term "allowance" brings to mind the amount given by a parent to a child. It had these paternalistic overtones in the diaconate, too. As daughters of the motherhouse, deaconesses were considered members of a family and received an allowance like children. As such, they did not control money as autonomous adults. For example, the House Rules of the Lutheran Philadelphia motherhouse stipulated, "Sisters and Candidates are not allowed to borrow or lend money. In case of need Sisters will apply to the Oberin [directing sister], Candidates to the *Probemeisterin* [sister in charge of candidates]."[13] Methodist regulations required that deaconesses not accept personal gifts; anything received was to be "gratefully accepted for the Home" and turned over to the superintendent.[14]

Calling their money "allowance" instead of "wages," "salary," or "paycheck" differentiated deaconesses' money from money earned by a male breadwinner and linked it to other women's money, variously described as "pin money," "butter money," or "pocket money."[15] A deaconess brochure labeling the allowance "pin money" indicated that it was to be thought of like other women's money, as a sum gifted from a husband, ostensibly for nonessential trivialities.[16] Apart from its infantilizing implications, "allowance" had another resonance for Americans at the turn of the twentieth century. There was discussion in the middle-class popular press at this time about the advisability of a wife receiving an allowance from her husband's paycheck. Home economists and authors in women's magazines began criticizing the traditional method of the "dole," through which women were forced to ask their husbands piecemeal for every cent they handled. With a definite sum of money to call her own each month, it was argued, a wife could better manage the household affairs and effectively assume her new role as family purchasing agent. Likewise, women's missionary societies were cognizant of how married women's lack of access to money limited what they could contribute to benevolent causes. These missionary societies embraced the idea of husbands giving their wives allowances so that women could contribute as they saw fit.[17] Although a majority of women favored the idea of an allowance in the early twentieth century, only a minority of households ever adopted the system. Before midcentury the allowance had given way to a new domestic ideal: joint bank accounts. But the concept of the wife's right to a defined sum of money had entered the public consciousness in a powerful way.[18]

The deaconess allowance was an ambiguous category of money, because it was neither a payment equivalent to services rendered nor a gift.[19] It was, rather, like all women's money of the time, presumably linked to women's needs. Even wage-earning women's pay was not directly linked to the work they performed in the same way that men's pay was. According to Alice Kessler-Harris, "The women's wage, at least for the early twentieth century, rested in large measure on conceptions of what women needed."[20] And employers of the time did not think that women needed much. Because men were supposed to earn a family wage, every woman was ideally adequately clothed, housed, and fed by a husband or father. As one exasperated deaconess complained to another in a letter, "I don't know how your brothers are, but mine can never see that a spinster has any use for money."[21] It was assumed, quite wrongly according to statistics, that women's wages were always merely supplemental to the family income. Employers assumed that even women living alone were subsidized by their families. Industrialists, journalists, and clergy such as Catholic social theologian John Ryan had much to say at the turn of the century about the proper wage for a woman.[22] The consensus was that wages should be just enough for a woman to survive: any less might compromise her virtue; any more might encourage other women to leave their families and strike out on their own.[23]

In like form the deaconess allowance was unapologetically needs based. The allowance corresponded to necessary expenses, not to service rendered. By this logic, it made perfect sense that the deaconess nurse (who could have commanded a decent salary on the market) and the deaconess housekeeper (who could not) received the same allowance. As Rider Meyer tellingly phrased it, "The question always is not how much can you earn; but how little can you live upon?" She explicated further to a laywoman friend who asked, "Why do you deaconesses so insist that your absurd little mite of money be called an allowance, not a salary? Of course it's small, but you know some women do actually work for that, and since you do receive ever so little for your work, why not call it a salary?" Rider Meyer began her answer, "Our sister makes her mistake in assuming that the amount usually assigned to a deaconess for needful expenses is given for her work."[24] For Rider Meyer, and other Social Gospel–oriented (and possibly class status–anxious) Methodists, this distinction between salary and support could not be emphasized strongly enough.

According to deaconesses, to assume that the small allowance represented all a deaconess's service was worth would have two disastrous consequences. First of all, it would devalue the work done by secular women who relied on a salary, however small. Deaconesses were aware that their own allowanced work had the potential to exert downward pressure on working women's wages. As Rider Meyer explained, when a deaconess nursed for a wealthy family, the family was still charged the market value, which was then given to the deaconess home: "To ask less would place her in competition with salaried workers and tend to lower wages, a thing she has no right to do."[25] A Southern Methodist article echoed this concern, speaking out against those who wanted deaconesses to nurse for the wealthy, but at "half rates, thus depriving many poor women" of opportunities for employment and "making it more difficult for the regular trained nurse to command the price her service deserves."[26] Methodist deaconess Isabelle Horton agreed that the allowance was "no disparagement of salaries nor of salaried service. That the 'workman is worthy of his hire' is as incontrovertible now as in St. Paul's time."[27] These women, while arguing that the deaconess allowance was and ought to be needs based, were simultaneously advocating for a wage for secular women workers that reflected the true value of their services.

Furthermore, to understand the deaconesses' money as salary would devalue deaconess work. Deaconesses seemed personally affronted by the idea that their services were only "worth" a few dollars a month. To call a deaconess's eight dollars a salary was "unjust, when the same woman could earn . . . eight times eight dollars per month." The continuation of the quotation, from an 1893 Methodist deaconess report, revealed class tensions at play: "Unless a much larger sum than this is paid it should not be considered a 'salary,' as it would bring discredit upon many noble workers, and practically debar from entering the work the very class that is most desired."[28] Deaconesses recognized that the educated and talented women they sought to recruit could earn significant salaries, and recruiters did not want prospective deaconesses to view themselves as taking "a pay cut." Instead, acknowledging the comparatively large salary a deaconess could command highlighted all the more her sacrifice in giving it up. A 1918 Presbyterian pamphlet made explicit this connection between sacrificial consecration and the acceptance of the allowance: "Many of these women are highly educated and could earn good salaries in secular pursuits, but they willingly give up their lives, in answer to the call."[29] Deaconesses claimed that only consecration made it possible to accept a strictly needs-based sum of money, thus reinforcing the idea of a consecrated life as the highest manifestation of true womanhood. In reality, the needs-based wage reflected the underlying situation of all working women (within and beyond the home) in this era.

Proponents claimed that the allowance system ensured the purity of intention of those who entered the deaconess office. As a 1902 Lutheran author argued, "But the best attendants for the unfortunate and suffering *can never be hired for money*."[30] It was as if the presence of money tainted the integrity of the office, and money was spoken of in coarse terms. In the same year, a Southern Methodist woman contrasted the deaconess with the professional nurse, explaining that the deaconess "looks for her reward not in greenbacks, but in souls won for Christ."[31] By using a slang word, the author denigrated the very concept of money.

The professional nurse here provided a useful foil for deaconesses. Readers were exhorted to pity the poor secular nurse, who faced uneven employment, an uncertain future, overwork, and a diminished spiritual life. Furthermore, she did not have the same high ideal as the deaconess; the professional nurse was "simply working for the money or glory that she might obtain."[32] A deaconess receiving an allowance, on the other hand, fostered in those she served a sense of trust, giving "people confidence in the disinterested motives of the worker."[33] A Lutheran minister (who surely received a salary himself!) asserted that the allowance was simultaneously "a severe test of sincerity of purpose" of a candidate and "a real blessing to the cause, preventing to some extent at least, many undesirable young women from applying for admission to our Sisterhood."[34] If deaconesses were paid a salary, it would be impossible to separate those who were just "in it for the money" from those who were truly consecrated to the work.

To the modern reader, this argument begs the gendered question: why would a salaried deaconess nurse inspire distrust while a salaried doctor did not? Why was the salaried minister, the deaconess's professional exemplar in other cases, not the model followed here? The answer is found in tensions over the cultural relationship between women and money in this time period. Women in the United States still identified their moral purity with their lack of (male) desire and concomitant renunciation of ambition for money or advancement. Desire and wealth were linked with manliness, desirelessness with womanliness. The only womanly desire was the desire to serve, and any financial reward that came with that service was purely incidental.[35] Deaconesses appropriated this cultural assumption, emphasizing their altruistic motives and denouncing any self-aggrandizement, either by disavowing desire or recasting it as service.

Male deaconess supporters and first-generation deaconesses themselves sought to separate the deaconess vocation from the male world of striving and moneymaking. This can be seen in a universal distaste for the word "ambition." When an Episcopal minister discussed women's appeal for an official position in church work, he concluded, "The ministry of the deaconess offers the only real place in which this ambition, if I may use the word, may be realized."[36] His apology for even using the word "ambition" implies that such was an ugly thing in a woman. An early Methodist periodical went even further: "Bishop Littlejohn spoke of the [deaconess] order as existing in the early days of the Church, and said it was not a sphere in which women's ambition could be gratified; but a field for beneficent and quiet work among the sick."[37] Deaconess Susie Kreutziger, the preceptress of the German Methodist Dorcas Institute, explained, "To have this one great idea dominating our lives," which she named "the Christ motive," "will keep us from desiring the salary a trained nurse can demand, or the freedom other positions allow."[38] In this statement, Kreutziger promoted consecration as a means of suppressing any unseemly, or unwomanly, desires.

Within this context, it makes sense that salary was seen as incompatible with the deaconess office as the highest manifestation of true womanhood. As Methodist deaconess Vennard argued, "One other feature of the 'real Deaconess' must be mentioned. She is an unsalaried worker. There is no prospect whatever in Deaconess work for the woman who is ambitious to make money."[39] Ambition in a woman was bad enough, but ambition to make money simply would not be countenanced. Her use of the phrase "real Deaconess" reveals that Vennard was consciously shaping the idea of what the deaconess ought to be: ambitious women might slip in, but they would never be authentic deaconesses. A German Reformed author argued that consecration lifted deaconesses' desires beyond financial matters: the deaconess "has absolutely no selfish motive,—she is beyond all that. She is beyond salary."[40] In shifting the understanding of desire to desire for service, deaconesses formalized their disavowal of monetary gain by means of the allowance.

If financial ambition was deemed incompatible with middle-class women's gendered selfhood, then the diaconate was a way for these women to work without working for a salary. A woman who wanted to work while avoiding the censure of unwomanliness could find a comfortable middle ground in the diaconate. Through her relationship with the community she received the benefits that money bought, but she remained untainted by the money itself. She gained a home, food, and clothing—items necessary to her protected status as true woman—but no one could accuse her of unseemly greed or desire. In the Progressive Era, being manly meant being financially independent.[41] The converse was that being womanly meant being financially dependent. Deaconesses thus remained womanly by remaining financially dependent, not on their parents or on their husbands, but on the deaconess community. A middle-class deaconess could thus engage in a meaningful career without becoming a "working girl," with the small but dangerous amount of independence that position brought.

Despite all of the rhetoric against women's ambition, large numbers of women who entered the diaconate were in fact already working for wages. In 1890, 44 percent of first- or second-generation immigrant women worked outside the home for wages, and many more labored within their own homes or farms, so it is not surprising that a great many deaconesses from the German denominations had previous work experience.[42] Most of the applicants to the German Methodist deaconess home in Cincinnati, for example, had left school between the ages of fourteen and sixteen out of economic necessity. The majority were housekeepers, either at home or for others, or seamstresses, but there were also caregivers and a few factory workers and office clerks. These women were accustomed to hard labor, as their letters to the motherhouse reveal. To excuse her tardiness in correspondence, one described her long workday: "I work from five o'clock in the morning until late it is sometimes eight and after before we have supper so you see it is after nine and sometimes ten o'clock before I get through." Another described the situation of many working-class deaconess applicants, specifically, a lack of education leading to an unsatisfying life of labor: "When at the age of 14 left school and had to work to help my parents and been working ever since and now wish to go and work for the Lord the rest of my life. I would have like to written last week but am here alone with 4 children and did not get time their mother is in the Hospital and so it made it a little Hard. Well I guess I must close because it is already after 12 and I must go to bed."[43] For many working-class women, mostly Lutherans, German Methodists, Evangelical Synod, or German Reformed, hard work for low wages was a fact of life. These women may have seen the diaconate as a respite from their menial work. Or, if deaconess work was equally laborious, at least they hoped it would be more satisfying.

As Anna Schmidt's letter that opened this chapter reveals, the assumptions about working-class women and money were somewhat different. Their wage work did not threaten social expectations about women's role because they were not perceived to be working for personal gain or advancement. They were expected to work on behalf of their families, not themselves. A working-class woman helping to support her family faced less stigma for earning a paycheck, but as discussed earlier, she might have to overcome parental resistance in order to become a deaconess. Furthermore, working-class women were still constrained by gendered ideas of work, and deaconess advocates played on these assumptions. A Lutheran recruiting pamphlet explained, "Some choose vocations little suited to a woman's nature, merely to gain their living. . . . Behold He is now calling you into His vineyard; there you will find true woman's work."[44] This offer appealed to working women seeking labor that was both significant and womanly, such as Sarah Delilah Church, who explained, "Last year I became very dissatisfied with my work, and decided there was surely some thing more worthwhile in life for me to do than catering to women's whims and fashions, so I sold my shop."[45] Likewise, an Evangelical Synod pamphlet surmised that many of the jobs available to women were not rewarding: "Many young women who are obligated to earn a livelihood as servants, salesladies, dressmakers, teachers, etc. . . . are frequently not satisfied with their lot, whereas a deaconess has a vocation that is highly gratifying."[46] Working-class women who became deaconesses traded in an earthly boss, who might overwork them, treat them unfairly, or sexually harass them, for a perfect heavenly boss. One applicant contrasted her former mundane occupation with the lofty and noble service before her: "I'm a dressmaker and have spent most of my time sewing, but from now on the Lord shall have all of my time, the Lord alone, I'm going to serve."[47]

Sociologist Robert Wuthnow points to the late nineteenth century as a time when it became more difficult to integrate moral considerations into economic life, as "new scientific conceptions of work and money were being advanced by political economists." Within this evolving framework, "Work and money became more intimately linked to each other, but farther removed from those conceptions of the human spirit that had once constrained them."[48] As deaconesses, middle-class women found a way to work without working; likewise, working-class women found a job that was not a job. Being a deaconess provided both middle- and working-class women not only the necessities of life but also a significant Christian vocation.

The "Poor" Deaconess

As recipients of an allowance, deaconesses found themselves in a unique position in the wage economy. As noted, deaconesses, like wives, and to a degree all working women, received money that was separated from the market value of their services. But unlike their peers who frequented the new department stores and new places of commercialized leisure, deaconesses had so little money that they lacked the ability to spend discretionary income in these "temples of commerce." Their position in, but not of, the wage labor system gave them a unique point of view on American capitalist society. Deaconesses, especially those who worked among the poor, saw firsthand the negative effects of capitalism and adopted a wary, if not outspokenly critical, stance. The emphasis on the allowance could be cast as a protest against the inequities of the economic system. Noted above was deaconesses' special concern not to depress working women's wages. Deaconesses, and on this theme again the Methodists were the most outspoken, could use their allowance to critique capitalist greed:

> Deaconess work and the mode in which Deaconesses live is a protest against the utilitarian standard which pervades all our civilization. The poor appreciate it. It is a revelation to them that here are women who are working for the love of Christ, and who know something of the limitations of poverty as well as the people among whom they labor. "He became poor for our sakes." It is a voice in this modern age, saying to the multitude, there is something more precious than dollars and cents. There is a wealth of life more to be desired than silver and gold. Friend, let me give you a hint, do not waste sympathy on the "poor Deaconess." She has souls for her hire.[49]

As Iva Durham Vennard attested in this quotation, the poverty that deaconesses embraced through the allowance system placed them in solidarity with the poor. It also stood as a witness against the materialist excesses of wealthy America. Deaconesses became keen observers and critics of the waste and frivolity of the wealthy and middle classes. The talking deaconess bonnet, quoted earlier, "dreamed that all the rich folks in the world made up their minds that they would never wear feathers and flowers and jewels on their bonnets any more at all, so long as babies are dying and mothers are starving and heathen are without Christ; but would give the whole price of them to the deaconesses to use in their work."[50] In this "dream," Lucy Rider Meyer put forward her understanding of sacrificial giving, particularly women's sacrificial giving. (Certainly men were not wearing flowers on their bonnets.) In her story, God did not smite the rich women or take from them their feathers and jewels. Rather, the women themselves gave up their luxuries for the betterment of humanity. Women's sacrificial giving was key to the success of the diaconate.

A handful of deaconesses were radicalized through their experiences with economic injustice. Isabelle Horton uttered words of rebuke against capitalism that few would have dared: "If under the present system a 'righteous distribution' of profits is impossible, let the 'moral forces' be brought to bear, though the system be destroyed."[51] Methodist deaconess Winifred Chappell went further and "came to embrace socialism and many communist ideas as being consistent with Christian commitment."[52] Chappell was for fifteen years a teacher and then assistant principal at the Chicago Training School, no doubt a powerful influence on the deaconess students of the 1910s and early '20s. She was an outspoken advocate for workers, especially women workers: "Employers mean business when they throw women with children in their wombs, children at their breasts, children at their skirts, out of the only homes they have."[53] After her tenure at the Chicago Training School, Chappell became an integral staff member of the Methodist Federation for Social Service and a popular writer and lecturer.[54]

Chappell was exceptional; the vast majority of deaconesses never moved that far left. On the whole, the envisioned economic reform was moderate and voluntary, a bending of the existing inflexible system through the actions of individuals. The novel *Joy, the Deaconess* (published by both secular and Methodist presses) modeled an ideal capitalist system in which workers and owners cared for each other's needs. The fictitious wealthy owner of the company helped out a poor worker and his family, and in return "Jim Scott never 'struck' while in Mr. Seeley's employ."[55] While deaconesses deplored the hunger and want in the tenement houses, their remedies usually worked through the "Christianizing of industry" rather than through some radical revolution.

Despite the fact that deaconesses had barely any money of their own, they did not identify themselves as poor. Their basic needs were met; they were clothed, fed, and housed, and therefore better off than many of the people they attempted to help. Indeed, for deaconesses in the working-class German denominations, entering the diaconate could be a way of climbing up the socioeconomic ladder. The "Self-Examination for Deaconesses" booklet published by the conference of German motherhouses prompted deaconesses to ask of themselves, "Have I not exalted myself above any of my relatives who may be living quietly in poverty and obscurity?"[56] These deaconesses may have considered their families poor, but not themselves.

For Social Gospel deaconesses, who hailed primarily from the middle class, the situation was different. Although they may have forsaken their families' wealth or significant salaries, they did not see joining the diaconate as downward social mobility into the lower class. Vennard's quotation above argued that deaconesses "know something of the limitations of poverty" but rebuffed sympathy for the "poor deaconess," set in quotation marks to hold the phrase at arm's length. We have seen already that the look of their garb ensured that deaconesses would not be mistaken for inhabitants of the tenement houses (or Salvation Army "slum sisters"). Deaconesses preferred to think of themselves as outside the economic system and as "a bridge between the rich and the poor."[57] A Lutheran handbook emphasized that a deaconess was expected "to knock at the door and hearts of the rich modestly and yet confidently" as surely as she was to be "a mother to the poor, a friend to the wretched."[58] Deaconesses saw themselves as conduits through which money could flow from the rich (or even middling, as most of their donors were) to the poor. Deaconesses did not ally themselves with the poor on the basis of shared poverty. Rather, through their own efforts and example, deaconesses thought they could effect the necessary—voluntary—redistribution of society's wealth.

The Bonds of Money: Sisterly Giving and Taking

On first glance, it would seem that money would not matter very much to deaconesses who eschewed a salary and lived simply. Ideally, deaconesses would barely have to interact with money at all. But the evidence suggests that deaconesses, particularly the leaders in the Social Gospel denominations, had a very complicated relationship with money.

Institution administrators were forced to think a great deal about money because they needed a great deal of it. Their hospitals brought in some revenue but rarely enough to be self-sustaining, and other institutions like motherhouses, orphanages, and city missions were entirely dependent on outside income. Deaconesses relied on support from denominations and churches, but it was individual donors who kept them afloat. As Priscilla Pope-Levison has argued about this era's women evangelists, deaconesses became tireless and creative fundraisers.[59] They traveled around to churches and spoke to women's groups with the purpose of raising recruits and money, treading carefully lest their fundraising cross some line of decorum. A Southern Methodist journal protested that the deaconess was not "a church beggar," implying some suspicion that she was.[60] The 1893 Methodist General Deaconess Board warned that "no Deaconess shall solicit money unless duly authorized," ostensibly by the board itself. Instead, the Deaconess Board asked that "collection boxes be placed in public and conspicuous places in the cities where Homes or Hospitals are established, to receive offerings for the work," implying that passive fundraising was less objectionable.[61]

As constant fundraisers, deaconesses, especially deaconess leaders, were keenly aware of the power of money. Episcopalian Virginia Young was raised as a socialite before her family's fortune dwindled. She became a deaconess and used her remaining means to found a home for unwed mothers. A staunch proponent of "mental hygiene," Young had a strong sense of the power and self-respect money gives the individual, as apparent in this excerpt:

> "You think you don't care about money," she said once to an aspiring youngster, "but let me tell you being poor means that you think about nothing but money, day in, day out. You work for money because you must have it, not because you love and believe in your work. You are never free because you need money someone else must give you. . . . If you have money, take it and use it, make your own needs your own affair and oh, how fortunate you will be if all the asking you do in life is for others, not yourself."[62]

Although she "appreciated comfort" and "loved beauty and worshipped cleanliness above all," Deaconess Young maintained Beekman Place through times of financial need in a "rigidly economical manner."[63] Young, who knew both luxury and want, recognized that a lack of money meant a lack of control and autonomy.

Lucy Rider Meyer was the paradigmatic fundraiser for the cause, creating numerous schemes to harness the goodwill, and loosen the purse strings, of Methodist women. When Rider Meyer needed money to build the Chicago Training School, she raised three thousand dollars with the "Nickel Fund": "While many are asking a penny a day for missions, I will ask for 5 cents from each [Methodist woman] not ONCE a day, not ONCE a year, but ONCE in a LIFETIME! Soon there will be $50,000 in our hands!" Her chain letter plan two years later gained her ten thousand dollars—and an investigation by the Chicago chief of police. But Rider Meyer's most significant money-raising effort was the "Do Without Band." Women across the country pledged, as emblazoned on an armband, "I will look about for opportunities to do without for Jesus' sake."[64] This "doing without" highlights the importance of sacrifice in deaconess fundraising. Large donors were crucial: the Philadelphia Lutheran motherhouse would never have existed without the sizable endowment of businessman John D. Lankenau. Even Rider Meyer was not above "telephon[ing] Mr. Bush, a wealthy contractor, and point blank ask[ing] him for some money." (Her biographer reports that although Rider Meyer initially asked for three thousand dollars, by the end of the phone call she had a pledge for twenty thousand dollars.)[65] But the small donations of churchwomen, the nickels and two-cent postage stamps they donated, were the lifeblood of deaconess fundraising.

Even women who did not have access to cash were essential supporters of the movement. Laywomen offered their services and gifts-in-kind as well as their money. As Methodist Bessie wrote to her grandmother on the postcard in figure 4.1, "We (the Queen Esther girls)[66] are hemstitching a set of table linen for this home. The Deaconesses are all so good and sweet that live here." Not to be outdone, the Epworth League of Jefferson, Iowa, furnished a room in the Chicago Training School in the 1890s.[67] In 1907, a proud donor sent Miss Molly Hohlstein an annotated postcard (figure 4.2) with the image of the German Deaconess Home and Hospital, commenting, "The room marked by cross was furnished in memory of grandmother [illegible]."

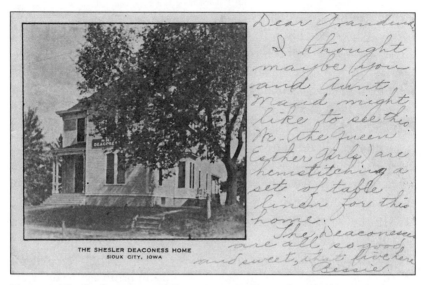

Figure 4.1. The Shesler Deaconess Home, Sioux City, Iowa, date illegible. Author's collection.

Figure 4.2. German Deaconess Home and Hospital, Cincinnati, Ohio, postmarked July 24, 1907. Author's collection.

Some deaconess bodies raised money themselves, through formal or informal appeals, but other deaconess institutions delegated their fundraising to an allied body, known variously as a Deaconess Aid Society, Board, Auxiliary, or *Verein* (society), consisting of married women, ministers, and, less commonly, laymen, unmarried laywomen, and deaconess representatives. Members paid annual dues and were charged with the task of promoting the cause and raising money. Deaconess periodicals were produced, and the revenue from subscriptions aided the cause. The role of associations of women, especially married women, in raising money for deaconesses was critical.[68] A 1918 newspaper clipping recorded the imbalanced fundraising for a Deaconess House for the Philadelphia School for Christian Workers of the Presbyterian and Reformed Churches: "The women's division reported $10,002; the men's division, $567."[69] This discrepancy, while comical, was not unusual. When the German Reformed Phoebe Deaconess Home reported its recent bequests in 1916, all four gifts were from women, three of the four from married women.[70]

A Mennonite example is illustrative of the pervasive women's influence in fundraising, even when men were the original administrators. When the Mennonites of Newton, Kansas, sought to build a deaconess hospital, nine men formed the Bethel Deaconess Home and Hospital Society in 1903. When the hospital was constructed in 1910, twenty-six enthusiastic women immediately organized a Women's Auxiliary. By year's end it had 136 members, each paying one dollar annually—all to support the work of only three deaconesses. In addition to their "regular work" of "sewing and mending for the institutions," the group's fundraising record was impressive:

> Plans for an addition to the hospital for the care of maternity cases were made almost immediately after this organization began. The Auxiliary contributed the first money for this, and assisted with the work of soliciting funds among friends and churches for its erection. They raised $10,715.00 for this purpose. At the same time (Christmas 1913) they presented sterling silver table ware for the Sisters' Dining Room. Next they solicited funds for a covered passage way (pergola) to connect the Hospital with the Deaconess Home, and they paid the entire cost ($1,200.00) for its construction.[71]

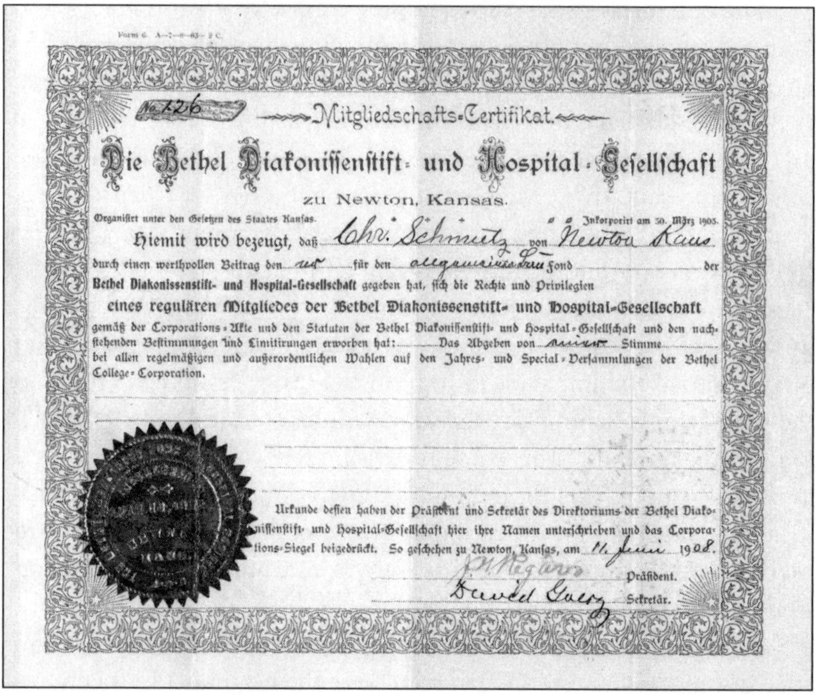

Form 6. A—7—8—03— 2 C.

No. 126 Mitgliedschafts-Certifikat.

Die Bethel Diakonissenstift- und Hospital-Gesellschaft

zu Newton, Kansas.

Organisirt unter den Gesetzen des Staates Kansas. Inkorporirt am 30. März 1903.

Hiemit wird bezeugt, daß Chr. Schmutz von Newton Kans durch einen werthvollen Beitrag den ______ für den ______ Fond der Bethel Diakonissenstift- und Hospital-Gesellschaft gegeben hat, sich die Rechte und Privilegien

eines regulären Mitgliedes der Bethel Diakonissenstift- und Hospital-Gesellschaft

gemäß der Corporations-Akte und den Statuten der Bethel Diakonissenstift- und Hospital-Gesellschaft und den nachstehenden Bestimmungen und Limitirungen erworben hat: Das Abgeben von ______ Stimme bei allen regelmäßigen und außerordentlichen Wahlen auf den Jahres- und Special-Versammlungen der Bethel College-Corporation.

Urkunde dessen haben der Präsident und Sekretär des Direktoriums der Bethel Diakonissenstift- und Hospital-Gesellschaft hier ihre Namen unterschrieben und das Corporations-Siegel beigedrückt. So geschehen zu Newton, Kansas, am 11. Juni 1908.

Präsident.

David Goerz Sekretär.

Figure 4.3. Christian Schmutz's membership certificate in Die Bethel Diakonissenstift und Hospital Gesellschaft, from 1908. Author's collection.

By the 1920s, the original male-founded Deaconess Home and Hospital Society itself boasted a membership that was approximately one-third female and included the deaconess sisters. Figures 4.3 and 4.4 show the certificates of membership preserved by one family who supported the Bethel Deaconess Home and Hospital for more than thirty years, from the father Christian Schmutz in 1908 to his daughter Miss Clara Schmutz in 1946.

Married women, ineligible for the diaconate themselves, were encouraged to contribute toward the training and support of other deaconesses. In that way, they became deaconesses by proxy, as suggested by the Episcopal pamphlet that asked, "Will not women, whose home ties prevent the dedication of themselves to the extension of Christ's Kingdom on earth, thus prepare and send forth other women as their substitutes?"[72] When Deaconess Anna Neiderheiser struggled to raise money

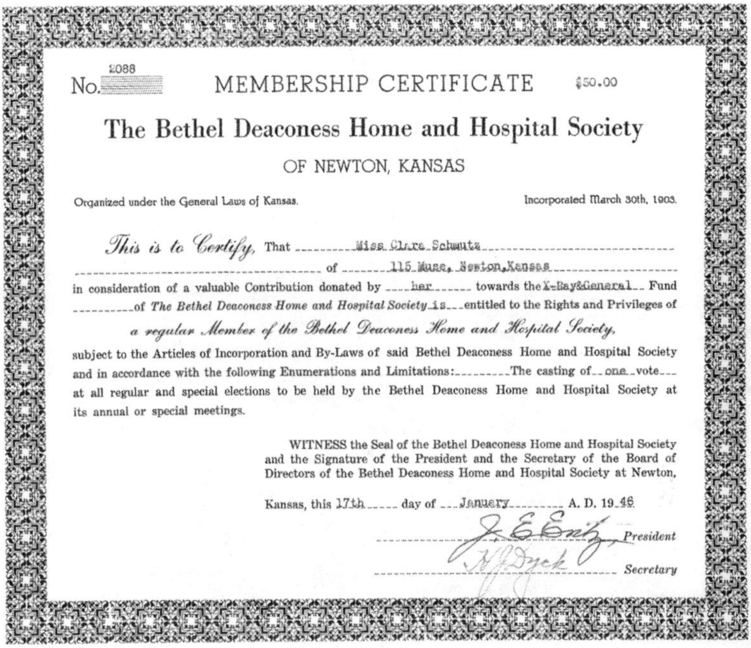

Figure 4.4. Clara Schmutz's 1946 membership certificate, reflecting her payment of fifty dollars. Author's collection.

for a new school building at the Kansas City Training School, it was five married women who came to her aid "during the difficult time attendant on the construction of Schoellkopf Hall." "They were staunch supporters of this work and understanding personal friends, all of them stalwart, far-visioned women," recalled Neiderheiser's biographer friends.[73]

Fundraising on behalf of the cause was another way in which the allowance system worked for the deaconesses by establishing and affirming their relationships with their nondeaconess sisters. Even though only a tiny fraction of Protestant churchwomen ever became deaconesses, fundraising is a key illustration of how the deaconess movement encompassed and affected a much larger segment of Protestant women, investing them in the success of the movement. Deaconesses and laywomen were linked together: laywomen supported and raised money for deaconesses, and deaconesses did the work that laywomen, constrained by

Figure 4.5. Deaconess Henrietta Pell-Clarke with friend Miss Frances White, undated postcard (after 1907). Author's collection.

their "home ties," could not. Figure 4.5 illustrates the friendship of a deaconess and her lay "sister." Just as the deaconesses consecrated their self-sacrifice, they encouraged the laywomen of their churches to make sacrifices of their own for the good of the cause.

The final piece of relational work the allowance system performed was to reinforce the deaconesses' sense of freedom by means of depen- dence. Deaconesses combined a traditionally female financial depen- dence with Christian faith in God's provision. Deaconesses' freedom rested on dependence on their diaconal communities, on dependence on donations from laypeople, but ultimately, they argued, on their de- pendence on the Lord. With trust in the Lord's provision, deaconesses were free to live out the gospel injunction to seek first the kingdom of God. From their position of constant need, deaconesses were forced to make good on their promises to trust in the Lord's supply. Although German American motherhouses often tasked their ministers with the financial affairs, thus providing an extra male buffer between the deaconesses and money, deaconesses were keenly aware of their precarious financial positions.

A historian of the Chicago Training School recorded the daily tests of faith of Lucy Rider Meyer and her Methodist deaconesses. Irva Colley Brown chronicled, "As the bills came in, they were made a subject of special prayer. . . . They sang the Doxology when cash and credit accounts seemed likely to balance." As the school's first Thanksgiving arrived, the students prayed for food: "Miss Holding has set her heart on a turkey, but after waiting until late in the afternoon, her face fell. Then after tea, came a smiling expressman, who, by the way, would take nothing for his services, with a barrel of apples, a great bunch of celery, a bag of cranberries, and a turkey that must be spelled with a capital, for as he held it up, it was as long as he." The deaconesses were so excited that, according to the story, "Mrs. Meyer said laughingly to the girls, 'We must not show so much emotion or people would see how little faith we had that our prayers for food would be answered.'"[74] Deaconesses argued that only consecration, the elevation of self-sacrifice for the Lord as one's highest goal, made possible this financial freedom that came from the allowance system.

For deaconesses, the allowance was enmeshed in ideas of consecration, the submission of the desires of self to the Lord. This was indeed a traditional Christian understanding of consecration, but in the deaconess movement it manifested itself in gendered ways. Pastors also consecrated their work to the Lord, but no one questioned their reception of a salary. True, some churches had a history of unpaid ministry, like Baptist "tent-maker" pastors or early Methodist circuit riders who worked for whatever collections the people would offer. But even the Methodist ministry was professionalized as quickly as possible; by this period ministers were perfectly comfortable with a salary and expected it as their right. Deaconesses, by contrast, were expected to do their work of Christian ministry with only the barest recompense, strictly because they were women. This gendered rhetoric served to conceal the fact that deaconess institutions could not afford to pay deaconesses a decent salary even if they had wanted to do so. What the rhetoric of self-sacrifice failed to address was the reality of running vast institutions and supporting lifetime workers without any money. Deaconess organizations perpetually struggled to keep the bills paid and deaconesses clothed, housed, and fed. In the end, there often simply was not enough money to go on. Although deaconesses professed allegiance to the principle of the allowance, they grumbled when they believed their allowances were too small.[75] Churches struggled to keep their promises to support deaconesses in their old age, such as when a church bureaucrat pleaded for a special grant for Presbyterian deaconess Amelia Hlavacek who was "faced with a desperate financial situation" upon her retirement in 1955, unable to live and support a dependent sister on her deaconess pension.[76] In reality, the deaconess ministry did not work without allowanced workers but, by the middle of the twentieth century, the allowance did not work well for deaconesses.

The allowance was the linchpin holding together the different facets of deaconesses' complicated relationship with money. It foregrounded consecration and self-sacrifice in a way that was explicitly gendered. It functioned to attract middle-class women to a career untainted by money, and it offered security to working-class women searching for meaningful work. The allowance set deaconess work apart from men's waged work, but it did not distance deaconesses so much from working women. Deaconesses, wives, and women workers all received money that was constructed as different from men's money: smaller in amount, called by different names, and linked to their needs rather than the value of the labor. Seen in this context, the allowance served to connect deaconesses to other women and their relationships to money. Their allowanced position and the charitable nature of their work ensured that deaconesses were always in need of money. This forced deaconesses into an awareness of the power of the very money they claimed to eschew. Deaconesses abhorred the poverty they saw around them, but their critique of the capitalist system that produced poverty was mild. They exalted self-sacrifice, but not poverty. Deaconesses envisioned that the sacrifices of men and especially women everywhere could both finance their own allowanced vocation and ameliorate the nation's poverty. Deaconesses argued that the allowance was possible only through consecration rooted in self-sacrifice. This idea of consecration will be further explored in the next chapter, especially as deaconesses used it to construct their vocation as a parallel to the ordained ministry.

5

Deaconesses and the Ordained Ministry

Contemporary authors have celebrated deaconesses as the "forerunners of the ordination of women in Protestant denominations."[1] "The deaconess calling became that of pastor," one United Church of Christ historian writes. The Episcopal Church's website reads, "The women's ordination movement in the Episcopal Church can be traced back to the 1850s, when women were first set apart as deaconesses in several dioceses."[2] But the links between the diaconate and the ordained ministry are far more complex than such easy statements suggest. Deaconesses compared their vocation to the ministry and attempted to place their office on as firm a biblical, ecclesiastical, and professional footing as the ministerial office. Like pastors, they claimed a divine calling, a consecration, and special training. But the on-the-ground relationship between deaconesses and clergy was complicated: just as the deaconesses used ministers to construct their vocations, ministers used deaconesses to buttress their own professional identities. In the end, most deaconesses sought to construct a vocation that had the same legitimacy and esteem as the ordained ministry but that was *not* the ordained ministry. What they sought to create was a consecrated Christian vocation of service specifically for women. When deaconesses considered seeking ordination for themselves in the 1920s and 1930s, the debate marked a paradigm shift in the diaconate.

The Professionalization of the Ministry

The nineteenth century had been a time of upheaval for the ordained ministry. Protestant clergy worried that their authority had been weakened by disestablishment and the proliferation of preachers from new evangelical sects. They worked in earnest to found seminaries, embrace masculine ideals of entrepreneurial competition, and cultivate the status of their profession. In the last two decades of the nineteenth century, pastors, as well as doctors, nurses, lawyers, teachers, and social workers, sought to standardize training and control access to their occupations, and individuals became more closely identified with their professions.[3] One result of the professionalization of the ministry was highlighting some aspects of the occupation at the expense of others. Deaconesses argued that the diaconate could serve as an invaluable resource for the busy modern pastor, performing some of the pastoral care tasks deemed less desirable. In so doing, they supported clerical professionalization and reinforced certain gendered assumptions about deaconesses.

Bolstering the professionalization of the ministry was a new emphasis on division of labor. The late nineteenth century, after all, ushered in not only the Progressive Era but also the "age of efficiency." The phrase "on time" entered the lexicon in the 1870s, and the time clock was invented in 1890. The deaconess movement flourished alongside Frederick Taylor's promotion of "scientific management."[4] A Presbyterian minister aligned the diaconate with these Progressive Era aims when he praised the creation of the Deaconess Home and Training School by saying, "It was a pressing necessity in church work to make it more effective. We live in a strenuous age. Old forms and methods will no longer avail. The spirit is progressive."[5]

The byword of the modern pastor was "too many responsibilities, too little time." When faced with the choice between emulating Jesus the Good Shepherd or Jesus the "founder of modern business" (so named by influential ad man and author Bruce Barton), clergy increasingly chose the latter. Ministers seemed especially excited about their new roles as businessmen and money managers but less enthusiastic about traditional pastoral labor: "A minister of the Gospel in this day if he is to be successful, in the generally accepted sense of the term, ought to be a good preacher, a splendid organizer, and a first-class financier. These so thoroughly occupy his time and attention that the real pastoral work is bound to suffer."[6] The roles of businessman and parish visitor were directly contrasted, as if mutually exclusive: "When so much of the responsibility of providing for the church finances devolves upon the pastor as it does here, it is impossible for him alone to do all the visiting that should be done."[7] The modern minister's responsibilities for "not only a pulpit and a pastoral staff, but an office, and a factory with a hundred wheels whirring" had "withdrawn him from the possible and useful intimacies of the other days."[8] Note how the role of chief financial officer and factory manager was not thought to preclude "good" preaching or "splendid" organization. It was only the face-to-face visitation that was eschewed so that ministers could "withdraw" to their offices.

Clergy also reserved for themselves public liturgical functions, and deaconesses facilitated this too. One United Brethren pastor was delighted that his parish deaconess even made funeral arrangements, "thus saving the pastor many times from any visit to the home prior to the hour of the funeral." Rev. Camp lauded rather than lamented this lack of contact with his parishioners; the service of a deaconess "gives the pastor of a large membership more time for the real movements of the church."[9] Thus, while conducting funerals was still deemed appropriate, having pastoral contact with the family ahead of time was not considered part of "the real movements of the church." One Episcopal deaconess characterized this not as the thrusting of parish work onto the deaconess by the pastor but as women drawing the lines and restricting the minister to his priestly function: "You are God's priests to administer to us the Holy Sacraments and to give us the inspiration that we need for our work and we count upon you to interpret God's love for His children of this generation, but we are not expecting you to take care of all the social activities of the parish or even of all the details of the religious education."[10]

In a familiar move, writers invoked the model of the apostolic church for this ecclesiastical division of labor. Citing the appointment of deacons in Acts 6:2, Lutheran minister Rev. Wenner argued that the "preacher cannot and ought not to serve tables," especially when the deaconess has "special training" to do it.[11] Clergy argued that not only was this model biblical, but it was also financially savvy. In his relished role as financier, Presbyterian Rev. William J. Dawson opined, "I should say that no investment which any church can make will yield such high returns of service as the employment of a deaconess."[12] An Episcopal author arguing for more women workers in the domestic mission field frankly admitted, "Another thing is to be remembered: a good woman can be secured for much less than what is required to pay an ordinary minister."[13] Volunteers might be free, but as a Presbyterian minister explained, the trained deaconess was far superior: "Every minister of the Gospel knows . . . the relative inefficiency of volunteers when obtained.

The trouble with most volunteer workers is that, whilst their intentions are good and unselfish, they don't know how to go about their work. It is a luxury for a minister to be freed from the necessity of personally instructing his workers in details of method."[14] The deaconess was the ideal volunteer: she was almost as cheap and more efficient.

Ministers of large churches were already calling on assistant pastors to help them in their many labors. One Presbyterian minister bluntly explained how a deaconess was superior to an assistant pastor, asserting that an assistant pastor was sometimes a source of "embarrassment" to the pastor, because he expected "to fill the church pulpit at some regular times, and to conduct funerals, and perform marriage ceremonies." But, the author explained, since the congregation preferred the senior pastor to do such things, the assistant pastor was left with only the visiting to do: "Therefore the Deaconess can do about all that an assistant pastor can do, and often can do it better."[15] It was as if a man in the role of ministerial helpmeet was unseemly. Deaconesses serving as assistant pastors, or "subpastors," according to one Southern Methodist, settled "the problem of the assistant pastor, which so very seldom is a success."[16] Some deaconesses who served as "pastors' assistants" recognized that they were doing the work of a pastor without the recognition, but Methodist deaconess Iva Conner was unusually candid when she reminisced in 1976 about her work: "If I'd been a man, I'd have been called Associate Pastor and had a better salary."[17] Because she was a woman and did not expect to "fill the pulpit," a deaconess was more helpful and more suitable—and cheaper—than an assistant pastor.

Women's historians have noted the role women played in fostering male professionalization on a broad scale in this era: "Only by recruiting a vast workforce of helpers, regarded as intellectually inferior but altruistically superior, could male-dominated professions pursue their course of abstraction and isolation."[18] Deaconesses certainly qualified as part of this vast workforce of helpers. As we have seen, friendly visiting, with its setting in the home and its attendant cooking, cleaning, nursing, and childcare, was seen as especially suited to woman's nature. It was especially eschewed by the male pastorate for the same reason. This benevolent work had already devolved to an extent to pastors' wives, as nineteenth-century ministerial manuals urged clergy to delegate pastoral work to their spouses. One author of an 1835 ministerial guidebook prescribed that the minister's wife take charge of parish visitation "as much as her family, health and degree of leisure would permit."[19] That was the challenge: how was the pastor's wife to take care of the visiting when she had to take care of the pastor and their family? A German Methodist pastor warned that the only way the minister's wife could reach "the innumerable homes practically closed to all but the mother love of some sister of the Church" was "to sacrifice children and home."[20] The deaconess was the ideal pastor's wife because she was not a wife at all. As deaconess, she combined the minister's manly freedom from domestic duties with the minister's wife's presumed womanly aptitude for visiting.

A German Reformed author claimed, "The Deaconess in a Congregation can go where no pastor can go, and she can come into closer touch with the individual family than any pastor can."[21] We would expect advocates to extol deaconesses' abilities in the home with women and children, but these writers went further by implying that ministers were especially poorly suited for relational work. "The fact is that good women can usually do this work with little children better than the men. They certainly do it better than the average clergyman," an Episcopal author opined.[22] Once with the family, in the home, the deaconess soared where the minister faltered: "She can alleviate suffering, she can comfort the disheartened, and bring sunshine where there has been darkness and despair, where many a minister would be in large measure helpless."[23] These and other accusations of the clergy's failure at pastoral care affirm and extend the conclusion reached by historian Karen Gedge that far from being allied with their ministers, nineteenth-century women felt disappointed and ignored by the men who were supposed to be their spiritual comforters.[24] Seminarians were urged to avoid women, and many women stayed away from ministers for fear of abuse or suspicion of misconduct. No wonder women saw clergy as ineffective counselors. Many deaconesses experienced this lack of ministerial support personally as they discerned their vocation to the diaconate.

When deaconesses recalled their decision to enter the vocation, often it was a visiting pastor or deaconess who introduced them to the cause, while their own ministers remained silent. When specifically asked whether their ministers encouraged them in their vocations, the nineteen elderly United Church of Christ sisters interviewed in 1981 reported that their ministers were indifferent at best. "Well, I wouldn't say [the church] encouraged me, but I wouldn't say they discouraged me. The minister was very surprised when I asked him about it" was one typical response.[25] Inspiration was more likely to come from someone other than the local pastor, such as the president of the church synod or "the pastor's wife's sister," who was a deaconess.[26] A Lutheran minister observed that pastors were reluctant to encourage women into the diaconate because they thereby lost their best parish volunteers. Rev. Bachmann extolled the "commendable and unselfish zeal in the cause of the Lord, when a pastor writes: 'Please add Miss so-and-so, one of my best Sunday-school teachers, to the list of your candidates,'" but lamented the larger number of his brethren who "would rather discourage than encourage the member anxious to become a deaconess."[27]

One Lutheran deaconess's story of discerning her calling poignantly confirms the isolation women felt: "So I went to my pastor, explained the dilemma; and—he simply looked at me, and his jaw dropped, and he said, 'I had no idea you were thinking about anything like that. *What am I going to do without you!?*' And that was the only answer I got. Several days later, why, he said he was sorry that he had responded in that way; but he just . . . so I had to struggle it through myself."[28] Instead of ministerial counsel, this woman experienced only betrayal. While pastors and women are often portrayed as allies in reform causes, the experiences of deaconesses reveal a more hesitant relationship. Pastors in the Methodist, Episcopal, and Presbyterian denominations were slightly more enthusiastic recruiters than their German brethren, possibly because there was a greater chance that a Social Gospel deaconess might return to her home church as a parish deaconess and continue her helpfulness to the local minister.[29] But advocates in these denominations still bemoaned ministerial apathy toward the deaconess movement.[30] Thus deaconess aspirants, especially those who were already active local church workers, could not rely on the support of the local minister for vocational counseling. As deaconesses, these same women sought to fill the void left by ministers who could not or would not meet the spiritual and emotional needs of women.

A German clergyman rhapsodized, "What can we imagine more beautiful than [a deaconess], at the side of the pastor and under his direction, to care for the souls of women and advise them in spiritual things."[31] The special work of the deaconess always remained carefully circumscribed. She was at the pastor's side but, more importantly, she was *under his direction*. The deaconess was never to usurp the role of the ordained clergy. This is why one Episcopal committee concluded that "secretarial work was of greatest value" lest deaconesses "duplicate the work of the clergy."[32] The deaconess manual of the African Methodist Episcopal Church, while it never governed any significant number of actual deaconesses, prescribed most strongly and plainly the separation of duties. In a section of special instructions to deaconesses in the sick room, the male author intoned, "Acquaint your pastor of all cases needing his attention. He can do his work much better than you. And do not argue about religion with the pastor; . . . be quiet and let him have the 'right of way.'" The deaconess was instead urged to "arrange the disordered room and the bedclothes."[33] Deaconesses' pastoral work buttressed the efforts of ministers to professionalize their office and affirm its masculinity. Given that they were doing some of the work of the ministry, it was only natural that deaconesses would link their office to the ministry as they sought to construct their own vocation.

Notwithstanding the lack of support they may have felt from their own pastors, when deaconesses looked for a professional model for their own office, they found it in the clergy. Deaconesses sought to sanctify the diaconal vocation by describing themselves as called by God to it. They established its legitimacy as a churchly office by emphasizing the consecration service. They strove to achieve their own professional identity by stressing their formal training. In these ways, deaconesses attempted to set their office on a par with the clerical office. Yet they reinforced the diaconate's womanliness and concomitant selflessness by assuming a gendered idea of consecration. By variously emphasizing call, consecration, and education, deaconesses fashioned the diaconate as a unique churchly vocation especially for women.

The Call and Consecration

Deaconesses believed themselves to be called by God to their office, and this call was essential to establishing the diaconate as a divinely sanctioned occupation. Advocates insisted that only women who were called to the work should enter, and that to take on the deaconess life without the certainty of a call was dangerous. "God's guidance and an inward call must lead you into the path upon which the half-hearted only too easily suffer ship-wreck," intoned a German Lutheran pastor.[34] But the call was defined very broadly and could manifest in myriad different ways. Lutheran Oberin Julie Mergner noted that the Lord called deaconesses both outwardly, through the church's invitation, and inwardly, through the Holy Ghost.[35] A German Methodist brochure urged women to listen closely for the beckoning of the spirit, sometimes mediated through other people: "The call may come through a great desire to do the work of a Deaconess, emphasized by a strong impression of the Spirit of God to enter this work; also through the conviction others may have received that you should give your life to this Cause. It would be a mistake for a young woman to look for any extraordinary divine demonstration urging her to accept this call. In most cases the call comes quietly."[36]

In their application letters, deaconesses confirmed receiving this call to the diaconate. Rare was the woman like Louise Higlin who reported hearing her "name called in a loud sweet voice, . . . and knew that it was no human voice" but "God and Jesus calling."[37] More calls were experienced as answers to prayers for guidance, often manifesting in the timely arrival of a visitor or piece of literature.[38] These human suggestions were interpreted as divine calls, such as the German Methodist woman whose minister suggested deaconess work to her. She prayed and concluded, "It is a call from God rather than man."[39] Some Methodist deaconesses linked their calls with their conversions. Clara Bay pointed to her conversion as sanctifying her previous call to nursing: "I have, always, intended to learn nursing when I became old enough but had not thought of entering a Home. Since my conversion, I feel that I must work for my Saviour. I feel that Jesus has called me to do this work."[40]

For this woman and others, the conversion experience included a conversion to a new purpose in life. Other women experienced their call as suddenly and forcefully as if it were a conversion. Methodist Anna Neiderheiser described her experience during the worship service at a convention for young adults: "I was sitting by myself at the end of the seat, lost in meditation. A great inner compulsion moved me to consecrate my all to Christ. When the invitation for dedication to full-time Christian service was given I did not wait to see if others were going forward. I arose at once and went to the altar. It seemed to me that Christ himself stood before me, and I said to him, 'Anything I have is yours. I am seeking to find what you wish me to do."' Leaving the service, Anna saw a magazine on a table, open to an article about the new Kansas City Training School for deaconesses, and interpreted this as the Lord's answer to her prayer.[41] Not surprisingly, the women who experienced these sudden call experiences were likely to be Methodists, with their emphasis on conversion and practices such as altar calls that enabled such experiences.

Highlighting the divine call linked deaconesses with male and female preachers before and after them.[42] A German Reformed pamphlet assured readers, "Just as clearly as God is calling men to the ministry is He also calling young women to consecrate their lives to the high office of the Deaconess."[43] Like women preachers, deaconesses believed this divine call endowed their vocations with the same spiritual legitimacy as that of the male clergy. The divine call worked for the diaconate on two levels. First, it placed the diaconate on a par with the ordained clergy as a divinely sanctioned office. Second, it was an especially effective tool for women to use because it minimized their apparent agency.

Invoking the divine call was one way deaconesses bolstered the idea of the diaconate as an appropriate woman's vocation. Like conversion stories that emphasize the work of God and the passivity of the convert, the agent of the divine call is God, not the woman. God converted her; God called her. Thus, a woman did not boldly choose the diaconate as her profession. Rather, God called her to it, and her only options were to heed God's call or ignore it. Indeed, the salient feature of a call was that it required a response. The German Methodist pamphlet quoted above continues, "In most cases the call comes quietly, but sufficiently clear to demand immediate obedience, and any delay may result in grieving the Spirit of God."[44] What Christian wanted to grieve the Spirit of God? When a minister told a young German Methodist woman, "Miss Albertsen you ought to be a Deaconess," her answer illustrated the substitution of agency: "'I know that' I said and I felt that I alone had not uttered the words but that the Spirit had prompted them."[45] Articulated this way, the call to the diaconate was, like the allowance, an effective defense against those who argued that deaconesses were displaying unwomanly ambition. Although women entering the diaconate were in fact selecting from a variety of career options, they emphasized that this was the one vocation for which they were not the choosers but the chosen.

Furthermore, heeding the call was obeying and surrendering to the call. Obeying and surrendering constituted familiar territory for Christian women. Through this surrender they found power. An Episcopal deaconess explicitly linked these, describing surrender to God's call as "your willingness to give yourself to Him, wholly, and without reserve, to be used or even not used, when and wherever He will." In exchange for this dedication, "You receive the gift of God's grace to help you make good your surrender, and to help you in all the work you are trying to do for Him."[46] Like contemporary evangelical women engaging in the "dialectic of submission and empowerment," analyzed by R. Marie Griffith in *God's Daughters*, deaconesses used their obedience to the call to find the power to exercise the diaconal ministry to which God had called them.[47]

The divine call alone did not make a deaconess. She also had to be consecrated. Consecration had multiple meanings, as illustrated in the following invitation by the German Reformed Church: God is "calling young women to consecrate their lives to the high office of the Deaconess. It is only the most consecrated womanhood that will respond to this calling." Consecration was both a spiritual condition and an intentional act, and both senses were essential for the deaconess. First, consecration was a character trait, and within this too there is a double meaning. Consecration was the spirit of dedication to God already present in a woman called to the diaconate. A list drawn up by the Methodist Church of Canada and reprinted by the Methodist Episcopal Church, South in 1902 lists "consecration" alongside "a trained mind, good health, common sense, and tact" as qualifications desirable in a deaconess.[48]

In addition to consecration as an innate disposition, consecration was also understood as a spiritual discipline to be pursued throughout a deaconess's life. The pamphlet entitled "Self-Examination for Deaconesses" contained close to one hundred soul-searching questions intended to assist deaconesses in practicing consecrated lives. The sister was directed to examine her personal spiritual state, asking herself, "Do I cast all my anxiety trustingly and confidentially upon the Lord?" and scrutinizing her devotional practices: "Do I seek daily the forgiveness of sins, and do I not neglect asking Him for it every evening before going to sleep?"[49] The manual exhorted the deaconess to a committed prayer life, participation in the sacraments, and Bible reading as means of continually consecrating herself to the Lord and to her work.

Consecration was also the deaconess's formal dedication of her life to the Lord in an official church ceremony. God's call gave the deaconess vocation divine sanction, but the consecration service gave it ecclesial sanction. The consecration ceremony served as the highlight of many deaconesses' lives.[50] Deaconesses, often practical to a fault, waxed rhapsodic when discussing the transporting beauty and holiness of the consecration service. "While the beautiful, impressive service proceeded there was a hush of intense interest upon the congregation, and a deep impression was made upon many hearts in that holy hour," a Southern Methodist wrote.[51] Episcopal deaconess Mary Truesdell described the transforming power of the ceremony at length for a recruiting pamphlet:

> The day dawned clear and lovely. It was late Spring. I remember the thrill I felt in putting on the Deaconess habit and veil for the first time. The Altar had white peonies and many candles for it was a major Holy Day. As I stood at the Altar rail as I was presented and the Bishop from his Episcopal throne put each question to me, I had a moment of feeling very much alone. But as I knelt and heard the Bishop say as he laid his hands on my head, "Take thou authority to exercise the Office of Deaconess in the Church of God, whereunto thou art now set apart, in the Name of the Father, and of the Son, and of the Holy Ghost," there came into my heart the warm feeling that I was not going to be alone any more. I was now His Servant. The Blessed Lord would be with me. The grace of the Holy Spirit had been given to direct and guide me as I would labor in this Office.[52]

A Lutheran deaconess writing under the initials S.A. described the preparation for her 1924 consecration as a similar time of transformation. Despite fearing that she was not ready, she spent a week with the other candidates in meditation and biblical study, led by older deaconesses and the motherhouse pastor. As the day of consecration approached, S.A.'s anxiety was transformed to joy as she "trusted that the God who had called me 'would make me perfect, strengthen and settle me.'"[53] Methodist Anna Neiderheiser's deaconess-biographers related that "her entire being seemed to take on an inner radiance" at consecration.[54] For all of these deaconesses, the consecration service linked together divine and ecclesial blessings and an inward and outward metamorphosis of the diaconal self.

Deaconesses likened the ritual of consecration to the ordination ceremony: "The deaconess differs from the missionary in that she has the official recognition of the church. . . . This is one of the most beautiful and impressive ritualistic services of the church. It is similar to the ordination of deacons and elders," explained Methodist deaconess Vennard.[55] Deaconesses felt that the legitimation and spiritual benefits imparted in their consecrations set them apart from all laypeople and placed them in a category shared only by the ordained ministry. Consecrations and ordinations were structurally similar. The consecration ritual was conducted in the church by a male officiant, either a minister or a bishop. Prayers were offered, and hymns like "Take My Life and Let It Be [Consecrated, Lord, to Thee]" were sung. Female biblical exemplars were invoked, sometimes Miriam and Deborah, Hannah and Huldah, Mary, and always Phoebe. Often deaconesses selected or were given a scripture verse to take as their motto for life.[56] The officiant asked candidates a series of questions committing them to the service of the Lord. Candidates knelt and the officiant laid hands on the deaconess candidates or prayed over them and then took each woman by the hand. The ceremony ended with prayer and with the presentation of the newly consecrated deaconesses.[57] As the liturgy of the Southern Methodist consecration service enjoined, "No doubt in the sacred stillness of the sanctuary of the heart you have already consecrated yourselves to this office and work. What you have done alone with God, you now do formally and publicly in the presence of the Church."[58]

Consecration, as both a formal ceremony and a spiritual discipline, linked deaconesses to the ministry but also set them apart in certain gendered ways. The Evangelical Synod consecration service exemplified the emphasis on feminine traits. Deaconess probationers were asked, "Will you especially consecrate yourselves to the Lord with self-denial, humility and love, to serve Him by ministering to the needy and helpless, endeavoring in all things to do what is well-pleasing unto Him?"[59] Self-denial, humility, and love were not the chief requirements of the male ministry. Episcopal historian Mary Sudman Donovan notes that while obedience to superiors was required of both Episcopal deacon-

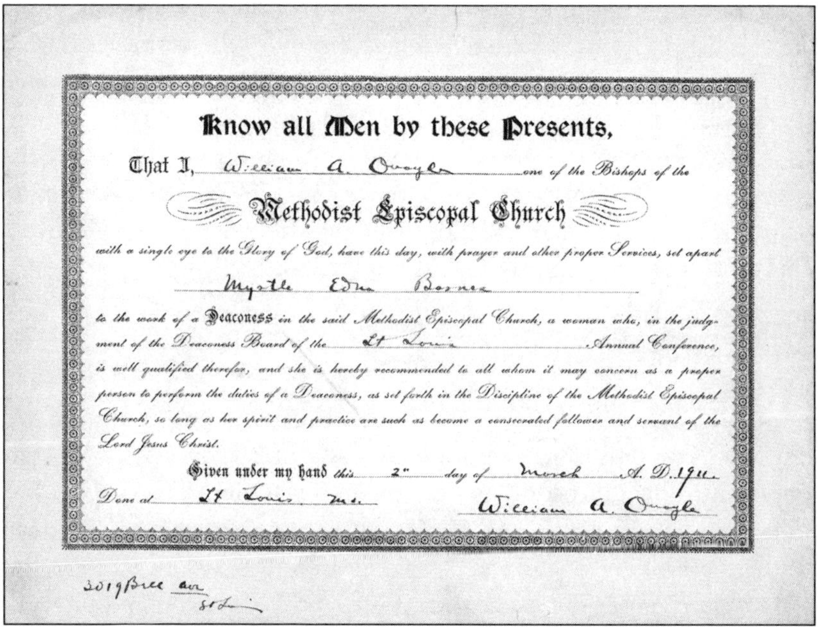

Know all Men by these Presents,

That I, William A. Quayle one of the Bishops of the

Methodist Episcopal Church

with a single eye to the Glory of God, have this day, with prayer and other proper Services, set apart

Myrtle Edna Barnes

to the work of a Deaconess in the said Methodist Episcopal Church, a woman who, in the judgment of the Deaconess Board of the St Louis Annual Conference, is well qualified therefor, and she is hereby recommended to all whom it may concern as a proper person to perform the duties of a Deaconess, as set forth in the Discipline of the Methodist Episcopal Church, so long as her spirit and practice are such as become a consecrated follower and servant of the Lord Jesus Christ.

Given under my hand this 2" day of March A. D. 1911.

Done at St Louis Mo. William A. Quayle

3019 Bell ave St Louis

Figure 5.1. Methodist Episcopal deaconess license. Author's collection.

esses and priests, it was the first promise a deaconess made at her consecration but the last promise a priest made at his ordination.[60]

The self-examination manual quoted above reveals that deaconesses' ongoing spiritual discipline was specifically coded as feminine. For deaconesses the pursuit of consecration entailed curbing an ostensibly female greed for frivolities—"Have I acquired the habit of wanting things unnecessary?"—and female tendency to gossip—"Do I murmur against my fellow-sisters and consider them as a burden?" Especially promoted were feminine attributes such as humility—"Am I not proud of my deaconess garb?"—and modesty—"Have I observed strict propriety toward men when meeting them was unavoidable?"[61] Consecration was gendered, as deaconess organizations continually endeavored to demonstrate "the fact that women lose none of the modesty, docility, tenderness, sympathy, nor other womanly quality, by being called and set apart to an office in the Church."[62] The heart of feminine consecration lay in self-sacrifice. Consecration was the way deaconesses were able to endure their arduous labors; consecration was why they donned the garb every morning; consecration was why they received an allowance instead of a salary. Consecration as feminine self-sacrifice was what set the deaconess apart from the minister. Women called to consecrate their lives to the diaconate were called not just as children of God but *as women*—as women were understood by Americans at the turn of the twentieth century. This gendered construction of the deaconess vocation helped make it acceptable to those who questioned women's place in a church office and circumscribed its scope accordingly.

Training and Education

As one Southern Methodist deaconess warned, "Let no one think, however, that only consecration is necessary for such work."[63] Just as important in the deaconess's understanding of her vocation was her training. Consecration and education were often linked as the crucial features of the diaconate, such as in this definition given in a Presbyterian Training School catalogue: "A Deaconess is a woman of devout Christian character and approved fitness who gives herself wholly to the service of Christ in connection with His Church and who has received special training for the work."[64] Advocates argued fiercely for education for deaconesses. They pointed out that a calling was a necessary but not sufficient qualification for the clergyman. Deaconesses, called like ministers, consecrated in a ceremony like the ordination of ministers, had both a right and a duty to receive training like ministers. In this way, the deaconess training school served as the female equivalent of the divinity school and was occasionally touted as such: the Presbyterian Training School "is seeking to do for women what the theological seminary is doing for men—equip them for their own special work."[65]

This nexus of consecration and training could be a source of conflict for deaconesses. In emphasizing their divine call and consecration, deaconesses distanced themselves from secular professions. Yet, at the same time, they sought the professional status that special training conveyed. Just like doctors, lawyers, and ministers, deaconesses claimed that standardized training was essential to their professional identities. They were especially keen to argue for the necessity of training any time they felt that their consecration to the work was being taken for granted. As one Episcopal author complained, "It is as little reasonable to expect an untrained girl to do the work of a parish visitor because she comes here to learn how, as to insist that a young man shall act as rector of a city parish because he has just entered the Divinity School."[66] Again, deaconesses invoked the example of the ministry as a career dedicated to God while still deserving of the respect due to the professions.

Deaconesses claimed that training differentiated them from ordinary women workers, who, although their hearts were in the right place, could not carry out their work in an organized and efficient manner. Deaconesses valued efficiency just as their ministerial brethren did. As early as 1899 one author declared, "Twenty five years ago, if a young woman was willing to teach, fitness was taken for granted and training was not considered." But now, "The day of the expert has come, and in every department of education, the first object is to train the student, to give the student the best training possible, to fit him for his work, to make him an expert."[67] Another Episcopal woman boasted the same year, "Wherever we find a member of a Sisterhood or a Deaconess at work, we are struck at once by the clear plan and direct method which governs all her efforts." In contrast, among "our great army" of women volunteers, "great forces are being wasted and splendid capabilities are lying dormant, for lack of system and discipline."[68] Deaconesses took professional pride in the training that equipped them to achieve this admirable efficiency, just as their ministerial counterparts did.

Specialized training did not always correlate with formal educational achievement. Particularly in the first few decades of the movement, fledgling deaconess institutions could not afford to set the educational bar too high. In all denominations college experience was rare; female college graduates were still scarce in the general population. In 1880, only 1.9 percent of women aged eighteen to twenty-one in the United States were enrolled in institutions of higher learning. In 1878, when Lutheran Rev. F. B. Meyer wrote of requirements for deaconess training, he listed first "knowledge of way to salvation," then Luther's Small Catechism, Bible verses, and hymns. He finally advised she be "acquainted with liturgy, reading, writing, arithmetic, geography."[69] Applications to the Cincinnati German Methodist Deaconess Home at the turn of the twentieth century reveal that low expectations were justified: almost all the applicants left school for work between the ages of fourteen and sixteen.[70] A few had difficulty writing their applications; Amelia Kenzler confessed, "Writing is quite a task, only what my parents taught me," which she followed with, "Have always been accustomed to labor."[71] Although lack of a high school degree was the norm, at least one applicant was encouraged by the Oberin to stay in school and apply again in a few years. The frustrated young woman replied, "I would like to go to school another year so bad but I do feel as I can not do this. A girl that has to earn every cent and gets no help from home is quite hard to go to school."[72] Working-class women of the German and Scandinavian denominations were not able to obtain as much education before beginning deaconess training as middle-class Episcopal, Presbyterian, and Anglophone Methodist women.

Educational levels of deaconess candidates rose in the twentieth century, and by the 1920s, deaconess training institutions were raising their educational standards. The Episcopal deaconess movement consistently attracted the most college students and graduates, due both to the higher socioeconomic level of Episcopalians and to the proximity of their deaconess institutions to colleges.[73] In the 1920s the Presbyterian Training Schools required applicants to have a high school education "or its equivalent," and added, "A college training is desirable."[74] A 1920s Methodist pamphlet echoed this ideal: "While a High School preparation is good, a College course is better. The best preparation is none too good for Christ's service."[75] By 1928, the Methodist Personnel Committee boasted that "only a few deaconesses have entered with less than high school requirement" and noted an increasing number of college graduates taking the course of study for deaconesses.[76]

While the Presbyterian and Methodist Episcopal churches were trying to raise their educational requirements, the German Methodists retained their more modest expectations. A 1922 recruiting pamphlet stipulated, "It is necessary that she should have finished the graded school and have at least one year of High School work." But there were exceptions even to this humble standard: "Where this is lacking a young woman of average intelligence and willingness to study hard need not to be discouraged. The year of High School work can be gotten at the Dorcas Institute."[77] Evangelical Synod deaconesses were in a similar position. An Evangelical recruiting pamphlet stipulated that candidates should have "*eine ziemlich gute Schulbildung*" (a fairly good education), and a 1921 application blank asked, "Where and how long did you go to school?"—inviting answers involving duration rather than degrees.[78] The St. Louis deaconesses of the former Evangelical Synod, interviewed in the early 1980s, downplayed their own educations and academic abilities and stressed physical or technical skills. Sisters Henrietta Lutten and Flora Pletz both reported that, in addition to their twelve-hour days of deaconess training, they had to take night school classes because they had not had any high school education.[79] Sister Betty Kunze recalled that all she could do was "hand work," and Sister Elsie Jungerman explained that she "was more for the daily routine" than for school.[80] Lutherans also downplayed formal education. Sister Julie Mergner, Oberin at the Philadelphia motherhouse, had this advice for deaconess candidates: "You do not need to feel badly if, on entering the deaconess house, you may not know much, nor be able to do much." "But," she concluded, "you must be ready to put forth all your strength, and be willing and diligent in learning wherever you are deficient."[81]

By 1930, the percentage of US college-age women attending school had risen to 10.5 percent.[82] The roughly four hundred deaconesses who appear in the 1940 census provide a snapshot comparison of educational achievement at the apex of the deaconess movement. Almost half of the Episcopal deaconesses in the 1940 census were college graduates, and 71 percent had some college. Anglophone Methodists followed in educational attainments: 60 percent had at least some college, 21 percent were high school graduates, and 19 percent had not finished high school. Even the German Methodists by now had a majority of deaconesses who were high school graduates. The numerous Lutheran deaconesses had a range of educational experiences: 21 percent had at least some college, and 25 percent were high school graduates, but the majority had not graduated high school. The Evangelical Synod remained at the bottom: three-fourths of the Evangelical Synod deaconesses had not finished high school.

Once women arrived for deaconess training, the education they received took varying forms in the different denominations and institutions. For the German denominations, the locus of training was in the hospital, where classes were mixed with practical nursing work. The 1901 curriculum for St. Louis Evangelical Synod deaconess probationers, for example, included classes in anatomy, physiology, nursing, German, English, Bible study, singing, and the history and principles of deaconess work, known as "diaconics." In Lutheran hospitals, physicians and deaconesses gave lectures and demonstrations.[83] Deaconess training in hospitals could be as short as two years but commonly lasted as long as seven years, after the European pattern.

The Methodists pioneered a different educational route, the religious training school, and the other Social Gospel denominations soon followed suit.[84] Dozens of training schools were founded in the last decades of the nineteenth century to train the lay men and especially women who were needed in YMCAs, settlement houses, missions, and, of course, deaconess work. Generally deaconess training in the training schools lasted for two years.[85] As in the hospitals, education in the training schools was eminently hands-on, combining lectures with applied learning in neighborhood visitation and institutional work. A Methodist curriculum published in 1922 included Methodist history and polity, evangelism, biblical studies and church history, comparative religion, Christian education, missions, "friendly visiting," and "Christian sociology."[86] The syllabus appears heavily influenced by the Social Gospel, but historian Priscilla Pope-Levison has convincingly argued that the training schools remained centrally focused on evangelism.[87] In the curriculum, Rauschenbusch's *Christianizing the Social Order* and Peabody's *Jesus Christ and the Social Question* are joined by F. D. Leete's *Everyday Evangelism*.[88]

Denominations without their own training schools came up with other ways of schooling their deaconesses. Several Mennonite deaconesses trained with the Evangelical Synod women in St. Louis.[89] Smaller institutions pooled their resources, such as the Presbyterian Training School in Philadelphia, which trained candidates jointly with the local Baptist Training School and the School for the Deaconesses of the Protestant Episcopal Church.[90] The United Brethren Church offered two avenues of training: a two-year self-directed course of study, including Bible studies, United Brethren and deaconess history, and Christian sociology, with the presiding elder or pastor administering examinations, or "an equivalent course in an approved training-school, or literary school providing such courses." Furthermore, "The deaconess desirous to become a nurse should take the course of training for that purpose in a school connected with a good hospital."[91]

The denominationally diverse training shared important features. First of all, the training was specialized. "This is the age of specialists; no one would hope to succeed in a life-work without special training for it. If this is true in our secular life, why should it not be true in our Christian service?" asked one deaconess.[92] As with secular training schools of this era, deaconess training was concise and practical and focused on the acquisition of certain skills. Classes were always connected with applied hands-on work in hospitals, in churches, or on the streets. A Presbyterian student applauded her training school for this balance: "The class-room work of the Home is especially helpful. The course of training is planned so that each class supplements the others, and is so practical that as surely as you meet a need in your work, something which you have learned in class comes to your mind—a friend in need."[93]

Deaconess training was also devotional. The quest to balance academics with the spiritual life revealed tensions between education and consecration. Deaconess advocates were wary of relying too much on practical training and not enough on God. Deaconess evangelist Vennard cautioned, "The point to be guarded in all our training for religious work is that we do not become so self assured in our book knowledge and human methods that we forget the absolute essential of the fiery unction of the Holy Ghost."[94] Thus classes were interspersed with chapel sessions, and Bible studies were intended to be both factual and devotional. Deaconess training was not designed to impart only knowledge and skills; it was meant to cultivate the deaconess spirit.

An article in the 1921 yearbook of the Kansas City National Training School described the school's regular devotional pattern. Daily, each student observed fifteen minutes of silent meditation and prayer in her room before attending a morning chapel service, which featured "heartfelt singing and [a] practical message" and a scripture lesson read by one of the students. Each evening after dinner there was family worship: "After singing a familiar hymn, we kneel, while two or three voice our prayer to God." In addition to these three daily prayer and worship times, there was a weekly class prayer meeting in the girls' rooms: "These prayer meetings add to the class spirit and draw the girls nearer to each other and to Christ, as nothing else can." Students highlighted the Saturday evening prayer meeting in the chapel, led by their superintendent, Miss Neiderheiser, as "an hour when all feel free to praise God and worship as the Spirit leads. The testimonies given always prove to be just what we are needing most."[95] In training schools, hospitals, and motherhouses, deaconess students' education was saturated with prayer, scripture, and worship. In this ideal balance, according to a German Methodist, "The nourishment of the spiritual life is coupled with every phase of the training school."[96]

Another important characteristic of deaconess education was that it was ongoing. Formally or informally, deaconesses continued their education throughout their careers. Significant numbers received college or advanced degrees after they were consecrated deaconesses. While not specifically asked about it, many of the St. Louis sisters interviewed in 1981 offered that they took various courses at neighboring Washington University or Barnes College of Nursing. One earned her master's degree.[97] German immigrant Elizabeth Lotz, who struggled with learning English during her deaconess training, proceeded to attend classes at Brookes Bible Institute and Eden Seminary, earn her B.S. in nursing from Washington University, and take a postgraduate course in psychiatrics at City Hospital—all while serving as a deaconess.[98] "We were proud to be R.N.s," enthused Sister Olivia Drusch, after she and her sisters passed their newly required state board exams. An older deaconess, Frieda Eckhoff, who instead of taking the board exam was "waived in," was "kind of sorry I fell for that," perhaps because she felt denied some legitimation of her educational attainments.[99] Deaconesses and their administrators encouraged this ongoing pursuit of education. In 1924, for example, the Methodist General Deaconess Board counseled that "there should be devised a plan by which a deaconess can gain increased knowledge of specialized fields of service. When a deaconess shows adaptation and has given a period of years in a chosen field she should be furnished with funds for advanced study in perfecting herself in a given work."[100] Of Methodist deaconesses surveyed in 1925, 104 reported that postgraduate work would better prepare them for their particular line of work, and only twelve disagreed.[101]

Education was a crucial component of a deaconess's life and professional self-understanding. What made deaconess education unique is that it was always viewed through the lens of consecration. The desires of self were to be sacrificed for the Lord's work. When a Lutheran applicant asked Sister Superior Julie Mergner if she could attend medical school as a deaconess, the Oberin consented, but with this caveat: "Should ability or circumstances prevent you from carrying out this desire in which you unite with us, then be prepared to serve the Lord among His needy ones in some other capacity. Place yourself entirely and with childlike obedience in the hands of the Lord."[102] An Evangelical Synod deaconess began a college course in dietetics but was called back to the mother-house before she could finish.[103] Education was valued, but it was assumed that education would serve the greater good of the Lord's work. As Lucy Rider Meyer passionately wrote, "But what my art, my literary pursuits, my society? May I not live for them? No, no, no! In a world full of souls with eternal life or death just before them . . . no one has a right to live for art, or for literature, or for science, or society, or wealth."[104] All endeavors, education especially, were to be sanctified and placed in the service of saving souls.

Call, consecration, and education all worked together to define the deaconess office as an analogue of the ordained ministry. Like ministers, deaconesses were called, trained, and given official recognition in a formal ceremony. Yet with consecration at its heart, the deaconess office was specifically gendered by the key role of self-sacrifice. All of these facets help explain deaconesses' ambivalence about ordination.

"But She Doesn't Preach"

Despite the lack of support they may have received from their own pastors, deaconesses linked their office with the ordained ministry in a myriad of ways. They were called, trained, and ritually initiated like ministers. In the Social Gospel denominations, they were praised for performing pastoral work better than the ministers themselves. But most deaconesses declined to rap on the stained glass ceiling of ordination.[105] Deaconesses sought to perform whatever functions they deemed necessary to the exercise of their office—pastoral work, public prayer, even preaching—while stopping short of demanding ordination. They viewed the diaconate, rather than the ordained ministry, as their unique calling as women. Pastors and deaconesses agreed that deaconesses excelled at pastoral visiting. When deaconesses sought to practice more highly valued tasks such as preaching or liturgical or sacramental duties, they were more likely to encounter resistance from their ministerial colleagues. Deaconesses found creative ways of using the role of pastor and preaching to accomplish their callings, when necessary, and negotiating with church power structures.

In the opinion of most churchmen, a deaconess's place in the Sunday worship service was in the pew with the rest of the women, not in the pulpit. Male church hierarchies had no desire to see deaconesses exercise liturgical functions in worship, which, as noted above, remained a respectably masculine part of the newly professionalized ministry. One deaconess recalled "playing church" as a child, "and going through each part of the worship. I did not know my father was watching me until I came to the end and started to put up my hand, as I had seen our minister do when he gave the benediction. My father stopped me and told me that I must never do that."[106] This staunch Presbyterian father apparently was amused until he saw his daughter begin to perform a liturgical act that, as a woman, she "must never do." Many Protestants, especially those in the German denominations, shared this antipathy to women's public role in worship. In his *Deaconess Calling*, used in training Lutheran candidates, Rev. Emil Wacker offered this alternate explanation of why the deaconess office in the early church declined:

> If the chief strength of the female diaconate of the early church, actually lay in its functions at the worship of the congregation, it was a mistake, and could not bear the test of time. A touching of the hem of the Lord's garment is the most that can be permitted to women. And extreme tact and discretion are required, to prevent even the small ministrations that may be allowed, from outraging churchly propriety. . . . The female diaconate of the early church approached too near the "altar"; withdrew too far from the "doors"; it took upon itself too much of the ministry in the church, at the expense of the ministry in the congregation.[107]

The women studying Wacker's textbook doubtless heard clearly the warning against approaching too near the altar.

In 1922, deaconesses and their advocates in the Episcopal Church attempted to regularize the deaconess's ability to participate in worship by amending the official Deaconess Canon to authorize the deaconess "to officiate in public worship as her office allows, and when licensed thereto by the Bishop."[108] The General Convention rejected the committee's proposed draft, arguing, "Officiating in public worship should be limited to occasions 'in the absence of a Priest or Deacon'; otherwise according to the provisions of the Canon it would be open to a Clergyman to employ a Deaconess to read or preach in the ordinary services, greatly to the displeasure and distress of many devout worshipers."[109] The failed amendment reveals the resistance against women performing these traditional priestly tasks. Yet, allowing deaconesses to officiate in the absence of a priest acknowledged the reality that deaconesses were already taking charge of Sunday worship when there was no clergyman available, and not just in the Episcopal Church. When the Philadelphia *Evening Public Ledger* ran an article about Presbyterian deaconess Bessie Buchanan in 1918, headlined "Woman Pastor of City Church," a bold-typed subheading declared, "But She Doesn't Preach" (figure 5.2). Buchanan had been the pastor's assistant for two years, and upon his departure, "The duties and authority of actual pastor fell upon her, with the exception of preaching, performing marriages, and pronouncing benediction."[110] Apparently Buchanan's "authority" did not include sacramental or homiletic authority, those very aspects of the professionalized ministry that had been deemed most masculine. Although the article does not mention it, this situation may have resulted from the wartime manpower shortage.

The specific issue of deaconesses preaching was handled quite differently in different denominations. Most denominations forbade it. In a 1902 Southern Methodist article entitled "What a Deaconess Is, and What She Is Not," the first two apophatic qualities were "1. She is *not a preacher*" and "2. She is *not ordained*."[111] A Lutheran brochure's lyrical invitation to the diaconate screeched to a halt at the issue of preaching: "The field for the Female Diaconate is as broad as sanctified human sympathy. Nothing to counteract sin and suffering is outside of the sphere of the Deaconess, except public preaching."[112] Denominations that did not forbid deaconesses from preaching, particularly the Methodists, were at best ambivalent about it, as illustrated by the postcard in figure 5.3. Titled, "Miss Knapp, the Deaconess," it pictures a garbed woman standing at or near the pulpit of the Middlesex Methodist Episcopal Church. Did she preach? We do not know. The large Bible on the pulpit is closed; the book of "Sacred Songs" on the adjacent lectern is open. Someone was at least comfortable enough with the image of her standing behind the pulpit to print it on a postcard. As Catherine Brekus pointed out of early-nineteenth-century women preachers, "The pulpit was not simply an elevated space at the front of the church, but a symbol of men's exclu-

WOMAN PASTOR OF CITY CHURCH

Deaconess Buchanan Is in Charge of Hollond Congregation

BUT SHE DOESN'T PREACH

Trained at the Presbyterian School to Conduct Meetings and Visit Sick

Hollond Memorial Presbyterian Church, Broad and Federal streets, has a woman pastor. This is one of the most important churches attached to the Philadelphia Presbytery.

Deaconess Bessie Buchanan is in charge of the church.

The honor was bestowed upon Deaconess Buchanan a year ago when the Rev. Gustav A. Briegleb, the pastor, accepted a call in Los Angeles, leaving the church in her charge. She had been his assistant for two years, having been graduated from the Philadelphia Dea-

MISS BESSIE BUCHANAN
Who fills the pastorate of the Hollond Memorial Presbyterian Church, Broad and Federal streets. She is a deaconess, graduate of the Philadelphia School for Christian Workers of

Figure 5.2. Newspaper clipping of "Woman Pastor of City Church: Miss Bessie Buchanan," *Evening Public Ledger*, March 29, 1918, p.m. edition.

Figure 5.3. "Miss Knapp, the Deaconess." Postcard, postmarked 1906. Author's collection.

sive authority to interpret Scripture."[113] Though Brekus wrote of early- and mid-nineteenth-century women preachers, a woman in the pulpit was still an unusual sight in 1906.

The history of deaconess preaching was characterized by periodic advances and retrenchments, as was the larger history of women preaching. The Methodist Church had issued local preachers' licenses to women beginning in 1869 but revoked all women's licenses in 1880 (coincidentally, or not, the same year the deaconess office was formally recognized).[114] Not until 1920 did women regain the local preacher's license.[115] The Methodist Episcopal Church cautiously recruited deaconess evangelists: "Some women—though not many—have gifts especially fitting them for this most delicate and important work; ability to use persuasive speech; power in appeal to individual or mass; a voice that, in song or speech, wings its way to the hearer's heart. Such women the church needs for evangelism."[116] By 1925, fifty-one Methodist deaconesses held local preachers' licenses, and at least one Episcopal deaconess and one African Methodist Episcopal Zion deaconess from this early period were licensed to preach.[117]

Licensed or not, deaconesses throughout the period served as evangelists, and there was slippage between evangelizing and preaching. Deaconesses tended to downplay their preaching. An Episcopal deaconess working with Native Americans confessed, "The ever faithful priest sends word that he is suddenly called away and in ten minutes you are in charge of the service and—shall I say—preaching a sermon."[118] Earlier we saw Methodist Lucy Rider Meyer soft-pedal the role of her "evangelistic" deaconesses: "Their work is far less ostentatious" than public preaching, she insisted.[119] United Brethren deaconess Mellie Perkins used self-deprecating humor to describe her homiletic efforts: "The one who teaches school five full days out of the week, keeps house, attends the sick, fills all the places in religious services, and writes from 60–110 letters and cards a month cannot do much at preaching."[120] Methodist Miss Buchanan (presumably no relation to the nonpreaching Presbyterian Bessie Buchanan) used the same strategy of self-effacement, along with emphasis on God's agency, to describe her own preaching: "It seems strange to me, even yet, to have charge of the Sunday morning services, for I have always dreaded public work, as you know. But the Lord helps me, and I always ask Him to give me thoughts that will help those who come to the service. Everything considered, it is surprising that so many come."[121] Deaconesses faced significant objections to their pastoring and preaching. Although some clergymen were loyal supporters, others policed the boundaries of their profession jealously, joining Rev. Emil Wacker in warning women not to approach too near the altar. When a hostile opponent accused Vennard of being a woman preacher, she appealed to the legitimation of her deaconess office, replying, "I am a consecrated and licensed deaconesses, but I have accepted invitations from pastors to assist them in evangelistic campaigns."[122] Much like their preaching foremothers, deaconesses used various strategies to render their preaching less objectionable to the church powers: highlighting an exigent situation, their own reluctance to preach, or a divine call that emphasized God's agency and their passivity. Although the deaconess office gave them some legitimacy in the church, these women were closed off from the regular access to the preaching profession afforded by seminary education and ordination. God's call was thus all the more important for legitimating their preaching. As Catherine Brekus writes of late-eighteenth- and early-nineteenth-century women, "Female preachers insisted that they had personally encountered the divine through dreams, visions, or voices. . . . They defended themselves against their critics by arguing that God had issued them an extraordinary call which could not be refused."[123]

These earlier preachers emphasized their personal reluctance to preach, and later deaconesses echoed the conviction that only God's direct call could overcome their opposition to women preaching. Iva Durham Vennard's biographer recalls her reluctance to begin preaching in the 1890s: despite feeling a call to evangelism, "She just did *not* approve of women preachers. It was all right to speak, to lecture, to give messages, but to come out in the open as a *woman preacher*—that did not appeal to her at all." Although Vennard prayed for guidance with the "secret hope that 'He would excuse me from preaching, and let me be perhaps a singer or a social worker,'" the divine commission to evangelize would not leave her.[124]

In another example, Dr. Willia Caffray emphasized that preaching was never her idea. As a brand-new Methodist deaconess, Caffray was assigned to do evangelistic work in Wisconsin. When asked to preach, she objected, and the pastor encouraged her simply to give her testimony—night after night. Caffray recounts suffering through two weeks of testifying, as souls were saved, only to travel to the next town and be asked to preach all over again. She protested to the Lord in prayer and received the answer, "'Ye have not chosen me, but I have chosen you and *ordained you.* . . .' 'Lord,' I replied, 'If you want me to preach I will preach.' The question was *settled* at last and my call to be an evangelist has never wavered." Caffray does not explain the provenance of the reply she received to her prayers—perhaps she thought it obvious—but the words are verbatim from the King James version of John 15:16, lending additional weight and authority to her direct revelation. Caffray eventually resigned from the diaconate so that she could widen her ministry, seeking and obtaining a local preacher's license "seven minutes after the new law went into effect" in 1920.[125] In the face of strong resistance, deaconesses Iva Durham Vennard and Willia Caffray both emphasized this personal divine encounter overturning their own objection to women preachers.

Deaconesses seem to have employed an "everything but" strategy in their work. Presbyterian Bessie Buchanan pastored a church, doing everything but preaching, marrying, and serving communion. Methodist Vennard led revival after revival but did not want to preach. Methodist Iva Conner did the work of an associate pastor but did not claim the title (or salary). Episcopalian Gertrude Jean Baker ran the Sunday service and preached the sermon, but only when the priest was absent. This strategy of leaving some function exclusively in ministerial hands, whether preaching or sacramental administration, may have helped deaconesses do the work they wanted to do without alienating their ministerial allies and fellow church members.

Of course, the biggest claim they left on the table was ordination itself. In the 1920s, a few deaconesses and their supporters began to advocate for women's ordination. Methodist deaconesses and laywomen workers surveyed in 1927 reported "a general desire and interest in an official relationship to the church for all full time women workers. Some think this should be the deaconess organization, others prefer ordination and equality with men in the Annual Conference."[126] A commission on "Women's Work in the Church as Related to Deaconess Work" was engaged to study the issue.[127] The discussions over women's ordination reveal the tensions over the gendered nature of the ordained ministry.

In the Episcopal Church, there was disagreement as to whether deaconesses were admitted to Holy Orders upon their consecrations. In 1921, an Episcopal priest denied the admissibility of women to Holy Orders, either in the diaconate or as priests, on the grounds that "we need a more virile presentation of Christianity, in the pulpit and elsewhere."[128] A deaconess speaking at the Methodist Deaconess Educational Conference two years later took this argument and turned it on its head: "There are those who think that the pulpit would lose its virility if women were allowed to enter it, but virility is not necessarily masculinity! It is vigor, sincerity, clear thinking, and the result of persistent, open-minded study, expressed through a personality alive and alert to life and its throbbing currents."[129] In a subversion of traditional gendered norms, this deaconess hoped to bring a feminine virility into the pulpit.

Rather than urging women's ordination, however, more deaconesses spent their pamphleteering energy promoting the diaconate as an appealing alternative to the ministry, specifically designed for women. In a 1952 tract, an Episcopal college student laments, "If I had only been born the boy that Father and Mother wanted, there would not be the slightest question in my mind as to what I would like to do. . . . Why the ministry of the Church, of course!" Her aunt's reply neither quashes nor encourages the young woman's ministerial ambitions but redirects them into a parallel vocation: "Anne, I think you should be a Deaconess!"[130]

In 1974, several Episcopal women deacons (as deaconesses were by then known) generated enormous controversy by seeking and receiving ordination from a sympathetic group of bishops, becoming known as the "Philadelphia 11." Nine other women deacons wrote a letter of remonstrance against the action, "extend[ing] their love and compassion" to their sisters but expressing their "profound regret at the action taken." The authors did not object explicitly to women's ordination but rather to the defiance of the Canons and Constitution of the church. It is illustrative of the diversity of diaconal opinion on women's ordination that the authors chose to side with the church authority and reaffirm their vows "to reverently obey their Bishops" rather than to support the Philadelphia 11's bold move on behalf of women's ordination to the priesthood.[131]

Deaconesses in the Social Gospel denominations often did the work of the clergy, certainly pastoral work and even preaching, so a discussion of women's ordination was a live issue for them. Deaconesses in the German denominations were less likely to equate their vocations with the ordained ministry because they usually served as hospital nurses and rarely as parish workers. The St. Louis United Church of Christ deaconesses revealed this when they were interviewed in their later years. When asked whether they would have attended seminary and sought ordination if it had been available to them, they almost unanimously demurred. They "never thought about it," were "interested in nursing," and "never felt [the ministry] was my life."[132] But from the perspective of 1981, they were almost all in favor of women's ordination, ranging from an "I guess it's alright" to an enthusiastic, "That's great. That's wonderful."[133]

This lack of deaconess consensus on the issue of women's ordination highlights the importance of listening to the sources before reaching facile conclusions about the movement. As we have seen, many scholars have hailed deaconesses as paving the way to women's ordination.[134] Other women's historians have dismissed the movement precisely because deaconesses did not demand ordination, instead occupying positions of "subordination and subservience."[135] In reality, most deaconesses did not broach the question of ordination, even as they were called, trained, and authorized like clergymen, and as they performed many ministerial functions. Instead they constructed their own vocation that expanded women's opportunities in the church even as it was grounded in an understanding of sacrificial female consecration. The relationship between deaconess and clergyman was multifaceted. Sometimes the two vocations were complementary, such as when ministerial advocates promoted the movement and when deaconesses supported the professionalization of the ministry. Sometimes the two were at odds, such as when pastors proved impediments to deaconesses struggling to realize their vocations or circumscribed the scope of their work. In the end, the ordained ministry was a model for the diaconate but an unreachable, and generally unsought, goal. Deaconesses in the twentieth century who began to question the gendered model of ordination for men and consecration for women portended a sea change in thinking about the female diaconate.

6

Differing Visions for the Diaconate

In 1927, Olivia Drusch entered her four-year training to be an Evangelical Synod deaconess. Interviewed in the 1980s, she recounted her experiences:

> One of the things which bothered me most during my probationary period was the attitude of the older sisters. Two of us of our class of five had been on our own and were used to making our own decisions. But the sisters treated us like children. This often led to friction and many conferences with the Superintendent, Rev. F. P. Jens. I remember one New Year's Eve, a group of six of us wanted to go out with an older nurse and her husband, to see the New Year in. The sisters were shocked and told us to see Rev. Jens for his permission. We told him all that we were going to do was to go to a late supper at a hotel, see a floor show, and then return shortly after midnight. We must have been quite persuasive as all he said was, "Take the Lord with you." We had a grand time, but some of the sisters felt we were not good material for the sisterhood.[1]

Sister Magdalena Gerhold, the superior with whom Sister Olivia clashed, entered the St. Louis motherhouse in 1891. Magdalena's father was a German immigrant, and her mother was the daughter of German immigrants. She probably grew up speaking German at home. For miles around her, aside from one schoolteacher and one minister, every man claimed his occupation as farming and every woman as "keeping house."[2] Six of her eight siblings became farmers themselves, a brother became a minister, and a sister followed her into the diaconate. Magdalena saw no examples of women living by themselves and working for wages or combining family and career. For Magdalena, entering the diaconate at age nineteen was an opportunity to have a vocation of her own. By age twenty-five, she was head of the motherhouse, a position she held for more than thirty years. Magdalena and the generation of women that founded the deaconess movement in the United States made use of the limited options available to them to create a life of consecration. They extracted a word from the Bible, "deaconess," and applied it to the ideal of a sanctified life devoted to Christian service, in which family, salary, ambition, romance, sexual relationships, and personal liberty were all sacrificed for the glory of the Kingdom.

Of course, the deaconess ideal was just that. The model of unmarried women in uniform dress living together in harmonious and self-sufficient community was difficult to maintain from the beginning. Into the twentieth century, the deaconess ideal became more difficult to sustain as new generations of women emerged who did not grow up under the same cultural constraints as their older sisters. The founders had woven the work of service tightly into a life of self-denial to create the tapestry of the deaconess vocation. It must have seemed to Magdalena and her sisters that Olivia's generation was determined to tear the fabric apart. Little did they know that yet another generation would emerge who would weave the tapestry anew.

Olivia Drusch, who entered the St. Louis motherhouse in 1927, was also the daughter of a German immigrant. Olivia grew up in a small town, rather than on a farm. "I had to earn my own way at an early age," Olivia explained, and when she did, she had some choices. She took a business course after high school and secured a position in payroll at the local factory that employed many of her neighbors. She was living not with her family but "on her own," and although she enjoyed her job, she began looking for something else, something in the field of nursing. After journeying to St. Louis and meeting Sister Magdalena, she "found [her] goal in life." Although she became a dedicated deaconess, Sister Olivia saw nothing wrong with secular entertainment, in the "mixed company" of men as well as women.[3] Both women chose the diaconate, but Olivia had choices that Magdalena did not, and Olivia sought to be a deaconess on her own terms. Sister Magdalena's and Sister Olivia's stories illustrate two themes as particularly important to the changing diaconate in the twentieth century: the impact of evolving expectations for marriage and family on women's community; and increased opportunities for working women enabling them to enjoy a new commercialized leisure culture.

Changing Ideas about Marriage and the Community of Women

Although Sister Olivia Drusch chose the single life of the diaconate, her peers were combining career and marriage in new ways, like her married nurse friend from New Year's Eve. Of course, deaconesses had been marrying from the earliest days of the movement, but at the cost of their deaconess relationship. In the twentieth century, women began to question whether the deaconess vocation required forsaking marriage. That shift in thinking came slowly and necessitated a new understanding of the deaconess community. Although there had always been a wide variation of living arrangements for deaconesses, particularly in Anglophone denominations and beyond the larger motherhouses, the diaconate was understood as a community of women and for women. Into the twentieth century, it became harder to argue that a homosocial community was "healthy" for women. In the founding decades, the language of health was deployed to differentiate deaconesses from anti-Catholic images of consumptive nuns. In the mid-twentieth century, discussions of deaconess health shifted, away from single-sex communities and toward heterosexual relationships.

In 1937, the Evangelical and Reformed Church (successor to the Evangelical Synod) surveyed current and former deaconesses as to their opinions on the "deaconess idea." The sixty-seven replies revealed great concern over the homosocial life of the deaconess. Of the current deaconesses, thirty-eight agreed that association with members of the opposite sex was essential to their happiness, and only fifteen disagreed. These women rejected the demands of modesty of their nineteenth-century foremothers, who were instructed to observe "strict propriety toward men when meeting them was unavoidable."[4] Several current and former deaconesses commented to this effect: "For persons of the opposite sex to associate is a perfectly normal thing, and any normal girl should take the opportunity occasionally in order to maintain a level and normal mind rather than to become narrow and sour on everyone and all modern ideas and customs."[5]

Here, the stand-in for "healthy" was the use, three times within the sentence, of the therapeutically inflected "normal." This period of suspicion of the traditional homosocial life of the deaconess maps onto the period within Protestantism of the construction of the "homosexual" as a deviant type, replacing earlier understandings of "sodomy" as a more diffuse and less specific sexual sin. Historian of religion and sexuality Heather White has argued that during this period, the development of pastoral counseling contributed to the construction of the homosexual and the distrust of same-sex bonds that were formerly regarded as benign.[6]

This evolving valuation of opposite-sex relationships as "healthy" and "normal" transformed the deaconess vocation. First of all, it was a notable reason given by women for leaving, or not joining, the order, contributing to the sharp dip in numbers at the mid-twentieth century. Moreover, it contributed to the most important development of this era, the new conceptualization of the married deaconess. In the 1920s and 1930s, Methodists explored the possibility of continuing their service as married women. The stories of three deaconesses reveal the poignancy of this transitional era. In 1921 Ida Marian Swett sorrowfully wrote the Deaconess Board to ask for honorable discharge after becoming Mrs. Treganza. She was ebullient about her new marriage but expressed her regret at losing her association with her deaconess sisters: "Nobody loves me any more at the Training School, I believe. At least I don't hear much. Maybe they think I have love enough. Well, I can always stand a <u>little</u> more."[7] Ida Marian recognized that her new marriage was an approved expression of love, but she resisted the idea that it could replace entirely her emotional need for her deaconess sisters.

Fifteen years later, Annie Raddin French wrote the deaconess board in the same circumstances but gently pressed the matter: "Unless some recommendation can be made to General Conference regarding the plan for married women to be continued in the deaconess relationship I shall have to ask for an honorable discharge. . . . I wonder if the Board will consider it?"[8] Apparently the board did not consider it. The records state, somewhat misleadingly, "Mrs. Annie Raddin French . . . requested honorable discharge, she having been married in February to Mr. Richard A. French of Westfield."[9] The next year, however, Martha Bowers Grant took a different approach with the Deaconess Board, writing, "I have no intention of requesting an honorable discharge from the deaconess work so long as I am in the active service. That I should be expected to do so seems to me very unfair and unjust." Grant concluded, "If I am dropped from the deaconess roster while I am in the active service, it will not be at my wish nor request."[10] Despite Grant's appeal to the bishop, the board stood firm and discharged her, informing her that her deaconess relationship was automatically severed the day she married.[11] It was another twenty years before the marriage prohibition was officially lifted in Methodism. In 1959, the Commission on Deaconess Work, consisting of men, laywomen, and deaconesses, agreed that there should be no discrimination against a married deaconess so long as she was available for appointment.[12]

Changing Ideas about Work and Allowance

The allowance system provided deaconesses the necessities of life without implicating them in the wage economy. But by the first decades of the twentieth century, deaconesses began to chafe at the paternalism of the allowance. In their fictive roles as "daughters," deaconesses were expected to leave money matters to the motherhouse *in loco parentis* (or as quasi-wives receiving a marital allowance). The flip side of the assurances of room, board, and care was the deprivation of the women's ability to make their own fiscal decisions. As the diaconate sought to maintain the allowance system, more American women were working for money in new ways, and many of the roles deaconesses played began emerging as professions of their own.[13] With the proliferation of nursing schools, nursing was no longer the sole province of religious sisterhoods, Catholic and Protestant. Social work was slowly gaining standing as a profession. Churches increasingly hired laywomen as church secretaries and directors of Christian education. And, although most churches remained reluctant to ordain female clergy, women continued to evangelize in disparate ways. In the 1900s, women who went to the cities had additional employment opportunities in department stores, offices, or large factories in addition to the traditional opportunities for domestic service or piecework.[14] These new jobs appealed to a woman who wanted to clock in and out on a defined work day, with pay envelope, albeit small, in hand, and the ability to spend both her discretionary money and her time as she pleased.

American women as a whole were gaining more access to money. Women workers' wages were slowly rising, and wives were gaining access to domestic money through allowances and joint bank accounts.

Even though society still clung to a needs-based ideal for women's wages, there was at least a grudging acceptance that women's needs were growing.[15] The heyday of the deaconess movement, 1880 to 1930, has been identified as "the crucial formative years" of American capitalist consumer culture.[16] With the increased availability of items such as pianos, stockings, and cosmetics, "General consumer expenditures expanded fivefold between 1900 and 1929."[17] In addition to the things money could buy were the pleasures of "commercialized leisure": a night spent at the nickelodeon or the dance hall.[18] For working women, even a small paycheck offered the promise of financial independence and the chance to participate in the economy as consumers of goods and leisure. Deaconesses were denied (or, as the founders insisted, sacrificed) this opportunity and increasingly many came to resent it. The assurance of one pastor in 1930 that "the Lord will not let you starve if you labor for him" was cold comfort for women presented with a smorgasbord of consumer pleasures designed for their delight.[19]

When, over the years, women exhibited a preference for a salary, allowance advocates took this as a sign of moral decline in the young women of America. A Methodist deaconess speaking in the 1920s insisted that the many secular, salaried opportunities for women were not per se a threat to the diaconate; the problem was that "the womanhood of America lacks spiritual fervor."[20] The deaconesses of the Methodist Woman's Home Missionary Society prepared a statement in the early twentieth century addressing the situation: "In recent years such an emphasis has been placed on the monetary rewards for service and on the power of position and preferment, in all lines of work, that the young people are in danger of becoming blinded to the real spirit of service, which ever has been and ever must be, sacrifice." These women sounded the clarion call of the diaconate, consecrated self-sacrifice. The statement continued, "The moment the emphasis is changed from the service to the personal reward for service, power is lost."[21] While the words are not explicitly gendered, "power" evokes the power gained by purity of female desirelessness.

Although the founding deaconess leaders found ways of coding their desire for money as acceptable, "personal reward" was never to be the goal. In a 1931 letter, an elderly Episcopalian declared herself flummoxed by the clamor for a significant salary by her younger deaconess sisters:

"I certainly desire to help you in any way possible, but I can not see how my life in the Order can be of any help to you, because I belong to the pioneer age, whereas you wish to 'memorialize' the Gen[eral] Con[vention] on the present condition of deaconesses, not the condition of a full generation ago, when things were so very different. . . . As to salary, about which you wish to 'memorialize,' I have no personal knowledge (see card) but I at least know it is very much better than any I received."[22] Younger deaconesses who desired a salary, rather than being fulfilled by the rendering of the service itself, were defining themselves according to a different standard of womanhood than their older sisters did. A 1921 Episcopal committee studying the decline in candidates came to the following terse and problematic conclusions: "value of women's work emphasized, but economic question loomed, few parishes can pay for women workers, but deaconesses need much better salaries than those that are available."[23]

Midcentury Crisis and Women's Ordination

In a 1939 *Deaconess Messenger* article entitled "Calls for Help Unheeded," Pastor E. F. Bachman rued, "New requests for deaconesses for parish and institutional work could not be filled because of lack of Sisters. We feel keenly that far too few of the capable young women of the Church respond to the plea for laborers in the Lord's harvest."[24] Voices from the Episcopal Church, the Methodist Church,[25] and elsewhere joined the Lutheran minister's lament. From the earliest days, deaconess advocates had bemoaned that their numbers did not grow as quickly as hoped, but by the middle of the twentieth century, these pleas reached fever pitch. In a 1945 story, "Lutheran Motherhouses Face Their Problems," another author lamented, "On all sides one faced the scarcity of workers; and the Church's institutions suffer. Motherhouses are sorely distressed by the heavy burdens this places upon the individual deaconess who strives to carry on. . . . They are asking of the young women of the Church, 'Is it nothing to you, all ye that pass by?' . . . WHAT CAN WE DO to increase the number of our workers?"[26] By the mid-twentieth century, the question was, would the deaconess movement survive?

In these uncertain decades, another development shook the diaconate: during the mid-twentieth century, almost all of the denominations that had established deaconess offices began to ordain women. The Evangelical and Reformed Church permitted the ordination of women in 1949. Although Methodist women had become eligible for local preachers' licenses in 1920, they gained full clergy rights in 1956, the same year the Presbyterian Church began ordaining women as ministers. The Lutheran Church in America (precursor to the Evangelical Lutheran Church of America) permitted women's ordination in 1970, and the Episcopal Church followed suit in 1976. Of the hundreds of deaconesses who were serving during these few decades, only about a dozen can be documented as leaving the diaconate for the ordained ministry, a fact that deaconess proponents took pains to point out.[27] Seven years after her church granted full clergy rights to women, Methodist Elizabeth Meredith Lee explained, "When a deaconess is accepted for full membership in an Annual Conference [as an ordained pastor], she thereby relinquishes her deaconess relationship. Few deaconesses have desired clergy rights."[28] Writing in 1984, Lutheran minister Frederick Weiser allowed that several deaconesses had left for the ordained ministry but emphasized the consequences of doing so: "Some [deaconesses-turned-pastors] would have liked to continue in the fellowship of the sisterhood, but the ministry of the word and the ministry of serving love are themselves disparate gifts. Wisely the Lutheran church insisted that they not be mixed."[29]

If, as some historians have argued, the deaconess movement was merely a transitional site, offering women access to vocations in the church in lieu of ordination, it should have disappeared by the 1970s, as its mission was complete. Some churches did in fact phase out the office. But in other church bodies, the late twentieth century provided the opportunity, catalyzed by alarmingly low recruitment numbers, to rethink and articulate anew the need for the office of deaconess. Deaconess bodies that survived and thrived into the twenty-first century made a number of modifications. Up to today, women have continued to adapt the deaconess office in creative ways to live out a distinctive Christian calling.

Fading Away: Evangelical Synod Deaconesses Disappear

The Evangelical Synod represents one path deaconess bodies took in the face of the changes of the twentieth century.[30] These deaconesses were prepared to make some changes and accommodations but eventually were willing to let the office come to an end rather than redefine it to an extent that made it, to them, unrecognizable. The St. Louis sisterhood was the most vibrant Evangelical Synod motherhouse, with a membership peaking in 1937 at 144 deaconesses. By then, these deaconesses had already begun redefining the emblems of their office. The most apparent changes were to the garb. In 1921, the sisters updated their garb to a plain, conservative version of ordinary women's street dress and exchanged the bonnet for a modern sailor hat. Sister Frieda Eckhoff, some sixty years later, remembered the awkward period of the hat transition: "We were consecrated on a Wednesday evening, during the Spring conference, it was April 13, and we were the first class consecrated without the bonnet. First class with the sailor hats. Well, we were almost ready to march down the aisle in the church before Sister Magdalene had definitely decided what we three should do, should we keep those sailor hats on or should we take them off? [Sister Frieda laughs.] So I don't know, I think some of the older sisters had kinda' encouraged her about the decision so we took the hats off [more laughter]."[31]

Another consecration controversy erupted in 1928, when Sister Elizabeth Lotz and her classmates visited a beauty parlor, without first asking permission, to have their hair "marcelled" (curled in the fashionable style with hot tongs) for the occasion. Superintendent Frederick Jens and Sister Superior Magdalene worried that these women were too frivolous to be deaconesses and almost denied them consecration.[32] These sisters' reminiscences are examples of how each small change to the prescribed details of the consecrated life required careful thought and negotiation among the deaconesses.

The 1940s and 1950s marked the turning point in the history of this deaconess group. In 1942, partly in answer to wartime demands, the Deaconess Society, composed both of deaconesses and their lay and clergy supporters, voted to open a separate training school for women who sought to become nurses but not deaconesses.[33] The resulting School of Nursing immediately, and permanently, attracted more students than the School for Deaconesses. Six years later, Beatrice M. Weaver became the first woman ordained a minister by the Evangelical and Reformed Church.[34] Two years after that, in 1950, Irma Williamson unknowingly became the final deaconess consecrated by this denomination. As the Deaconess Society observed the number of incoming deaconess probationers

Figure 6.1. Evangelical Synod 1921 street garb.
Courtesy of the Deaconess Foundation, St. Louis,
Missouri.

dwindle, they struggled with how much to accommodate the office to the changing expectations of women. Primarily, they debated the question of marriage. As a committee of male ministerial advisors reported in 1956, the older sisters, "and this is true mostly of those in retirement, maintain that a deaconess can give herself completely to her task only if she is single." On the other hand, the ministers "felt that a devoted nurse, for example, could continue to give consecrated service whether she remained single or chose to become married."[35] Unable to come to agreement, the Deaconess Society left the marriage prohibition in place. Despite marketing efforts, in 1960, no new students entered the School for Deaconesses, and it ceased operations. In 1979, twenty-nine deaconesses remained, and the last living deaconess, Sister Marie Lee, died in 2010 at age one hundred.

Sporadic efforts have been made to acknowledge the legacy of these deaconesses. In 1989, the United Church of Christ General Synod me-

Figure 6.2. Dolls dressed in Evangelical Synod/United Church of Christ garb. Courtesy of the Deaconess Foundation, St. Louis, Missouri.

morialized the hundredth anniversary of the St. Louis motherhouse with a proclamation "gratefully [acknowledging] the legacy of the Deaconess Sisters whose gifts and grace have abundantly enriched the life of the whole church," noting that the sixteen deaconess sisters remaining "continue their witness to consecrated service in retirement."[36] The deaconesses themselves sought to preserve the memory of their office in a tangible way. In 1942, perhaps sensing the irrevocable decline in the office, the sisters had purchased a set of ten antique dolls, and Sister Bena Fuch had fashioned for them miniature versions of the different garbs worn by the deaconesses from 1889 to 1942. These dolls were displayed in a "Heritage Exhibit" in the hospital lobby from 1943 until 1997, when the hospital was sold to a secular corporation.[37] When I personally saw the dolls in 2002, they were tucked away in a glass case in a small basement room in the Luhr Library of Eden Seminary, preserved as a quaint reminder of an age past.

Deaconess, Woman Deacon, Deacon: Presbyterians and Episcopalians

Other twentieth-century deaconesses ceased to be deaconesses by becoming deacons. The Presbyterian Church is unique for its tradition of ordaining within the local congregation lay deacons "whose business it is to take care of the poor, and to distribute among them the collections which may be raised for their use."[38] Although the Presbyterian deaconess movement emerged separately from this tradition, confusion and conflation were perhaps inevitable. The early-twentieth-century deaconess derived authority not from congregational election but from special training and consecration, and her field could be within or beyond the local congregation. Yet, the Presbyterian deaconess slowly became understood as a female equivalent of the congregational male deacon. Before 1915, the Constitution of the Presbyterian Church in the United States of America stipulated that both elders and deacons "must be male members in full communion."[39] That year the constitution added a line permitting the election of local congregational deaconesses: "Deaconesses may be elected to office in a manner similar to that appointed for deacons, and set apart by prayer. They shall be under the supervision of the session" (ruling elders of the local congregation).[40]

Melding the traditions of electing deacons and setting apart deaconesses caused confusion and surely consternation among the trained, consecrated deaconesses who had been at work for decades already. In 1920 the Judicial Committee sought to clarify: "The term 'deaconess' shall be reserved to desigante [sic], as at present, a woman properly prepared and set apart by prayer for the duties of a pastor's assistant in the broadest sense; but that a woman elected to serve on the Board of Deacons shall be designated merely as 'a member of the Board of Deacons.'"[41] And in 1924, the constitution was amended again to permit "that men and women shall be eligible to election to the office of deacon."[42]

In 1926, a leadership manual acknowledged the de facto situation that there were three categories of diaconal women in the Presbyterian Church: (1) trained deaconesses consecrated by the Presbytery for full-time work beyond the congregation; (2) deaconesses set apart by the congregation to work alongside the male deacons; and (3) women deacons, elected by the congregation and ordained along with their male counterparts.[43] Although trained, consecrated Presbyterian deaconesses continued their work through the mid-twentieth century at least, the Presbyterian deaconess faded from public view. In a poignant 1945 letter, her lay supervisor requested that a twenty-five-year service recognition pin be presented to Deaconess Marie Vacek: "She is an ordained [sic] Deaconess, a graduate of the old Baltimore Missionary Training School.

We hope you will find Miss Vacek eligible. She has had very little rec-ognition and I am sure it would please her to have one of these pins."[44] Vacek had been serving for thirty-three years by then.

Although consecrated Presbyterian deaconesses dressed in their blue garb were recognizable on the streets of Baltimore and Philadelphia in the first few decades of the twentieth century, the deaconess vocation never captured the imagination of this denomination's people in a last-ing way. Presbyterian women seeking an authorized ecclesiastical role increasingly chose the option that had deeper ecclesiastical roots in that church: service within the local congregation on the mixed-gender Board of Deacons.

Although it took several more decades, Episcopal deaconesses fol-lowed the same path as Presbyterians. They experienced the same strug-gles as other twentieth-century groups. Wrestling with changing the garb, Deaconess Anita Hodgkin lamented in 1924, "I feel all the time that the Church needs deaconesses who have the woman's point of view and she cannot have it and wear a veil."[45] They debated marriage, with prominent dean of the New York Training School Susan Trevor Knapp against, and her bishop William Huntington in favor.[46] Furthermore, they suffered from the confusion of deaconesses with sisterhoods and from inaction and frequent reversals by the Episcopal governing body. In 1970, the General Convention repealed Canon 50 on Deaconesses and replaced it with one ordering women as deacons.[47] Episcopal dea-conesses became deacons, indistinguishable in name and function from their male counterparts.

Not all Protestant deaconesses disappeared in the twentieth century. Using different approaches, several Methodist and Lutheran deaconess groups found ways to preserve their unique role by adapting it to the changed culture.

United Methodist Church: Love, Justice, and Service

As the largest Protestant denomination throughout the heyday of the deaconess movement, Methodism was able to harness its numbers, its publishing enterprises, and the enthusiasm of the training school move-ment to produce by far the greatest number of consecrated deaconesses in the United States, although most were not lifelong members of the office.[48] Methodists also proved flexible in adapting the office over time, though not without considerable introspection on the part of deaconesses and administrative trial and error. They devoted the early to middle part of the twentieth century to untangling the deaconess work from its distinctive lifestyle. In 1920, the wearing of the prescribed garb was made optional. In 1927, the Methodist Episcopal Church, South, abolished the garb altogether.[49] In the 1930s and '40s, the allowance ideal held sacrosanct by Lucy Rider Meyer and other Methodist founders quietly gave way to a model of equal pay for equal work. In 1948, the new deaconess executive secretary, Mary Lou Barnwell, argued that young people considering the diaconate "have a right to demand fair employment practices on the part of the church just as the church has a right to demand higher standards of its workers."[50] By 1960, the Commission Deaconess Work affirmed that "the salary of a deaconess should be commensurate with that paid to any other person in the community with similar training, experience, and responsibility."[51] As noted above, in 1959 Methodist deaconesses were permitted to continue in their office after marriage.

Rethinking garb, allowance, and marriage was only part of a larger effort of soul searching for midcentury Methodist deaconesses. In 1965 and 1970, the Commission on Deaconess Work solicited statements from deaconesses on how they understood their role. The commission received hundreds of answers from women who were passionate about their vocation yet who struggled to articulate what made the deaconess office unique. Women's ordination forced the rethinking of the gender-specific office of deaconess: since both men and women could be ordained, why could only women be diaconal? In the 1968 union that created the United Methodist Church, Methodist deaconesses were joined by another category of commissioned lay worker: (mostly male) home missionaries from the United Brethren Church. In the 1970s, Methodist deaconesses encountering emerging feminist theology questioned whether the office promoted women's oppression: "In today's world where we are fighting for the equality of women, I am not sure that she has, or should have, a unique role. The deaconess relationship sets women off, and permits them to be the low-paid servants of the church."[52]

The creation of "diaconal ministers" was an attempt to institute a gender-neutral version of the diaconate but pleased few. Deaconess

Betty J. Letzig complained in 1977 about the "nebulousness" of the new name and the "loss of the term 'deaconess,' with its Biblical basis and long history." She added that "the reference to 'minister' in the term 'diaconal minister' still has for most, the image of male and clergy." Letzig protested that no one even knew how to pronounce correctly the word "diaconal."[53] Furthermore, the United Methodist Church offered women plenty of jobs in churches that did not require the deaconess designation. The proliferation of alternative Methodist forms of service in the second half of the twentieth century—mission associate, lay worker, US-2 (young adults who devote two years to missions in the United States), lay person in service, and eventually diaconal minister—did not help the cause of clarity. Consecrations slowed to a bare trickle from 1980 to 1995 while committees studied the issue, and the number of active United Methodist deaconesses reached a nadir of sixty-nine in 1996. The 1996 General Conference restated its support for the deaconess office, and the movement slowly began to grow once more, claiming its unique mission as the only order of lay people consecrated to the full-time vocation of love, justice, and service.[54]

To twenty-first-century Methodist deaconesses, opening the diaconal office to men has been important but complicated. Because the term "deacon" has traditionally marked a step in the Methodist ordination process, that term is not available as a male or gender-neutral naming option for the lay diaconate. In 2004, the position of "home missioner" was created as a parallel diaconal opportunity for men, and today there are close to a dozen in full-time service nationwide.[55] When in 2017 I asked United Methodist deaconess Cindy Andrade Johnson what the office of deaconess meant to her as an order specifically for women, her first response was to object and point to her home missioner counterparts. Then she paused and reflected, "Although I don't want ever to get rid of the name 'deaconess' because of Phoebe, from the Bible. They wanted a neutral [name]. Some of us would not be happy with that because we like the 'deaconess' because of the historical [sic] and Phoebe, in Romans."[56]

Today, Methodists who identify as queer are challenging this parallel structure for men and women. Deaconess Robin Ridenour expressed a similarly conflicted sentiment: "The problem is I like the name 'deaconess'! Mainly because of the history. I love the history of the deaconess movement. And you know, way back. I wouldn't necessarily want to change it." But later in our conversation she stated, with resolve, "I would give up the name, if they went to a gender-neutral name," explaining, "You can't be in community with people and not see where people are suffering, or being treated unjustly, and not advocate for that as well."[57]

Helen Ryde is just such a person in the Methodist community who has struggled with the naming issue. Ryde is a member of the Order of Deaconess and Home Missioner who identifies as agender, or nonbinary. She explained that she felt drawn to the order, but that the name "deaconess" was a stumbling block for her: "I couldn't fathom the idea of having the title 'deaconess' attached to me because it just was far too gendered, for me."[58] When it came time for consecration, Ryde and the administrators worked collaboratively to construct the ceremony so that Ryde was not consecrated as a deaconess per se, but as a member of the Order of Deaconess and Home Missioner. Instead of receiving a pin and a stole that read "Deaconess" or "Home Missioner," they found for her an older version of the pin that said "Diaconate," and her stole was blank. Ryde was satisfied, feeling "that they were affirming my identity, affirming my desire, and doing everything they could within the bounds of what they thought the Discipline could do."[59] Today's Office of Deaconess and Home Missioner, administered by the United Methodist Women, represents a compromise, perhaps not the final one, between valuing the tradition of deaconesses in biblical and Methodist history and offering men a parallel consecrated lay vocation.

As of 2019, there were 172 active United Methodist deaconesses and home missioners in the United States, with another 108 in retirement. Most deaconesses first sense a calling to a particular career, and then, recognizing that their vocation aligns with the mission of love, justice, and service, seek out a relationship with the Office of Deaconess and Home Missioner. United Methodist deaconesses serve as firefighters, court-appointed children's advocates, chaplains, community organizers, and nonprofit administrators, to name a few roles. Some are outspoken advocates for immigration justice and detention issues along the US/Mexico border, such as Cindy Johnson, pictured in figure 6.3, who engages in community organizing and advocacy in her hometown of Brownsville, Texas.[60] At least two deaconesses, including Helen Ryde, have worked for the Reconciling Ministries Network, which works for the inclusion of people of all sexual orientations and gender identities.[61]

Figure 6.3. United Methodist Cindy Andrade Johnson of Brownsville, Texas. Paul Jeffrey/kairosphoto.com.

Although not all Methodists in the United States are liberal, many deaconesses embrace liberal social causes, heirs to both their foremothers' Social Gospel commitment and the twentieth-century social justice tradition of mainline Protestantism.[62] Robin Ridenour explains, "Deaconesses and Home Missioners may not all agree with social progressivism, but they're all committed to justice. So even if they didn't particularly understand me or where I'm coming from as a lesbian, they understand the justice part. And they will all stand up for me, no matter what, if they saw an injustice occurring." Ridenour has experienced this support from her diaconal sisters and brothers as they have walked alongside her in her public role as the spouse of the United Methodist Church's first openly gay bishop, Rev. Karen Oliveto.[63]

United Methodist deaconesses, along with their home missioner counterparts, seem to have successfully reenvisioned their office as an opportunity to join a community of laypeople, recognized by the church and committed to love, justice, and service. In an interview, Helen Ryde pointed to a further key aspect of the movement, possibly highlighted by the timing of our conversation in the weeks after the 2018 Parkland, Florida, school shooting, as "thoughts and prayers" had become a ridiculed shibboleth for inaction on gun control legislation. When asked about the role of prayer in the community, Ryde paused and reflected her belief that deaconesses and home missioners are "a group of people who are committed to walking their prayers. . . . I know that there is a lot of prayer that goes on, but generally it is a community that is extremely hands-on with their work, sort of feet-on-the-ground-type of people."[64] Not unlike their nineteenth-century foremothers, who contrasted themselves with the contemplative but useless Catholic nun and the out-of-touch ordained minister, today's United Methodist deaconesses and home missioners point to the embodied, active character of their ministry. They see themselves as "feet-on-the-ground-type" people, walking the walk of the Gospel.

Evangelical Lutheran Church in America: The Deaconess Community and a New Roster

Deaconesses in the Evangelical Lutheran Church in America have also spent the past century reenvisioning their office. Beginning in the 1920s, new Lutheran deaconesses, like their sisters in other churches, asked for more concessions to popular culture, particularly in issues of personal liberty. In 1929, Oberin Julie Mergner instructed Sister Edith Baden to stop waving her hair, adding that a little self-denial would not harm her. Marshaling her biblical training in her defense, Sister Edith invoked the Jewish woman who "washed our Master's feet with her tears and wiped them with her . . . abundance of wavy hair" and challenged, "Is the Philadelphia motherhouse style of parting the hair in the middle, drawing it tight back off the head and putting it up with hair pins in accordance with the Biblical hairdressing of the women in the days of St. Paul?"[65] Sister Edith's letter questioned how a mutable cultural issue such as hair styling could be essential to her deaconess vocation. We do not know whether Sister Edith continued waving her hair, but we do know that she remained a deaconess until her death in 1977, living her vocation in various Lutheran outstations, rather than under the watchful gaze of the sister superior in the Philadelphia motherhouse.

By the 1940s, Sister Edith's more expansive views on the deaconess lifestyle had won the day. In the same decade that the Evangelical Synod deaconesses put their memorial dolls on display and watched the School for Deaconesses enrollment drop precipitously, the Lutheran deaconesses realized their need to adapt in order to survive. Articles in the *Deaconess Messenger* reveal these changes, particularly changes in leisure culture as the homosocial home-based sociality of late-nineteenth- and early-twentieth-century deaconess groups gave way to a mixed-gender public commercial culture. In the winter of 1946, deaconess sisters reported attending a performance of the Ice Follies.[66] A new spirit of fun and shenanigans was in the air, such as in 1947 when the student deaconesses celebrated Friday the Thirteenth with a "Topsy Turvy Party," including playing games in reverse and lampooning parliamentary procedure.[67] In 1948, Lutherans again revamped their garb in an effort to update the uniform and standardize it across the Lutheran motherhouses. As reported in the *Deaconess Messenger*, the "modern blue garb is a comfortable and suitable one for the constant service expected of them. The change to a modern garb with simple lines results in a saving of material and of time."[68]

Sister Mildred Winter was recruiting young Lutheran women for the diaconate during this era. She presciently urged her sisters to adopt modernized language to appeal to young women who thought and spoke differently from their elders. After she spoke at length to college students, a young woman had asked her, "But what is the diaconate?"—prompting Sister Mildred to realize that this key word "meant nothing to them. It was not in their vocabulary." So she answered, "It is a type of sorority—an organized fellowship of Christian women." Sister Mildred advised, "We may not like this language ourselves; it may be much less ecclesiastical in sound, but if it is the only way we can reach their understanding, then let us use it." She recommended replacing "motherhouse"—too authoritarian and institutional—with "deaconess fellowship center." "ALLOWANCE," Sister Mildred reported, "is another term which grates upon the ears of any young adult who likes to think of herself as self-sustaining." She suggested changing it to "dividend," "as any business firm calls the sharing of profits."[69]

The generational communication failure that Sister Mildred hoped to solve with a simple vocabulary change went far deeper. The deaconesses would have to rethink not only the emblems of their office but its very nature if they were to appeal to a new generation. Here, Lutherans decided they could reenvision the diaconate in a way that the Evangelical Synod was unwilling or unable to do. In 1952, the United Lutheran Church instituted a parallel track for deaconesses who chose to wear "civilian clothes" instead of the garb and chose to be paid a salary instead of receiving the allowance. Such deaconesses were instructed to take out private health insurance in lieu of relying on the motherhouse for care in old age or illness.[70] We can almost see the older deaconesses shudder. Private health insurance! In the nineteenth century, joining the deaconess community *was* health insurance. With one policy change, the diaconate was recast as a job, instead of a way of life. Yet the new policy mandated that these women were still to be addressed by the title of "sister"; these were still deaconesses, just modern ones. In 1978, the traditional "cooperative plan" was phased out, and all new deaconesses received a salary.[71] Lutheran deaconesses slowly warmed up to the idea of permitting women to continue to serve as deaconesses after marriage. Although disagreement persisted, in 1969, the following carefully worded policy was adopted: "Deaconesses who marry may be privileged to continue to serve in their office as deaconesses as long as in the opinion of the Sisters' Council they are available for full time service." It was not until 1982 that this policy was amended to allow for part-time service.[72]

One of the more sweeping changes to the Lutheran deaconess community has been the transformation from the motherhouse model to a covenanted community of geographically dispersed women. In 1953 the Philadelphia motherhouse had moved from downtown into the mansion known as Skylands on a lush piece of land in the suburbs of Gladwyne, donated to the order by friend and supporter Mary Ethel Pew. In 1963, deaconesses from the Baltimore motherhouse moved in with their sisters in Gladwyne, and in 1966, the Omaha sisters did the same.[73] For the next thirty years, the Evangelical Lutheran Church of America (ELCA) deaconesses were consolidated in this one motherhouse. A monumental change came in 1998 when the deaconesses decided to sell the multi-million-dollar property.[74] Facing a 1.5-million-dollar renovation just to bring the aged estate up to code, directing sister Nora Frost explained, "For us, the whole impetus for the move came from our desire to be able to free up monies for mission and ministry in the church. We have been saddened for a very long time that funds needed for ministry were being used to maintain buildings."[75] The ELCA deaconess community now has an office in Chicago alongside the headquarters of the denomination, but, outside of retirement homes, its individual deaconesses no longer live in community.

Despite their geographical dispersion, community has become perhaps the defining feature of the current ELCA deaconess office. If the Lutheran diaconate was founded as a way of life, and reenvisioned as a job, it has now emerged as a commitment to an intentional community. Every official statement of the Deaconess Community of the ELCA (as well as its very name) emphasizes the importance of community to the deaconesses. During her candidacy, a potential deaconess is required to discern, "through her experience, interactions, and prayer that her call is diaconal and also to life within the Deaconess Community."[76] Deaconesses do enact the tradition, dating back to the early twentieth century, of meeting together as a body in conference once a year. Yet, just as important seems to be the virtual community, linked together through the intertwined practices of prayer and digital media. The practice of praying for each other is in continuity with the past; deaconesses have always affirmed the strength that comes from having a community of praying sisters behind them. Today, this tradition of intercessory prayer is manifest in the frequent uses of the #prayingsisters hashtag on the Deaconess Community's online Facebook page. This digital presence provides daily scripture quotations, community news, photos, and, of course, prayer concerns. In a new online ritual, "likes" serve as digital amens to the prayers posted on Facebook.

ELCA deaconesses now also live in the tension of holding a gender-neutral office in a gender-specific community. Although still members of the Deaconess Community, in 2017 ELCA deaconesses officially became "deacons" when the church merged three rosters of lay workers (deaconess, associates in ministry, and diaconal ministers) into a unified roster with the gender-neutral title of "deacon." When I asked Sister Louise Williams how she was dealing with the name change, she responded with a sense of equanimity: "I've been a deaconess for fifty-one years now. I'm not likely to cease to be known as a deaconess, but I also embrace the title deacon because I think it's more ecumenically recognized. It's also a little more representative of a more contemporary and forward-looking sense of ministry. But I'm happy with either title."[77] As of March 2019, there were sixty-three active sisters in the ELCA Deaconess Community and an additional fourteen in retirement. This number is growing as eighteen candidates prepare for consecration. The story of deaconesses in the ELCA will evolve with them.

Lutheran Church–Missouri Synod: Supporting the Ordained Ministry

The Lutheran Church–Missouri Synod (LCMS) was a latecomer to the American deaconess movement. The most theologically and socially conservative of the many US Lutheran bodies, the Missouri Synod remained suspicious of Romanism lurking in the deaconess office throughout the nineteenth century and into the twentieth. It was not until 1919 that five ministers and three laymen independently organized the Lutheran Deaconess Association, which, although founded by and for LCMS members, has never been formally affiliated with the Missouri Synod, or any other Lutheran church. From its inception, the LCMS emphasized more explicitly than other denominations the circumscription of woman's role. Rev. F. W. Herzberger, a city missionary in St. Louis, had witnessed the work of the Evangelical Synod sisterhood and became a vocal early advocate for training LCMS deaconesses.[78] In the first issue of the *Lutheran Deaconess* he insisted, "The office, as we all know, is limited in its scope by the physical nature of woman and certain limitations of Holy Writ. Within these limitations our Society purposes to carry on its deaconess work."[79] Writers from other denominations were more oblique about the scriptural limitations of women's role in the church, but for the LCMS, this was, and remains, a key part of their confessional identity.

The mid-twentieth century witnessed increasing financial, administrative, and doctrinal struggles between the Missouri Synod and the LDA. In the 1970s, LCMS deaconesses and their supporters became unhappy with liberalizing theological positions of the LDA, including "resolutions supporting sisters preparing for the ministry" and allowing an ordained woman from the American Lutheran Church to celebrate Holy Eucharist at the 1978 annual deaconess conference in Valparaiso, Indiana.[80] The LCMS disaffiliated with the LDA in 1979 and created its own confessional deaconess training program at the synodical colleges and the new Concordia Deaconess Conference (CDC). As in other contemporary diaconates, LCMS deaconesses live independently, receive a salary, and are permitted to marry. Yet, in contrast to other deaconess groups that have abandoned the wearing of the garb in favor of, at most, a designated lapel pin, the new Concordia Deaconess Conference reinstated the full deaconess uniform: a navy-blue suit or dress with jacket. The cross pin is worn on the lapel, and the left sleeve is marked by a cross insignia, newly designed to be "sufficiently feminine as well as rich in symbolism."[81]

Lutheran Church–Missouri Synod deaconesses have participated in the crafting of an office that upholds their theological distinctiveness. The LCMS affirms that because man and woman were created individually, "the identities and functions of each are not interchangeable; they must remain distinct."[82] Woman's subordination to man is neither a result of Adam and Eve's fall nor a relic of a foreign past culture. Thus, all the Pauline proscriptions against females speaking in church or holding authority over men remain binding today, and the church does not ordain women to the clergy. The LCMS's most recent teaching on gender, the 2009 "Creator's Tapestry," confirms that "a human being is not an independent soul or mind that just happens to be encased in a male or female body"; rather, a person's entire identity is gendered.[83] The confessional position of the LCMS is co-constitutive of the gendered hierarchy in Missouri Synod polity, families, and society, where men are the leaders and women play supporting roles. In 2005, the CDC created and adopted a code of ethics that clearly articulates the deaconess's role supporting the ordained ministry. She promises to "point others to Word and Sacrament provided by the Office of the Public Ministry" and to refrain from performing the distinctive works of the clergy: preaching and administering the sacraments. The code also ensures that a deaconess's behavior comports with the church's doctrine and stance on certain social issues. The deaconess promises not only to "aptly express the faith in word and deed" but also specifically to uphold the sanctity of life "from conception to death" and to "limit sexual intimacy to heterosexual marriage as instituted by God."[84]

As part of their understanding that men and women are created differently by design, LCMS deaconesses argue that women are divinely created with special gifts for diaconal service. Missouri Synod deaconess Kristin Wassilak affirmed, "We do believe the Lord has created women with by and large some unique skills and perspective on life," elsewhere defining deaconess work as "a uniquely feminine care, perceiving need and responding with gentle helpfulness, expressing the compassion of Christ in a tender nurturing way."[85]

Because Missouri Synod clergy are all male, deaconesses argue that they play a crucial role in the pastoral care of women. In 2017, LCMS deaconess Grace Rao described her role as a parish deaconess as especially helpful for the women of the congregation. Deaconess Rao explained that some women felt more comfortable going to her, a woman, than to the pastor. She spoke of counseling women in situations of domestic abuse, depression, and difficult family situations. She explained, "I think that women get a little . . . it's not intimidating going in to talk to the pastor, they do go and talk, but still . . . certain things they cannot share. Certain important issues and which are very delicate." She affirmed her special ability to counsel women, concluding that sometimes "a woman-to-woman talk is necessary." Rao's explanations evoke the earlier understanding that deaconesses were especially effective at the spiritual care of women. Rao took pains to point out that she was not supplanting the role of the ordained minister; in counseling women she always encouraged them to seek out the pastor as well, "pointing out to them that he's the one that gives you the sacrament."[86]

The LCMS emphasis on male headship and the order of creation reinforces a structure of strictly defined gender roles in church ministry: as men and women are seen as complementary, so deaconesses understand themselves as complementary to the male pastorate. Chaplain deaconess Margaret Anderson writes that she "complements her male counterparts." She explains that as a woman she has a unique bond with female patients, especially when dealing with "female surgeries" and the death of children. She speaks of women being linked together by the maternal role, presumably whether or not the deaconess herself is a mother. Furthermore, since a "woman's emotions and tears are accepted by most of society," deaconesses are uniquely situated to encourage "male patients to release their deepest emotions."[87]

As these examples demonstrate, the twenty-first-century female diaconate of the LCMS retains strong connections to the movement's founding era, employing rationales of gender complementarity, maternalism, and the efficacy of female suffering. LCMS deaconesses serve in roles that do not conflict with traditional commitments to male headship, such as church musicians; missionaries; teachers of youth or women; workers in confessional institutions for children, women, the disabled, or the elderly; and prison ministries. As of 2019 there were 306 deaconesses on the roster of the Lutheran Church–Missouri Synod.[88]

Lutheran Deaconess Association: Forming the Diaconal Identity

Despite parting ways with the Lutheran Church–Missouri Synod in 1979, the Lutheran Deaconess/Diaconal Association continues to thrive.[89] Headquartered at Indiana's Valparaiso University, the LDA remains open to Lutherans from different confessional branches and focuses on forming deaconesses and deacons to exercise their ministry in secular or church settings. The LDA constructs diaconal ministry as an identity rather than a vocation. The distinction becomes apparent when one considers that two ordained Lutheran ministers have recently completed diaconal training and added "deaconess" to their titles. In other times and expressions of the Lutheran diaconate, the ordained ministry and the diaconate have been seen as discrete vocations, mutually exclusive. Codirector of education and formation Valerie Webdell explained in 2016 that both women discovered "that their identity is as a deaconess, as one who serves, and that 'pastor' plays a role in that identity. They very clearly, both of them, said, 'that [pastor] is one of the roles I play as deaconess.'"[90] The LDA is reinterpreting diaconal formation as recognizing how to be a diaconal presence in whatever job one has been called to by God, whether that be pastor or "burrito chaplain" (as one deaconess who works at Chipotle Mexican Grill and ministers to her coworkers and customers has named herself).

In 2014 the Lutheran Deaconess Association began training men alongside women for the diaconate and in 2018 changed its name to the Lutheran Diaconal Association. As of 2019, the LDA claimed 778 deaconesses and five deacons, of whom 450 are currently active, making it the largest contemporary diaconal body. Deaconess Jennifer Clark Tinker shared her conviction that men becoming deacons, in a way, "validates the office itself." She sees the training of men as a way of reclaiming the shared male and female diaconate of the early church and affirming the idea that the diaconate is a ministry in its own right, not just a second-class status given to women. "Why wouldn't men want to be in this role as well?" she asked.[91]

Echoing other contemporary deaconesses with whom I spoke, Tinker articulated two commitments that are sometimes in conflict: she is dedicated to the idea that a diaconal identity transcends gender while also being devoted to the diaconate as her community of women. Tinker explained that the (then exclusively) female community of the LDA "wasn't the draw" for her when she became a deaconess in 2001, but that her community of sisters has become increasingly meaningful and important to her over the years. She explained that despite feminism's accomplishments, "Women still face challenges. . . . Even if on paper they can do whatever they want, there are ways that they are kept down, [sometimes] because of systems that prohibit them." Tinker described the LDA as sustaining a culture of empowering women, including women in the LCMS who are not permitted ordination in their denomination. Tinker and other LDA deaconesses are dedicated to their community of sisters and to affirming the diaconal gifts of men. She concluded, "Even though it makes things a little bit messy in terms of the sisterhood, I affirm the idea of us training men. But I would still want to be called 'deaconess.'"[92]

One way in which the LDA is redefining the diaconate as gender neutral is by broadening the biblical imagery of diaconal service. The paramount biblical image for the deaconess founders was Phoebe. But in the LDA formation process, Phoebe steps aside to make room for five different images of diakonia (the anglicized version of the Greek word for service): foot washing, table serving, storytelling, door keeping, and light bearing.[93] Each of these has its own biblical origin in the life of Jesus and the early church. Former executive deaconess Louise Williams explained that she adapted these five images over decades of training LDA deaconesses. The images represent a spectrum of service, moving from the most personal, embodied service of foot washing out to the public, prophetic leadership of bearing the light of hope. It spans serving on lowly bended knee to stretching up to serve on tiptoe.[94] In emphasizing images other than Phoebe and expanding the vision beyond images of care of the body, the LDA contributes to the construction of a less gender-bound vision of the diaconate.

Like the other Lutheran and UM diaconates, the LDA uses tech-
nologies old and new to creatively reenvision community. LDA deaconesses join together on a conference call each Monday evening to
pray the Deaconess Litany, a fifty-year-old call and response prayer.[95]
There is a growing social media presence on Facebook, Twitter, Ins-
tagram, and YouTube. Deaconesses also participate in a very active
e-mail chain, sharing news and prayer requests several times a day.
As Tinker described, this geographically far-flung community remains
essential to her: "I need them in my life, the people I can be real with.
I feel like that is something that we are to each other. Come as you
are, and we're in this together. That depth of caring for one another is
something that I cherish." Community and forming the "servant heart"
at the center of diaconal identity are the essentials of the Lutheran
Diaconal Association.[96]

The Heart of the Diaconate

In the twentieth century, deaconesses shed certain aspects of the consecrated lifestyle, such as the allowance, almost effortlessly. Although
it required more incremental steps, most deaconesses shrugged off
the garb with few regrets. Furthermore, there is almost no discussion among deaconesses today of their distinctions from their Roman
Catholic counterparts. The Catholicism of Protestant imagination no
longer plays the constitutive role it did in the late-nineteenth- and
early-twentieth-century deaconess movement, and today's deaconesses
no longer feel the need to define themselves against Catholic sisters.
Interestingly, the place where the diaconate and Catholicism inter-
sect today is in heated conversations over the possibility of ordaining
women to the diaconate within the Roman Catholic Church.[97] The
possibility of combining marriage with the deaconess office proved a
greater challenge to resolve, although it too has been settled. How the
diaconate relates to the ordained ministry is still being worked out,
with different results for different groups. Deaconesses continue the
process of working out the relationship of the office to constructions
of gender. Most diaconates have had to address the question of what
it means to be in a gender-specific ministry once all the other church
offices have become gender neutral.

If the work of the twentieth century seemed to unravel the tapestry of diaconates woven by the nineteenth-century founders, perhaps the twenty-first century is the time of weaving the tapestry anew. Taken together, these four groups of contemporary deaconesses illustrate different aspects of the reimagined vocation. Although all of the groups have creatively reimagined community, the ELCA Deaconess Community is a remarkable example of how, in one generation, deaconesses have adapted from living together in one traditional motherhouse to living separately around the country, meeting periodically in person and regularly online and in prayer. The Lutheran Diaconal (formerly Deaconess) Association best articulates a new understanding of the diaconate as an identity that transcends job, synod, and even gender. The Lutheran Church–Missouri Synod has also left behind the nineteenth-century commitments to singleness, communal living, and allowance but holds fast to the traditional understanding of the diaconate as the female expression of ministry complementary to the male pastorate. With the slogan of "love, justice, and service," the United Methodist Office of Deaconess and Home Missioner extends its nineteenth-century Methodist roots, linking service with social justice.[98]

Though their numbers remain small, women in several American churches have reclaimed the diaconate for the twenty-first century. Nineteenth- and twentieth-century deaconesses understood themselves as women called by God to a life entirely devoted to service. Although specific aspects of the consecrated life have changed, deaconesses' stated purpose remains largely intact. After a nadir in the second half of the twentieth century, the deaconess movement, or what today would best be called the diaconal movement, appears to be growing again. Chaplaincy scholar Wendy Cadge argues that in the United States today, a person may be more likely to meet a religious professional in a secular setting than in a place of worship.[99] Deaconesses are well positioned to respond to this phenomenon, attempting to meet people out in the world, people who may never darken the door of a church. Deaconesses draw on their history of ministry at the margins, and the flexibility of the diaconal vocation encourages a ministry of service in secular settings. Methodist Cindy Johnson argues that the church needs deaconesses because, "I still feel we're very focused on the structures of our churches—

almost the physical structures of the churches—instead of going out into the world where the people are."[100] Lutheran Valerie Webdell points to a deaconess who teaches math in a public school, where she cannot even talk about her faith but where "her presence and her being . . . is very much diaconal."[101] Drawing on a century and a half of presence in the United States, deaconesses argue that they are poised to meet the needs of the world today.

Conclusion

In 1902, Anna Pfeifer wrote to the Cincinnati German Methodist deaconess home, "Every now and then for years, a feeling of dissatisfaction has come over me, a feeling that seemed to say that I was not doing all I could and should for God, and I realize more and more every day that it is not all He asks of me to save my own soul."[1] In 2006, United Methodist Susan Hunt reported the same feeling: "During those years I was uneasy about what I was doing. I felt God calling me into full-time Christian service. And so I prayed and looked around for opportunities to answer my call."[2] More than one hundred years apart, these women made the same choice: they became deaconesses.

Beginning around 1880 and continuing through the 1930s, the American deaconess movement flourished. Inspired by one particular verse from the New Testament and European examples, American women sought a new way of being Protestant Christians. Different theological heritages of the Inner Mission, the Oxford Movement, and the Social Gospel all compelled deaconesses to service to the whole person, situated in society. They capitalized on and subverted prevalent gender norms to create their vocation. They agreed that woman's role was motherhood but broadened that category to include all sorts of caregiving roles. They subscribed to the idea that women belonged in the home but expanded that understanding beyond their own family homes. Deaconesses took advantage of entrenched anti-Catholic prejudice and harnessed it in their defense. Although they did little to dismantle anti-Catholicism, they could not help but call attention to the sincerity of the Catholic faithful they encountered and the beneficial work of Catholic women religious in particular. Deaconesses created an allowance system that enabled them to work for a living without implicating them in the wage economy. The allowance changed the way deaconesses related to both the rich and the poor, providing deaconesses independence through dependence. No longer financially beholden to fathers or husbands, these women still relied on their deaconess community and on the giving of others, mostly fundraising laywomen. Deaconesses assumed a unique place relative to the ordained clergy. They supported the professionalization of the male ministry by assuming duties that clergymen viewed as feminine, such as visitation in the home, work with children, and secretarial work. While some deaconesses were content with their parallel female vocation, others began to resent their exclusion from ordination.

By the 1930s, institutions had been built and bylaws had been codified. Yet by the time the tapestry of the deaconess movement was finally completed, loose ends were already unraveling. The Northern and Western European immigrants who had provided so much of the womanpower for the movement were arriving in fewer numbers. Higher education for women continued to expand, and Bible training schools had a difficult time competing with colleges and universities for women's attendance. Employment opportunities for women increased, both outside and inside the church, as denominations began ordaining women. Should a woman who felt called by the Lord become a consecrated deaconess or a social worker? Maybe she should become an ordained pastor or a director of Christian education?

As the number of candidates dropped precipitously, deaconesses committed to the uniqueness of their vocation reshaped the office to address these changes. The allowance no longer served its purpose of getting women into the diaconal workforce and seemed counter to ideas of fairness and equal pay. The allowance system was jettisoned. Respectable single women could roam the streets more freely; the "protective" garb was discarded and communal living deemphasized. Deaconesses struggled longer with whether their office was compatible with marriage; eventually they concluded that it was. Churches that do not ordain women have doubled down on the idea of the diaconate as the female expression of ministry, the complement to the male clergy. But in other churches, competing vocations and avenues of service forced late-twentieth-century deaconesses to articulate what made their office distinctive and necessary. Women still felt the need to consecrate their actions and their lives in a significant way. Emphasis shifted from the diaconate as especially womanly to the diaconate as a unique lay ministry, particularly outside the church walls. Nineteenth-, twentieth-, and twenty-first-century deaconesses have all sought to set their hands to God's work, but today's deaconesses understand consecration as setting themselves apart not through their dress and living arrangements but rather through a vocation that transcends their "job" and a commitment to their community of sisters—and brothers—in service. Today deaconesses are found not only in church-related organizations but also in public schools, law firms, border communities, and Chipotle restaurants. Many are affirming the social justice heritage of the movement, working with people at the margins. Deaconesses today are at once a very old and a very new face of Protestant churches in the United States, and in the larger world.

This book has argued for the necessity of understanding the American deaconess movement in order to tell a better story of US religion. Married Protestant women reformers cannot be seen as the only parallel to Roman Catholic women religious; deaconesses manifest a third category of women church workers: not quite Protestant laywomen, but not nuns either. The entire concept of a "Protestant sister" forces a rethinking of the story of Catholic/Protestant relations in the late-nineteenth/early-twentieth centuries. It also helps to explain how and why Catholic women today are arguing for their own place in the diaconate, arguing with such energy that in 2016, Pope Francis established a commission to begin studying the historical roles of women deacons—or deaconesses—in the early church. This is a fascinating new chapter to the story, one that demands new research. The way deaconesses have constructed their vocation calls for a rethinking of the gendered roles of church women. The deaconess movement compels an acknowledgment of the ways in which women took the messages they heard from the pulpit about their essential womanhood and pushed and pulled on them to construct new versions of gender. The deaconess story offers a new picture of Americanization. It is readily apparent that native-born American deaconesses used their mission to Americanize the immigrants around them, attempting to manipulate their homemaking, child-rearing, and commercial practices. But the movement also made Americans out of many deaconesses themselves. This book suggests that becoming a deaconess was a way for young women arriving from Europe to learn the language and customs of the

United States within a community of sister immigrants. The history of women's ordination looks different through the lens of the deaconess movement.

Understanding the role the diaconate played in the construction of the professional ministry as male offers insight into the necessity of deconstructing the male clergy in order to create a new, gender-neutral model of ministry. So far, more women have been ordained as clergy than men have been consecrated as permanent deacons or home missioners. But the rising number of male deacons (in Protestant and Catholic churches) suggests a need for further research into how these men understand the contemporary diaconate, with its roots both in the Bible and in the women's deaconess movement, as related to their own conceptions of Christian manhood. Gender did not disappear from the church with women's ordination, as the current debates over same-sex marriage and gay and lesbian ordination demonstrate. Today's deaconesses offer a range of understandings of gender and ministry. While one LCMS deaconess explains that she "brings a uniquely feminine care" to the church, a Methodist member of the order describes the idea of gender essentialism as "nonsense." An LDA deaconess offers a nuanced alternative, explaining that because of their history as a marginalized group, women see the world through a different lens, a lens that helps them identify "the least of these."[3] Gender in the church demands even more careful study today, and the study of the diaconate points the way.

* * *

People have regularly asked me as the author to render a verdict on the deaconess movement: "So, was the deaconess office good or bad for women?" To which my answer must be, "Yes." Did the movement deflect attention and pressure away from women's struggle for equal rights of representation, voting, and ordination in the churches? Yes, I believe it did. I do not believe it was a coincidence that the same Methodist General Conference in 1880 that approved the deaconess office denied women the right to serve as voting delegates. But did the (re)creation of the deaconess office broaden women's opportunities by offering them a new vocation? Yes, I believe it did that too. Women seeking to answer a divine call to service found in the deaconess office a unique opportunity for a season, or a lifetime, of meaningful work, embedded in a supportive Christian community of women. The deaconess movement was broad and flexible enough to be used as a tool by women and men with feminist and antifeminist (to use anachronistic terms) aims. Today's diaconal movements are equally capacious, encompassing women with varying reasons for seeking to weave the deaconess tapestry anew.

ABBREVIATIONS

COLLECTIONS
AEC: Archives of the Episcopal Church, Episcopal Seminary of the Southwest

AELCA: Archives of the Evangelical Lutheran Church of America

CMC: Nippert Collection of German Methodism, Cincinnati Historical Society Library, Cincinnati Museum Center

DF: Deaconess Archives, Deaconess Foundation, St. Louis, Missouri

MAHC: Methodist Archives and History Center of the United Methodist Church, Drew University

PHS: Presbyterian Historical Society, Presbyterian Church (USA)

DENOMINATIONAL NEWSLETTERS, NEWSPAPERS, SERIALS, AND OTHER PUBLICATIONS

CPC: *The Constitution of the Presbyterian Church in the United States of America*

CR: *The Christian Recorder*

DA: *The Deaconess Advocate*

DB: *The Deaconess Banner*

LC: *The Living Church*

LCW: *Lutheran Church Work*

LR: *The Ladies' Repository*

OH: *Our Homes*

PDQ: *The Presbyterian Deaconess Quarterly*

PHM: *The Phoebe Home Messenger*

PR: *The Presbyterian Review*

TME: *The Messenger*

WE: *Woman's Evangel*

OTHER CITATIONS
BHHD: Board of Hospitals, Homes, and Deaconess Work

KI: Interviews by Sister Velma Kampschmidt, tape recordings and supplemental materials located in the Deaconess Archives, Deaconess Foundation, St. Louis, Missouri

GL: Letters to Louise Golder and related correspondence located in Nippert Collection of German Methodism, Cincinnati Historical Society Library, Cincinnati Museum Center

MJD: Publications and papers by the Mary J. Drexel Home and Philadelphia Motherhouse of Deaconesses

USFC: United States Federal Census

NOTES

INTRODUCTION

1 Sister Ella Loew, June 1, 1981, KI, DF. In quotations from deaconesses I have used the indication "*sic*" only when absolutely necessary in order to preserve as much as possible the flow of the women's words, eccentric syntax, and word choice.

2 Louise Epkerrs, Letter to The members of the official board of The German deaconess work, March 16, 1904, box 2–16, folder 1, CMC.

3 The median age of first marriage for a native-born white woman in 1900 was twenty-two. Fitch and Ruggles, "Marriage Formation," 63.

4 The office of deacon itself has been extremely plastic throughout church history and among the different Protestant denominations. The Reformed churches sought to follow Calvin's lead in redirecting deacons toward service. The Presbyterian Church insisted that deacons were instructed by scripture to care for the poor but added that they could also legitimately manage "the temporal affairs of the church." Presbyterian Church in the USA, *CPC*, 1896, chapter 6. Episcopalians and, in turn, Methodists retained the medieval model of the sequential diaconate, wherein becoming a deacon was a step toward becoming an ordained minister. Olson, *Centuries*, 18. For instance, in the Methodist Episcopal Church, deacons had "authority to preach; to conduct Divine Worship; to solemnize Matrimony; to administer Baptism; and to assist the Elder in administering the Lord's Supper." Episcopal deacons exercised both service and liturgical roles. Donovan, *A Different Call*, 89. Lutherans in the United States adopted a hybrid model, with both lay deacons and ordained clerical deacons on their way to priesthood. Olson, *One Ministry, Many Roles*, 172. Although early Baptist churches had deacons and elders, deacons eventually added the governing functions of elders to their own role of service. Olson, *One Ministry, Many Roles*, 162; Deweese, *Baptist Service*, 69.

5 Although most American Catholic women religious were not technically "nuns" according to canon law, I use this term because my sources, and most nineteenth- and twentieth-century Americans, used it.

6 Cynthia Jurisson's encyclopedia entry comprehensively summarizes the secondary literature but fails to draw any conclusions. Jurisson, "Deaconess Movement." Priscilla Pope-Levison is an exception. Her most recent book includes deaconesses, and she is attuned to the possibilities and limits of the vocation. Pope-Levison, *Old Time Religion*.

7 For example, the Lutheran minister studying deaconesses considers any diaconate not centered in a motherhouse as a corruption of the original ideal. Weiser, *Love's Response* and *To Serve*. And a scholar studying only Methodists comes to the conclusion that deaconesses were mainly social workers. Scott, *Natural Allies*, 88. Olson takes the opposite approach with her *Deacons and Deaconesses throughout the Centuries*, which is admirably broad and encyclopedic but cannot give more than a cursory description of deaconesses in the United States in this era.

8 More accurately, they identified as Presbyterian, Norwegian Lutheran, or German Methodist, etc. I am grouping them together as Protestants in a way that they rarely articulated—except when distinguishing themselves from Catholics. I use "Protestant" in this book to mean non–Roman Catholic.

9 Fitzgerald, *Habits of Compassion*.

10 Pope-Levison, *Old Time Religion*, 5.

11 For example, see Griffith, *God's Daughters*; Butler, *Sanctified World*; Brekus, *Strangers & Pilgrims*, 14–15.

12 Dougherty, "Religious Feminism." Even the titles of articles on deaconesses betray the conviction that the female diaconate was but a preamble to women's ordination, with titles such as "From Deaconess to Bishop" by Jacqueline Field-Bibb and Mary Sudman Donovan's "Paving the Way."

13 SenGupta, *From Slavery to Poverty*; Goldstein, *Price of Whiteness*; Jacobson, *Whiteness*; L. Gordon, *Arizona Orphan Abduction*. Judith Weisenfeld's *New World A-comin'* (New York: NYU Press, 2016) is a brilliant exception to the blind spot for religion in recent histories of race.

14 Moody, "Introduction," in *Deaconess Stories*.

15 "Ich befehle euch aber unsere Schwester Phöbe, welche ist im Dienste der Gemeinde zu Kenchreä, daß ihr sie aufnehmet in dem HERRN, wie sich's ziemt den Heiligen, und tut ihr Beistand in allem Geschäfte, darin sie euer bedarf; denn sie hat auch vielen Beistand getan, auch mir selbst."

16 Thuesen, *Discordance*, 45.

17 Meyer, *Deaconesses, Biblical*, 13.

18 A small number of training schools for deaconesses, such as Iva Durham Vennard's Chicago Evangelistic Institute, did teach biblical languages. Pope-Levison, *Old Time Religion*, 122.

19 Meyer, *Deaconesses, Biblical*, 13. Of the biblical scholars who weighed in on the deaconess idea in their denominational periodicals, that seems right. See Warfield, "Presbyterian Deaconesses," *PR*, BX9428.A1, PHS. At least one, McGill, claimed the translation should be "deacon," without any feminine suffix, but his opinion did not carry the day. McGill, "Deaconesses," *PR*, BX9428.A1, PHS.

20 For two examples, see the epigraph in Lucy Rider Meyer, *Deaconesses, Biblical* (1892) and Jubilee Committee, *Deaconess Program: A Great Door and Effectual* (1929), box 2–14, folder 26, CMC.

21 Prelinger, *Charity, Challenge, and Change*, 2–3.

22 Ohl, *Inner Mission*, 12.

23 Weiser, *Love's Response*, 40; Meyer, *Deaconesses, Biblical*, 32. Sioban Nelson points out that mention of the Catholic impetus is conspicuously absent in most histories of the Kaiserswerth deaconesses. Nelson, *Say Little, Do Much*, 134.

24 Prelinger and Keller, "Female Bonding," 319–23.

25 Fritschel, *One Hundred Years*, 14–15; Golder, *History of the Deaconess Movement*, 604.

26 Allchin, *Silent Rebellion*, 59, 37–38, 49–50.

27 Prelinger, "Female Diaconate," 170–71.

28 Prelinger, "Female Diaconate," 167; Cooke, *Mildmay*.

29 Cooke, *Mildmay*, 43, 51, 53–54.

30 For example, the Methodist Woman's Home Missionary Society sent a member to live and work with the English Mildmay deaconesses for two years and to report on her experience. The result of Harriet Cooke's stay was her book *Mildmay; or, The Story of the First Deaconess Institution*.

31 Periodicals such as the Methodist Episcopal *Ladies' Repository*, the Reformed *Mercersburg Review*, the A.M.E. *Christian Recorder*, the *Congregationalist*, the *Lutheran Quarterly*, and the *Presbyterian Review* all carried articles in the mid- to late nineteenth century discussing the deaconess movement, including "Deaconesses," *CR*; "Selected Deaconesses—or Sister Phebe," *CR*; Fry, "Ancient and Modern Deaconesses," *LR*; Hurst, "Charitable Institutions in Europe," *LR*; "Women's Record at Home," *LR*; Warfield, "Presbyterian Deaconesses," *PR*; McGill, "Deaconesses," *PR*.

32 "The Mary J. Drexel Home and Philadelphia Mother-House of Deaconesses," *Harper's Bazar*, April 13, 1889, 265–67. (The magazine originally spelled its title "Bazar," without the double *a*.)

33 Historians have spilled much ink debating and defending periodization in US history. I use the terms with a light touch, recognizing that much of my discussion overflows any periodization: I invoke the Gilded Age when it aligns with deaconesses' concern for consumerism; I refer to the Progressive Era when it is relevant context for deaconesses' reform efforts that appealed to new ideals of efficiency and scientific charity; and I point out when the Depression maps onto concerns over money.

34 Meyer, *Deaconess Stories*, 238–39.

CHAPTER 1. A TAPESTRY OF DIACONATES

1 Cook, *The Life of Florence Nightingale*, 1:57.

2 McGill, "Deaconesses," 285.

3 J.U.S., "How Can We Best Adapt the Biblical Deaconess Ideas to Our American Conditions?" 3, 121–5 Es 7, DF.

4 Keller, Moede, and Moore, *Called to Serve*, 26; Keller, "Protestant Tradition," 326. Previous estimates have ranged from "almost 2,000" Protestant women to more than 5,000 Methodist women alone who were consecrated deaconesses between 1885 and 1920, with no reliable empirical basis for denominational comparison.

5 Fritschel, *One Hundred Years*, 15–17; Weiser, *Love's Response*, 54.

6 Fritschel, *One Hundred Years*, 22–27, 64.

7 Ohl, *Work in Philadelphia*, 4.

8 Some partisans frowned on such endeavors: "The disastrous experience of a number of American deaconess houses organized on an inter-denominational basis amply demonstrates the futility of endeavoring to do effective Inner Mission work on any other than that of confessional agreement and a correct and sound churchly practice." Ohl, *Inner Mission*, 100.

9 Divided into no less than twenty-four ecclesiastical groups by 1900, "throughout the 19th century, Lutherans in America concentrated on what distinguished them not so much from other Christians as from other Lutherans." Gaustad and Barlow, *Historical Atlas*, 108; Weiser, *Serving Love*, 128.

10 I use "German denominations" loosely to include the German and Northern European denominations, including German Lutherans, German Methodists, German Reformed, and Evangelical Synod, as well as Swedish, Danish, and Norwegian Lutherans.

11 Bettin, "History of Miss Martha Bettin," 1903, box 2–15, folder 16, CMC.

12 Lagerquist, *Mothers' Arms*, 69.

13 Gaustad and Barlow, *Historical Atlas*, 61.

14 Ayres, *Muhlenberg*, 188.

15 Donovan, *A Different Call*.

16 Schnorrenberg, "Alabama Deaconesses," 468–90.

17 Brown, *In Their Time*, 6.

18 Golder, *History of the Deaconess Movement*, 321.

19 Pope-Levison, "Exposing Complexities," 101–8. Priscilla Pope-Levison offers an incisive critique of the myopic focus on Meyer and her deaconess model in Methodist historiography, arguing that Robinson's model offered a more liberating option for women, utilizing a separatist strategy of female institution building.

20 Ahlstrom, *Religious History*, 795.

21 *First Annual Report of the New England Deaconess Home and Training School, 1889–1890* (Boston: McDonald, Gill, 1890), 5; New England Deaconess Association, *New England Training School for Christian Service, 1914–1915* (Boston: 1914), 12–13, 16–17; New England Deaconess Association, *Catalogue: Training School* (Boston, 1905), 8.

22 Heffner, *United Brethren Traditions*, 2.

23 Study Committee of the General Deaconess Board, *Directions and Helps: Course of Study for Deaconesses* (New York: Methodist Book Concern, 1922), 69–71, 168–70.

24 Edwards, "St. Margaret's House," 32.

25 Horton, "Womanhood and Service," 498. The *Presbyterian Deaconess Quarterly* approvingly reprinted Horton's lecture two years later as "Reaching the People."

26 *A Deaconess—Why Not?* Fourth edition (Buffalo, NY: General Deaconess Board of the Methodist Episcopal Church, ca. 1920), 10–11.

27 Thirteenth Annual Report of the Chicago Deaconess Home of the Methodist Episcopal Church (1901), box 2–30, folder 5, CMC.
28 Fitzgerald, *Habits of Compassion*, 119. Catholic women religious also conflicted with ideas of "scientific charity."
29 Meyer, *Deaconess Stories*, 21, 59.
30 For the story of Episcopal deaconesses selling dry goods at cost, see Howell, "The Deaconess and Home-Making," 5.
31 This argument is seconded by Lindley in *Stept out of Your Place* (144–45). Dougherty provides a more detailed treatment of Methodist deaconesses' participation in the Social Gospel, including their establishment of makeshift employment offices, in "The Social Gospel according to Phoebe."
32 Laceye Warner has pointed to the precedent to Methodist deaconess nursing in John Wesley's appointing women as sick visitors in his ministry in Georgia, possibly referring to them as deaconesses. Warner, "Paradigm for Evangelism," 178–82.
33 Meyer, "Social Service," *Deaconess Advocate* 29, no. 4 (1914): 8; "Services at Ocean Grove," *New York Times*, August 12, 1901; "Miss Verna McFerrin, Biographical Sketch," 1980, 2589-6-7:19, MAHC.
34 Robert, *Women in Mission*, 159; Pope-Levison, *Old Time Religion*. The most noted Methodist deaconess evangelist was Iva Durham Vennard, whom we will meet again in subsequent chapters. Vennard's insistence on the centrality of evangelism did rankle her Methodist colleagues. Pope-Levison has analyzed Vennard's hard-fought career as an evangelist and institution builder.
35 Deweese, *Baptist Service*, 69, 89.
36 Collier-Thomas, *Jesus, Jobs, and Justice*, 83.
37 Roebuck, "Limiting Liberty," 131–46.
38 Spaeth, "A Review."
39 Spaeth, "The Chicago Training School."
40 Spaeth, "Deaconess-Evangelist-Sister."
41 Rev. C. O. Pederson, "What Has the Diaconate to Offer to Solve the Moral and Religious Problems Confronting the Church Today?" in *The Twenty-Second Conference of the Lutheran Deaconess Motherhouses in America* (1936), 26–27. As Jean Miller Schmidt has shown, the Evangelical Synod, German Reformed, and General Synod Lutherans *did* develop a social Christianity influenced by the Social Gospel, but not until a later date. The Evangelical Synod and German Reformed churches were charter members of the Federal Council of Churches, which also had the early support of the Lutheran General Synod. More conservative Lutherans remained staunchly opposed. Schmidt, *Souls*, 179–85.
42 Sources hint that the German clergy were more concerned with distancing themselves from the Social Gospel than were the deaconesses. For example, the head sister of the Baltimore Lutheran motherhouse corresponded with muckraking journalist, Progressive reformer, and fellow Dane Jacob Riis, inviting him to visit their motherhouse. In his reply he expressed familiarity with the deaconess work. Jacob A. Riis to Sister Sophia Jepson, August 29, 1903, AELCA.

43 German Methodists occupied an in-between position, sharing the theology of their Anglophone coreligionists, while also sharing the motherhouse commitment and health care focus of their other German brethren.

44 Donovan, *A Different Call*, 94.

45 Bradley, "The Deaconess as Nurse," 14.

46 Of the 1499 known US-born deaconesses, 863 were from the Midwest. The Northeast claimed 427 deaconesses. And despite the fact that more institutions were located in the West than the South, 170 deaconesses were southerners, and the remaining 39 were westerners. USFC 1920.

47 It is important to note that many of these institutions did not survive as deaconess institutions for more than a decade or two. Into the twentieth century, many deaconess hospitals especially remained "deaconess" in name only. Institutions: Methodist 110; Lutheran 23; Evangelical Synod 15; Episcopalian 11; German Methodist 12; Midwest 102; Northeast 42; West 32; South 25; German Triangle 55.

48 Carroll, *Routledge Historical Atlas*, 90.

49 Herzberger, "Lutherischen Diaconissenheims," 131–33.

50 Additionally, Baltimore, Brooklyn, St. Paul, New York, Cincinnati, Cleveland, Philadelphia, and Milwaukee could all claim deaconess institutions of at least three different denominations.

51 USFC 1920.

52 Of the 2021 deaconesses whose birthplace is known, 522 were immigrants: Germany 213; Sweden 75; Norway 73; Canada 48; England 36; Switzerland 21; Russia 13. Ten or fewer deaconesses came from other countries: Austria, Belgium, Brazil, China, Denmark, Finland, Hungary, Iceland, India, Ireland, Italy, Liberia, Lithuania, Martinique, New Zealand, Palestine, Peru, Poland, Scotland, the West Indies.

53 The 549 immigrants and 583 second-generation immigrants together equal 1132. This is 54 percent of the 2101 deaconesses whose birthplace is known.

54 Thus, Rosemary Skinner Keller's conclusion that "a majority of the deaconesses came from old-stock Protestant homes" gravely mischaracterizes the movement. While that statement may have been truer of the deaconesses of the Methodist Episcopal Church, even there the European influence was significant. Keller, "Protestant Tradition," 273.

55 Douglass, *Immigrant Soul*, 141.

56 Sister Anna M. P. Goetze, "Reminiscences," n.d., DF.

57 Clara M. Bay, May 9, 1897, GL, box 2–15, folder 11, CMC.

58 Clara M. Bay, May 15, 1897, GL, box 2–15, folder 11, CMC.

59 MJD, *Hand-Book*, 1919.

60 Bertha Grollmus, KI, DF.

61 Bertha Grollmus, KI, DF.

62 Benz, "Short Sketch of My Life," 1903, box 2–15, folder 14, CMC.

63 Richard Preuter, "Bio of Mary Elaine (Nee Kluge) Preuter." In *LCMS Deaconess Biographies Project*. http://www.deaconessbio.org, accessed February 21, 2017.

64 MJD, *Hand-Book*, 1919.

65 MJD, *Hand-Book*, 1919, 20; Sister Margaret Schueder and Sister Grace Lauer, "Philadelphia Sisters Council Minutes," 1921–1940, 268–4 B2, AELCA.

66 Grant, *Deaconess Manual.*

67 Gibson, "Florence Randolph," 423.

68 I find evidence for a dozen black deaconesses consecrated before 1940.

69 Sister Martha Hansen to Rev. J. Frank Fife, December 20, 1945, AELCA; Roland W. Renkel to Sister Martha Hansen, May 2, 1946, AELCA.

70 "Anna Alexander, Deaconess," *LC*, AELCA.

71 Frickey, "The Deaconess of Today," 9, box 2–14, folder 34, CMC.

72 Schueder and Lauer entries for May 11, 1927, and November 30, 1927, in "Philadelphia Sisters Council Minutes," 268–4 B2, AELCA.

73 Rev. H. R. Gold to Charles E. Hay, April 21, 1919, AELCA.

74 The urban population in the United States increased from 40 percent in 1900 to 51.4 percent in 1920. USFC, II: Population 1920, General Report and Analytical Tables: 88, table 21.

75 While the census did not enumerate all the places classed as urban, it did track population data for cities having twenty-five thousand inhabitants or more. I use this classification here as a proxy for "urban." USFC, I: Population 1920, Number and Distribution of Inhabitants: 82–86, table 48. Two hundred and eighty-seven out of 812 American-born deaconesses (of known birthplace) were from cities of twenty-five thousand or more.

76 One hundred and forty-four out of 195 deaconess institutions were in cities of twenty-five thousand or more.

77 "Don't Come to the City, Girls, to Seek Your Fortune."

78 Brown, *In Their Time*, 11. The specter of girls being confined against their will replays Protestant fears and fantasies of Roman Catholic convents that will be explored in chapter 3.

79 Sister Sophie Damme, interview by Mary Pellauer, March, 19, 1989, AELCA.

80 Fogelstrom, *Greatest Need*, 20.

81 *A Deaconess—Why Not?* 14–15.

CHAPTER 2. NEGOTIATING GENDER

1 Horton, *Builders*, 158.

2 Johnston, *White Ties*, 6.

3 Rev. William Muir Auld, letter in the Deaconess House Campaign Scrapbook of the Philadelphia School for Christian Workers of the Presbyterian and Reformed Churches (Philadelphia, 1918), VAULT BV4180.P53A4, PHS. Jeanne Boydston, in "Gender as a Question of Historical Analysis," emphasizes that scholars of women's history must understand gender as a historical process rather than a static category of analysis.

4 Dorsey, *Reforming Men and Women*, 38. Dorsey traces the nineteenth-century emergence of "influence" as the quality seen as suiting women for reform work, supplanting the more ambiguously gendered eighteenth-century idea of "virtue."

5   Morris, *At Our Own Door*, 16.

6   Krauth, "Woman's Work," 18.

7   "The Homer Toberman Deaconess House," *OH*, MAHC.

8   Welter, *American History*; Helsinger, Sheets, and Veeder, *Woman Question*.

9   Philadelphia School for Christian Workers of the Presbyterian and Reformed Churches. "Deaconess House Campaign Scrapbook," scrapbooks 227, PHS.

10 McGill, "Deaconesses," 286–87.

11 Golder, *Mission and Aim of the Deaconess Movement in the United States*, box 2–14, folder 38, CMC.

12 Fry, "Ancient and Modern Deaconesses," 110.

13 "Where Are the Nine?" 25–26.

14 Johnston, *White Ties*, 9.

15 Ess, *What Is Deaconess Work?* (St. Louis: Evangelical Deaconess Home and Hospital, n.d.).

16 Edward A. Ross, "The Causes of Race Superiority," *Annals of the Institute for Political Science* 18 (1901): 67–89.

17 Roosevelt, *Theodore Roosevelt: An Autobiography*, 177.

18 Golder, *History of the Deaconess Movement*, 446–47.

19 Bachmann, "Peculiar Difficulties," 269.2 B2 F2, AELCA.

20 Fogelstrom, *Greatest Need*, 20.

21 Lears, *Rebirth*, 94.

22 Biennial Report to the German Central Deaconess Board by the General Superintendent (n.d.), box 23, folder 15, CMC, 7.

23 Jens, *Evangelical Faith*, 15.

24 Lydia E. Froebe, September 9, 1900, GL, box 2–16, folder 19, CMC.

25 Sister Sophie Damme, interview by Mary Pellauer, March, 19, 1989, AELCA.

26 Helm, "What a Deaconess Is."

27 J.U.S., "How Can We Best Adapt the Biblical Deaconess Ideas to Our American Conditions?" 3, 121–5 Es 7, DF.

28 Meyer, *DA*, June 1888: 1.

29 Fitch and Ruggles, "Marriage Formation," 85.

30 Holding, *Joy, the Deaconess*, 92.

31 Jens, *Evangelical Faith*.

32 Fitch and Ruggles, "Marriage Formation," 83. Averaging the available data for 1880–1940, 25 percent of these women were married by 19.14 years of age, 50 percent married by 21.72, and 75 percent, by 25.15.

33 N=939. Note that this data does include immigrant deaconesses, unlike Fitch and Ruggles's data, which only includes native-born Americans.

34 N=1426. Evangelical Synod women were the youngest at entrance (twenty-four) and consecration (twenty-seven), and Episcopalians were the oldest (thirty-three at entrance, thirty-seven at consecration). Methodists and Lutherans mirrored the averages.

35 Sister Frieda Eckoff, June 22, 1981, KI, DF.

36 Of the pre-1940s women for whom I have enough information to tell, I can identify 848 lifelong deaconesses (who either died in active service or retired due to old age or disability) and 476 deaconesses who left the office. There were almost certainly many more "leavers" than these numbers suggest. I can account for the service duration of only 1324 of the 3347 known pre-1940s deaconesses. Unaccounted-for deaconesses were more likely to be "leavers" than "lifers." Deaconess groups loved to celebrate the stories of lifers, whereas leavers seem to have been swept under the rug. It appears that many deaconesses simply ceased communicating with the central organization rather than formally severing their ties with the diaconate. They simply faded from the records. Internal statistics kept by the Methodists and United Church of Christ confirm that at least one-quarter of deaconesses who left informed the administration that they were leaving for marriage. For statistics on the United Church of Christ, see reports of the Committee to Study Deaconess Idea and Work of the St. Louis Evangelical Sisterhood, 1937 and 1957, DF. For the Methodist Episcopal Church: Dr. C. S. Woods, Report of the Personnel Committee to the Annual Meeting of BHHD (February 14–15, 1928), 2085-7-1:03, MAHC. That data reveals a much larger percentage of women marrying soon after their departure, which suggests a reluctance by deaconesses to admit that they were leaving for marriage.

37 Sisterhood Roster: Original Ledger from the Executive Deaconess, Sisterhood Lists/Data Folder, DF.

38 Fisk, "Deaconess Home."

39 McGill, "Deaconesses," 286.

40 Holding, *Joy, the Deaconess*, 213.

41 Hall, in *The Deaconess*, October 1927, RG300, AELCA.

42 Ninth Annual Report of the Church Training and Deaconess House of the Diocese of Pennsylvania (1900), 16, PP183 acc.92.92, AEC.

43 Wacker, *Deaconess Calling*, 97–98.

44 Joan Likness, "[Dellema King] Observes 50 Years of Service," *Times*, 1973, AEC.

45 Seventy-five percent lifers, 12 percent leavers, 13 percent of unknown fate.

46 The other two denominations for whom there is enough evidence to draw meaningful conclusions are the Mennonites (52 percent lifers, 25 percent leavers, 23 percent unknown) and the Evangelical Synod (26 percent lifers, 23 percent leavers, 51 percent unknown).

47 Hall, "Women and Holy Orders," 20. Only passing references to deaconesses marrying doctors were found. Perhaps deaconesses saw marriage to a minister as a legitimate extension of their calling in a way that marriage to a doctor would not be.

48 Grindal, *Sister Elisabeth Fedde*, 167.

49 Hazel B. Blanchard to the Deaconess Board, August 13, 1926, Correspondence 1925–1926, 2595-7-1:08, MAHC.

50 Ida Marian Swett Treganza to the New England Deaconess Association, March 12, 1921, 2595-7-1:04, MAHC.

51 In *Mothers of All Children*, Clapp reviews maternalism as defined by Molly Ladd-Taylor, Theda Skocpol, Linda Gordon, and Seth Koven and Sonya Michel.

52 Ladd-Taylor, "Defining Maternalism"; Clapp, *Mothers of All Children*, 48.

53 Smith, Tibbetts, and Pike, *There Was One Anna*, 68.

54 Wathen, *A Gallant Life*.

55 F. B. Meyer, *Their Calling*, 32.

56 Green, "Woman's Work in the Church."

57 "Tributes."

58 Kaufman, *Inasmuch*, 10.

59 Minutes of the Ninth Annual Meeting of the National Methodist Hospitals and Homes Association in Convention with the Methodist Deaconess Association and the National Deaconess Convention, 1926–1927 (Chicago, February 16–17, 1927), 2079-4-6:05, MAHC.

60 Johnston, *White Ties*, 26–27.

61 L. M. Zimmerman, "World's Need of Deaconesses," *DB* 7, no. 6 (March 1928): 2.

62 Jens, *Evangelical Faith*, 13.

63 *A Deaconess—Why Not?* 21.

64 *How Will I Spend This Life?* (General Deaconess Board of the Methodist Episcopal Church, ca. 1923), 3, box 2–22, folder 18, CMC. Likewise, for a deaconess who mothered not three, but "more than a hundred times three," see Smith, Tibbetts, and Pike, *There Was One Anna*, 68.

65 Zimmerman, "Glory," *LCW*, 6, 269.1, B2, F4, AELCA.

66 Howell, "The Deaconess and Home-Making," 5.

67 Howell, "The Deaconess and Home-Making," 5; Clapp, *Mothers*, 12–14.

68 Meyer, *Deaconess Stories*, 26, 75.

69 Fisk, "What the Deaconesses Are Doing."

70 Mergner, *The Deaconess and Her Work*, 186–87. Refer also to Lutheran pastor Rev. G. U. Wenner's injunction: "To such [servant girls] the deaconess is as a mother, and one of the church rooms or some other suitable place may be a gathering-place and home, and a centre of all good influences" (*The Office of Deaconess*, 11).

71 Yursik, "Work for the Immigrant Children," 14. Likewise, the immigrant mothers in Johnston's novel take a "childish" pleasure in inspecting the deaconesses' kitchen-garden. Johnston, *White Ties*, 27.

72 Mergner, *The Deaconess and Her Work*, 188.

73 Molly Ladd-Taylor categorizes these two kinds of appeals as sentimental maternalism and progressive maternalism in "Maternalism as a Paradigm." Weiner et al., "Maternalism as a Paradigm," 110. Lori Ginzburg argues that after the Civil War, women activists began advocating a professional standard over moral suasion as their best technique for social amelioration. Ginzburg, *Work of Benevolence*, 208–9. And Daniel Walkowitz argues that female social workers in the 1920s were challenged by contradictory messages to adopt both a traditional feminine nurturing role and the masculine dispassionate objectivity of the new professions. Walkowitz, "Feminine Professional Identity," 1056.

74 Wathen, *A Gallant Life*, 23, 26.

75 Green, "Woman's Work in the Church," 3.

76 Sister Magdalene Krebs, *The Motherhouse—a Home* (Milwaukee: Lutheran Deaconess Home), Lutheran Deaconess Folder, DF. Sister Olivia recalled her resentment at the meddlesomeness of her older deaconess sisters in a 1982 interview. Sister Olivia Drusch, January 26, 1982, KI, DF.

77 Jens, *Principles of Deaconess Work*, 33.

78 Coburn and Smith, *Spirited Lives*, 77. For the comparison of a Methodist deaconess home to a boarding school, see Johnston, *White Ties*, 14. For another example of a family of women, see Carolyn De Swarte Gifford's analysis of Woman's Christian Temperance Union founder Frances Willard, who visited a deaconess institution in France and created a unique home for herself and her fellow workers. Instead of "the dominant mid-nineteenth-century ideal of a home containing a family of close kin with husband as its head, surrounded by his wife and their children," Willard created a "family of women who chose to live with each other, and who might or might not be kin." Willard, *Writing Out My Heart*, 16.

79 USFC 1930.

80 Donovan argues that Episcopal deaconesses were reluctant to form communities because of the risk of confusion with Episcopal sisterhoods, which were suspect because of their high-church association. *A Different Call*, 120.

81 "In Memoriam," *Deaconess*, May 1941.

82 Golder, *Mission and Aim*, 579.

83 Johnston, *White Ties*, 13–14.

84 Deaconess hospitals were often built alongside of, or before, deaconess homes, and more postcards survive from hospitals than from homes. Rev. Golder warned deaconess communities not to get too caught up in building hospitals, but to give priority to the motherhouse itself. Golder, *History of the Deaconess Movement*, 494.

85 Sister Magdalene Krebs, *The Motherhouse—a Home* (Milwaukee: Lutheran Deaconess Home), Lutheran Deaconess Folder, DF.

86 Joselit, *Jewish Culture*, 135–39.

87 McDannell, *Christian Home*, 25–28.

88 Sister Elizabeth Lotz, September 14, 1981, KI, DF.

89 Rasche, *Deaconess Heritage*, 284.

90 Sister Velma Kampschmidt, oral review, May 1981, DF.

91 Johnston, *White Ties*, 14–16.

92 Donovan, "Paving the Way," 495.

93 Johnston, *White Ties*, 14–16.

94 McDannell, *Christian Home*, 45, 134, 152.

95 Smith, Tibbetts, and Pike, *There Was One Anna*, 100.

96 Deaconess Theodora Beard, "Letters from Alumnae," *New York Training School for Deaconesses*, October 1913, 5, AEC.

97 MJD, *A Call*, 23.

98 Pauline Becker, "Preparation for Deaconesses for Consecration," 1934, Consecration Services folder, DF.

99 MJD, *A Call*, 23.

100 Jens, *Evangelical Faith*, 12. For similar advice, see Wacker, *Deaconess Calling*, 88–89.

101 "Deaconesses," 23.

102 Sister Ella Loew, June 1, 1981, KI, DF.

103 Tentler, *Wage-Earning Women*, 88–89.

104 Bachmann, "Peculiar Difficulties," 9.

105 Anna D. Schmidt, July 13, 1896, GL, box 2–17, folder 30, CMC.

106 Jubilee Committee, *Deaconess Program: A Great Door and Effectual* (1929), box 2–14, folder 26, CMC.

107 Jens, *Evangelical Faith*, 13.

108 Jens, *Evangelical Faith*, 13. However, Jens chose the milder words of Matthew over the harsher teaching of Luke 14:26: "If any man come to me, and hate not his father, and mother, and wife, and children, and brethren, and sisters, yea, and his own life also, he cannot be my disciple."

109 Jens, *Principles of Deaconess Work*, 32.

110 According to Woods, *Personnel Committee*, between 1888 and 1928, 226 deaconesses left for marriage and only 42 left for "care of family."

111 Margaret Van Dyck to Sister Olivia Drusch and Sister Hilda, May 9, 1952, DF.

112 "Sarah Delilah Church," 1975, MAHC.

113 Bertha Conde to "My dear friend," April 6, 1921, RG-289, box 3, folder 6, AEC.

CHAPTER 3. USES OF CATHOLICISM

1 According to canon law, the term "nun" designates only women religious who have taken solemn vows, and in the nineteenth-century United States very few Catholic sisters were actually nuns. Deaconesses, however, followed Protestant convention and applied the term to all Catholic women religious. I retain their broad usage of the term but recognize its technical inaccuracy.

2 Lears, *Grace*, 184–203.

3 Strong, *Our Country*, 53.

4 Leigh Eric Schmidt points out how the Enlightenment project of unmasking the oracles went hand in hand with Protestant disavowal of popish priestcraft. L. Schmidt, *Hearing Things*, 86–101.

5 Ewens, *Role of the Nun*, 301. As Maureen Fitzgerald argues, this Protestant trope of the victimization of nuns at the hands of priests masked the more complicated dynamics of power among Catholic men and women religious. Although their interest was in discrediting the Catholic gender system in which nuns were victimized by priests, deaconesses also praised the sisters (rather than the men, and especially bishops, lauded in traditional Catholic histories) for building up the system of Catholic charities that emerged in this period. Maureen Fitzgerald, *Habits of Compassion*, 8.

6 Franchot, *Roads to Rome.*

7 Ewens, *Role of the Nun*, 183. The best, though by no means only, example of this genre is the story of "Maria Monk" in *The Awful Disclosures of the Hotel Dieu Nunnery of Montreal* (New York: Howe & Bates, 1836).

8 Horton, *Burden.*

9 "Die römisch-katholische Kirche hat es trefflich verstanden, den Dienst christlich gesinnter Jungfrauen für die Hebung ihres Ansehens aufs beste zu verwerthen, denn es ist nicht sowohl die Thätigkeit ihrer Priester direkt, wodurch sie den Massen imponirt, als vielmehr der stille, selbstverleugnende Samariterdienst, den ihre barmherzigen Schwestern den Kranken und Armen erweisen." "Rathschlaege für Christliche Jungfrauen, die mit dem Gedanken Umgehen, in die Deutsche Methodisten Diakonissen Anstalt Einzutreten" (Pittsburgh, PA: City Mission Publishing, 1896).

10 For example, the Sisters of Charity of Cincinnati. Kraman, "Women Religious," 26. Also, the Irish Sisters of Mercy took up nursing in Chicago's 1849 cholera epidemic. Hoy, *Good Hearts*, 37.

11 Coburn and Smith, *Spirited Lives*, 63.

12 Ewens, *Role of the Nun*, 222, 36, 50.

13 Fry, "Ancient and Modern Deaconesses," 110.

14 Meyer, *Deaconess, Biblical*, 122.

15 Horton, *Builders*, 99–100.

16 "Immanuel Deaconess Institute, Omaha, Nebraska" (1932), 270.1 B2 F1, AELCA; H. Anderson, *Immanuel Deaconess Institute*, 9. Interestingly, nineteenth-century Catholic priests complained that they were debarred from visiting their parishioners in public hospitals and used these arguments to promote the same Catholic hospitals of which the ministers complained! See Cetina, "In Times of Immigration," 89.

17 Dickey, "Why Wear the Costume," *OH*, MAHC.

18 "One Century of Protestant Deaconess Work," 121–1K Sai 2, DF.

19 Fogelstrom, *Greatest Need*, 4.

20 "The Deaconess and the City," *OH*, MAHC.

21 "The Difference between a Deaconess and a Nun," box 2–22, folder 7, CMC.

22 Fry, "Ancient and Modern Deaconesses," *LR*, 109.

23 Rigg, "Wesley Deaconess Order."

24 Ewens, *Role of the Nun*, 281.

25 "The Mary J. Drexel Home and Philadelphia Mother-House of Deaconesses," *Harper's Bazar*, April 13, 1889, 265, 67.

26 Rasche, "The Deaconess Garb," pre-1983, Deaconess Garb Folder, DF.

27 The pursuit of simplicity of dress was thoroughgoing: the Presbyterian training school catalogs of Philadelphia and Baltimore both stipulated that candidates bring "plain underclothing." *Deaconess House and Training School for Christian Workers of the Presbyterian and Reformed Churches (Catalogue)* (Philadelphia, 1909); Presbyterian Training School, *The Presbyterian Training School (Cata-*

logue) (Baltimore, MD, 1913–1914), 38. A German Methodist deaconess candidate inquired specifically of the head deaconess, "Can we have trimming on our underwear or do you want them made plain?" Clara M. Bay, May 15, 1897, GL, box 2–15, folder 11, CMC.

28 Bachmann, "Peculiar Difficulties," 11–12.

29 Bothilda Swenson to A. E. Fogelstrom, July 1887, AELCA.

30 Meyer, *Deaconesses, Biblical*, 148. As evidenced in figure 3.2, some Episcopal and Lutheran deaconesses did wear veils, but they did not completely cover the hair.

31 M. Scott, *Convent Life*, 86.

32 Horton, *Builders*, 77–78.

33 Vennard, "The Deaconess of Today," 11, box 2–22, folder 7, CMC.

34 "The Wesley Deaconess," 2.

35 Meyer, *Deaconess Stories*, 25, 125.

36 Richelsen, "Protestant Deaconesses," 2; Dickey, "Why Wear the Costume."

37 Winston, *Red-Hot and Righteous*, 87.

38 Kaufman, *Inasmuch*, 10.

39 Dickey, "Why Wear the Costume."

40 Mogle, "Deaconess Work in the South," 21–24.

41 Jepson, *Where Lies the Sacrifice*, 153; *Why I Am Glad*.

42 *Why I Am Glad.*

43 Cooke, *Mildmay*, 52.

44 "The New Woman."

45 Golder, *Motherhouse*, 109.

46 Jens, *Principles of Deaconess Work*, 37.

47 Meyer, *Deaconess Stories*, 213.

48 Fischer, "Dressing to Please God," 57.

49 "Objections Considered," *Message* 5 (February 1890): 6.

50 Withrow, "Dr. Withrow on Deaconesses."

51 Bowie, *Alabaster and Spikenard*, 106.

52 Winston, *Red-Hot and Righteous*, 85–88.

53 Withrow, "Dr. Withrow on the Deaconess Costume."

54 Cooke, *Mildmay*, 52.

55 "The Wesley Deaconess," 2.

56 *Why I Am Glad*, 5.

57 Meyer, *Deaconesses, Biblical* (1892), 234.

58 Bushman, *Refinement*, 69–74.

59 Deaconesses pointed out that "while the first cost of good black is higher than colors, it continues to look well until worn out." Deaconesses of the Woman's Home Missionary Society, *Present Day Outlook*, 6–7. Meyer, *Deaconess Stories*, 207.

60 Bushman, *Refinement*, 65.

61 Meyer, *Deaconess Stories*, 15.

62 Jens, *Principles of Deaconess Work*, 37.

63 Meyer, *Deaconess, Biblical* (1892), 235.
64 Methodists' class status had been rising throughout the nineteenth century. See Hatch's *Democratization of American Christianity*, 193.
65 Gordon, "Fossilized Fashion," 53.
66 Holding, *Joy, the Deaconess*, 113.
67 Jepson, *Where Lies the Sacrifice*, 153.
68 Sister Anna, "An Open Letter by a Deaconess."
69 Wathen, *A Gallant Life*, 155.
70 Ewens, *Role of the Nun*, 123, 15, 76, 304.
71 Fry, "Ancient and Modern Deaconesses," 109.
72 Ewens, *Role of the Nun*, 166–67.
73 Spaeth, Manhart, and Goedel, *An Appeal*, 2, 269.2 B2 F1, AELCA.
74 "The Difference between a Deaconess and a Nun," box 2–22, folder 7, CMC.
75 "The Difference between a Deaconess and a Nun," box 2–22, folder 7, CMC, 1–2.
76 Jens, *Principles of Deaconess Work*, 17–18.
77 Meyer, *Deaconesses, Biblical*, 148 (1889); Withrow, "Deaconess Costume."
78 Fry, "Ancient and Modern Deaconesses," 109.
79 Cooke, *Mildmay*, xviii, 56.
80 Withrow, "Dr. Withrow on Deaconesses."
81 Wathen, *A Gallant Life*, 32.
82 What is not revealed in the promotional literature is the extent to which deaconess work taxed the health of deaconesses, who often asked for leaves of absence or reassignments on account of poor health.
83 Jubilee Committee, *Deaconess Program: A Great Door and Effectual* (1929), box 2–14, folder 26, CMC.
84 Meyer, *Deaconess Stories*, 69.
85 M. L. Gibson, "The Ideal Deaconess."
86 Students of the Kansas City National Training School for Deaconesses and Missionaries, *The Shield* (1921), 62.
87 Golder, *History of the Deaconess Movement*, 446.
88 Johnston, *White Ties*, 24.
89 Johnston, *White Ties*, 14.
90 Meyer, *Deaconess Stories*, 234.
91 MJD, *Hand-Book*, 1913, 4.
92 *General Information about Deaconess Work*, n.d., Organization of Sisterhood folder, DF.
93 Martin Luther, "The Freedom of a Christian," in *Three Treatises*, trans. W. A. Lambert (Philadelphia: Fortress Press, 1970), 277.
94 Fry, "Ancient and Modern Deaconesses," 109. Fry here quotes from liberal Anglican Thomas Arnold's 1856 *Christian Life: Its Course, Its Hindrances, and Its Helps*.
95 "The Difference between a Deaconess and a Nun," box 2–22, folder 7, CMC.
96 Franchot, *Roads to Rome*, xxv.
97 Jens, *Principles of Deaconess Work*, 38.

98 McGill, "Deaconesses," 283–84.
99 Hall, "Women and Holy Orders," 20.
100 Hall, in *The Deaconess*, October 1927, RG300, AELCA.
101 "Deaconess Margaret Booz," *Living Church*, June 8, 1958, Margaret Booz Folder, National Center for the Diaconate, AELCA.
102 Fitzgerald, *Habits of Compassion*, 23–24.
103 Kaufman, *Inasmuch*, 8.
104 Kaufman, *Inasmuch*, 8.
105 "Sister Velma Kampschmidt Wanted to Be a Missionary," *Focus* (August 1989): 5.
106 Jennie Christ, tagebuch [diary], 1894–1895, AELCA.
107 Meyer, *Deaconess Stories*, 16.
108 Meyer, *Deaconesses, Biblical* (1889), 123.
109 Meyer, *Deaconesses, Biblical* (1889), 74, 65.
110 Jens, *Principles of Deaconess Work*, 68.
111 Bendroth and Brereton, *Women and Twentieth-Century Protestantism*, xiv–xv.
112 For one example of this: "Einweihung des Evang. St. Lukas-Diakonissenhauses und Hospitals zu Faribault, Minn."
113 "Deaconess House Campaign Scrapbook," PHS.
114 *Deaconess House and Training School for Christian Workers of the Presbyterian and Reformed Churches (Catalogue)* (Philadelphia, 1909), 6.
115 *Thirty-third Annual Report of the Fall River Deaconess Home of the Methodist Episcopal Church* (Fall River, MA: Baggett Printers, 1927), 11, 2083-4-4:06, MAHC; Elizabeth S. Whitehouse to Sadie Hagen, January 17, 1927, 2595-7-1:10, MAHC.

CHAPTER 4. DEACONESSES AND THE ALLOWANCE

1 Schmidt, July 13, 1896, GL, CMC. Grammatical, syntactical, and spelling errors in original.
2 Some deaconesses, mostly Episcopal and Presbyterian deaconesses, were salaried from the beginning. But this "salary" was set at a sacrificially low amount, like the allowance.
3 Vennard, "The Deaconess of Today," box 2–22, folder 7, CMC.
4 Vennard, "The Deaconess of Today," box 2–22, folder 7, CMC.
5 Rasche, *Deaconess Heritage*, 33.
6 Rasche, *Deaconess Heritage*, 33; Schueder and Lauer, "Philadelphia Sisters Council Minutes," 16, 268–4 B2, AELCA; Report of the Corresponding Secretary of the General Deaconess Board to the Board of Hospitals, Homes, and Deaconess Work (December 16, 1924), 3, 2085-7-1:02, MAHC.
7 Report of the Corresponding Secretary of the General Deaconess Board to the Board of Hospitals, Homes, and Deaconess Work (December 16, 1924), 3, 2085-7-1:02, MAHC.
8 Methodist Episcopal Church, BHHD (1927), 5, MAHC. The same paper reported that Brooklyn deaconesses received much less, but that they were currently raising the amount.

9   A. Z. Mann, Meeting of Commission on Deaconess Work in Methodist Episcopal Church, BHHD (Cincinnati, March 10, 1925), 3, 2085-7-1:02, MAHC.

10 Edward W. Young to Rev. Foster U. Gift, March 6, 1933, 296.6 B1 F4, AELCA.

11 Sister Martha Hansen to the Sisterhood, February 1943, AELCA.

12 Zelizer, "'Special Monies'"; Zelizer, *The Social Meaning of Money*.

13 *House Rules of the Philadelphia Motherhouse of Deaconesses (Mary J. Drexel Home)*, rev. ed., 268.2 B1 F1, AELCA.

14 *Report of the Sixth Deaconess Conference of the Methodist Episcopal Church Held at Cincinnati, Ohio, February 24–27, 1893* (Message and Deaconess World Press, 1893), 9.

15 The phrase "pin money," for example, arose from the money husbands gave their wives to buy pins, expensive in centuries past. Zelizer, *The Social Meaning of Money*, 42.

16 MJD, *A Call*, 26. As late as the 1970s, a Methodist historian persisted in calling the allowance "pin money." Also, Heffner, *United Brethren Traditions*, 9.

17 Yohn, "Protestant Women's Organizations," 217. With or without allowances, lay women were the fundraising backbone of the deaconess movement, as will be explored in detail below.

18 Zelizer cites a 1938 survey that reported that 88 percent of women were in favor of an allowance, but only 48 percent of wives reported receiving one. Zelizer, *The Social Meaning of Money*, 48–52; Henry F. Pringle, "What Do the Women of America Think about Money?" *Ladies Home Journal* 55 (1938). Although the effects of the Great Depression may have factored in these numbers, scant evidence exists that the uxorial allowance was actually practiced, but there was plenty of discussion that it should be, e.g., "The Wife's Empty Purse: Though a Co-Earner She Often Is Not a Sharer," *Cincinnati Enquirer*, September 24, 1892, 13; "Living on a Good Income: The Expenses of a Well-to-Do Family," *New York Times*, July 6, 1884, 3; "Managing a Household Efficiently: Mrs. Robert A. Franks Says Running It Is a Business Obligation and Should Be Done Well by Every Woman Who Undertakes It," *New York Times*, January 31, 1915, SM6.

19 Zelizer, *The Social Meaning of Money*, 53, 65.

20 Kessler-Harris, *Woman's Wage*, 7.

21 H. R. Goodwin to unknown, n.d., AEC.

22 For example, Ryan dealt with these ideas chiefly in John A. Ryan, *Distributive Justice: The Right and Wrong of Our Present Distribution of Wealth* (New York: Macmillan, 1916). Catholic social thought strongly advocated a family wage, as codified in the papal encyclicals *Casti Connubii*, 1930, paragraph 117, and *Quadragesimo Anno*, 1931, paragraph 71.

23 Zelizer, *The Social Meaning of Money*, 27.

24 Meyer, *Deaconess Stories*, 238–39.

25 Meyer, *Deaconess Stories*, 239.

26 Aikens, "The Nurse Deaconess and Her Work."

27 Horton, *Builders*, 24.

214 | NOTES

28 *Report of the Sixth Deaconess Conference of the Methodist Episcopal Church Held at Cincinnati, Ohio, February 24–27, 1893* (Message and Deaconess World Press, 1893), 8.

29 "Deaconess House Campaign Scrapbook," PHS.

30 Fogelstrom, *Greatest Need,* 5.

31 Aikens, "The Nurse Deaconess and Her Work."

32 Feutz, *My Experiences as a Deaconess and a Nurse* (St. Louis, MO: Eden, n.d.); Sisterhood Lists/Data Folder, DF. For more, see W[illiam] A[lfred] Passavant, *The Deaconess and the Professional Nurse,* n.d., box 2–14, folder 36, CMC.

33 Deaconesses of the Woman's Home Missionary Society, *The Present Day Outlook,* 7.

34 Bachmann, "Peculiar Difficulties," 9.

35 Satter, *Each Mind a Kingdom,* 47, 150–51.

36 Edward Lambe Parsons to Frederick Burgess, March 11, 1916, AEC.

37 "Women's Record at Home," *LR* 1, no. 3 (1875): 267.

38 Kreutziger, "Problems Confronting the Deaconess Work," 16.

39 Vennard, "The Deaconess of Today," box 2–22, folder 7, CMC.

40 "A Call to the Young Women of the Church," *PHM* 1, no. 4 (1916): 1, DF.

41 Lears, *Rebirth,* 65.

42 Ruether, *Christianity,* 107.

43 Ida Huebscher, December 8, 1898, GL, box 2–16, folder 42, CMC; Anna Elizabeth Flesner, May 15, 1907, May 15, 1907, GL, box 2–16, folder 17, CMC.

44 "Will You Become a Deaconess?" *TME* 1, no. 2 (1890).

45 "Sarah Delilah Church," 1975, memorandum. 2591-5-7:22, MAHC. Also: "I had been working in a very large, industrial corporation in the offices, in an accounting department, and I discovered that much of the work that we did really went into the waste paper basket as the procedures were changed or somebody got a new idea, and that much of the work that you did simply disappeared. I wanted something that had, seemed to have, more value in life." Eleanor Stelzner Spohn, *Interview with Sister Louise Burroughs* (Gladwyne, PA: Archives of Cooperative Lutheranism, Lutheran Council in the USA, 1983), 1–2, AELCA.

46 Jens, *Principles of Deaconess Work,* 39.

47 Minnie B. Horlitz, December 27, 1899, GL, box 2–16, folder 40, CMC.

48 Wuthnow, *Poor Richard's Principle,* 5.

49 Vennard, "The Deaconess of Today," box 2–22, folder 7, CMC.

50 Meyer, *Deaconess Stories,* 213.

51 Horton, "The Coming Billionaire."

52 Crist, "Everybody on the Left Knew Her," 362.

53 Winifred L. Chappell, "Embattled Miners," *Christian Century,* August 19, 1931, 1044.

54 The Methodist Federation for Social Service (MFSS) was founded in 1907 as "an unofficial Methodist organization dedicated to speaking out on social issues and to pushing official church bodies to act prophetically." As Miriam Crist has argued, Winifred Chappell never received full credit for her work in the male-

dominated MFSS, and her memory was buried in the anti-communist scare of the mid-twentieth century. Crist, "Everybody on the Left Knew Her," 431, footnote 1.

55 Holding, *Joy, the Deaconess*, 155.
56 *Self-Examination for Deaconesses* (Protestant Deaconess Conference), 12, Consecration Services Folder, DF.
57 *Why I Am Glad.*
58 F. B. Meyer, *Their Calling*, 53–54.
59 Pope-Levison has documented women evangelists' uphill struggle to fund their evangelistic efforts and institutions in the Progressive Era. Pope-Levison, *Old Time Religion*.
60 Helm, "What a Deaconess Is," 1.
61 *Report of the Sixth Deaconess Conference of the Methodist Episcopal Church Held at Cincinnati, Ohio, February 24–27, 1893* (Message and Deaconess World Press, 1893), 14.
62 Wathen, *A Gallant Life*, 65–66.
63 Wathen, *A Gallant Life*, 130, 64–65.
64 Brown, *In Their Time*, 9–10, 17.
65 Brown, *In Their Time*, 22.
66 Queen Esther circles were established in 1903 by the Woman's Home Missionary Society for girls ages fourteen to twenty-one.
67 The Epworth League was a Methodist Episcopal organization for young adults. Smith, Tibbetts, and Pike, *There Was One Anna*, 11.
68 Morgan, in her study of St. Margaret's House, agrees: "Support, both financial and spiritual, for women church workers came chiefly through the lay women and their organizations." Morgan, "Vocational Formation," 109.
69 "Deaconess House Campaign Scrapbook," PHS.
70 "Recent Bequests," *PHM*, DF.
71 *Silver Anniversary Memorial: The Bethel Deaconess Home and Hospital, Newton, Kansas* (Newton, KS, 1933), 5–6.
72 *Sixth Annual Report of the Church Training and Deaconess House of the Diocese of Pennsylvania* (Philadelphia, 1897), 11, PP183 acc.92.92, AEC.
73 Smith, Tibbetts, and Pike, *There Was One Anna*, 44.
74 Brown, *In Their Time*, 15, 12.
75 For an example, see Report of the Corresponding Secretary of the General Deaconess Board to the BHHD (December 16, 1924), 2085-7-1:02, MAHC.
76 Laurence W. Lange of the Department of Missionary Personnel to Dr. Walter K. Clark of the Board of Pensions, November 30, 1955, Amelia F. Hlavacek File, Biographical Vertical Files, RG414, PHS.

CHAPTER 5. DEACONESSES AND THE ORDAINED MINISTRY

1 Ruether and McLaughlin, *Female Leadership*, 24.
2 Rasche, *Pioneer Professional Women*, 109; Pamela W. Darling, "The Struggle to Authorize Women's Ordination: A Long Road," The Episcopal Church, July 1, 2007, www.episcopalchurch.org."

3   Wiebe, *Search for Order*, 111–32.

4   Lears, *Grace*, 8, 10, 11.

5   Jones, "Reaching the People," 15.

6   "A Call to the Young Women of the Church," *PHM* 1, no. 4 (1916): 1, DF.

7   "Opportunities for Deaconess Work," *WE* 31, no. 9 (1912): 323.

8   Radcliffe, "The Presbyterian Deaconess," 3.

9   Camp, "The Importance of Our Deaconess Work," *WE* 34, no. 10 (October 1915): 378.

10 Anita Hodgkin, *The School for Christian Service: A Statement of Its Plans for Expansion* (Berkeley, CA: St. Margaret's House, pre-1928), box 11, folder 2, AEC.

11 Wenner, *The Office of Deaconess*, 15–16. Likewise, a Presbyterian minister assures readers, "The Presbyterian deaconess carries to the Church the promise of a more scriptural organization." Radcliffe, "The Presbyterian Deaconess," 4.

12 Presbyterian Training School Baltimore, "The Presbyterian Training School of Baltimore: A Bulletin of Information" (Philadelphia), Pam. Fol. BV4176.M31.P7D, PHS.

13 "More Women Workers," *Church News: The Journal of the Thirty-Second Annual Convocation of the Church in the Missionary District of Spokane* (1924): 16.

14 Donald Guthrie, "First Presbyterian Church, Baltimore." *PDQ* 4, no. 1 (1909): 15.

15 Kerr, "What the Pastors Say," 22.

16 "Deaconess Items"; Camp, "The Importance of Our Deaconess Work," 378.

17 Iva P. Conner [biography], 1976, Records of the Women's Division of the General Board of Global Ministries, 2591-5-7:25, MAHC.

18 Brumberg and Tomes, "Research Agenda," 288.

19 Miller, *Letters on Clerical Manners*, 329–31.

20 Golder, *History of the Deaconess Movement*, 467.

21 "A Call to the Young Women of the Church," *PHM* 1, no. 4 (1916): 1. DF.

22 "More Women Workers," *Church News: The Journal of the Thirty-Second Annual Convocation of the Church in the Missionary District of Spokane* (1924): 16.

23 "A Call to the Young Women of the Church," *PHM* 1, no. 4 (1916): 1.

24 Gedge, *Without Benefit of Clergy*, 220.

25 Sister Pauline Becker, July 28, 1981, KI (1981), DF.

26 Sister Edna Stoenner, June 8, 1981, KI, DF; Sister Mary Kramme, July 20, 1981, KI, DF.

27 Bachmann, "Peculiar Difficulties," 13.

28 Sister Sophie Damme, interview by Mary Pellauer, 19 March, 1989, AELCA.

29 In 1925, almost half of the 140 Methodist deaconesses surveyed responded that their pastor had a large influence on their decision to become a deaconess; the other half reported that he had no influence. Margaret M. Brooks, *Report of the Personnel Secretary to the Annual Meeting of the Board of Hospitals, Homes, and Deaconess Work for the Year December 1924 to December 1925*, BHHD, Records of Health and Welfare Ministries Division of the General Board of Global Ministries, 2085-7-1:02, MAHC.

30   A Methodist committee in 1925 blamed decreasing numbers of deaconess recruits partly on the objections of pastors. Margaret M. Brooks, *First Meeting of the Committee on the Study of Training Schools of the Methodist Episcopal Church*, May 8, 1925, BHHD, Records of Health and Welfare Division of the General Board of Global Ministries, 2085-7-1:02, MAHC.

31   Rev. Wilhelm Löhe in Mergner, *The Deaconess and Her Work*, 140.

32   Records of St. Margaret's House, 1908–1966, RG289, AEC.

33   Grant, *Deaconess Manual*, 28–29.

34   F. B. Meyer, *Their Calling*, 12.

35   Mergner, *The Deaconess and Her Work*, 148–49.

36   *Would You Like to Be a Deaconess* (Cincinnati, OH: Bethesda Hospital, 1922).

37   Louise Higlin, February 24, 1902, GL, box 2–16, folder 36, CMC.

38   Benz, "Short Sketch of My Life," CMC.

39   Dora Eisley, application, 1910, box 2–16, folder 8, CMC.

40   Clara M. Bay, n.d., GL, box 2–15, folder 11, CMC. Also, Louise Epkerrs, Letter to The members of the official board of The German deaconess work, March 16, 1904, box 2–16, folder 1, CMC.

41   Smith, Tibbetts, and Pike, *There Was One Anna*, 12.

42   Brekus, *Strangers & Pilgrims*, 181–82. While Brekus found that female preachers emphasized the supernatural aspects of their call more than male preachers, I found a wider spectrum of call experiences among the deaconesses.

43   "A Call to the Young Women of the Church," *PHM* 1, no. 4 (1916): 1.

44   *Would You Like to Be a Deaconess* (Cincinnati: Bethesda Hospital, 1922).

45   Anna Dorothy Albertsen, application, 1900, box 2–15, folder 2, CMC.

46   Mary P. Truesdell, *The Deaconess Office and Ministry* (New York: National Conference of Deaconesses, 1952), 9.

47   Griffith, *God's Daughters*, 199.

48   "A Call to the Young Women of the Church," *PHM* 1, no. 4 (1916): 1; "Qualifications Desirable for a Deaconess," *OH* 11, no. 12 (December 1902): 6–7.

49   This is the same pamphlet that reminded deaconesses not to disdain their impoverished relatives, quoted in the previous chapter. *Self-Examination for Deaconesses* (Protestant Deaconess Conference), 3, 4, Consecration Services Folder, DF.

50   Cox, "Set Apart," 1918, Anna Grace Cox folder, National Center for the Diaconate, AEC.

51   "Form for Consecration of Deaconesses."

52   Mary P. Truesdell, *The Deaconess Office and Ministry* (New York: National Conference of Deaconesses, 1952), 9.

53   S.A., "My Consecration."

54   Smith, Tibbetts, and Pike, *There Was One Anna*, 19.

55   Vennard, "The Deaconess of Today," box 2–22, folder 7, CMC.

56   Deaconesses such as Evangelical Synod Sister Elsie Jungermann recalled how these verses sustained them throughout their lives. When interviewed

at age seventy-eight, Sister Elsie explained, "My memory verse meant a lot to me when I was taking care of a patient that would be a little difficult," and then recited Hebrews 1:1–2: "Wherefore seeing we are compassed about with so great a cloud of witnesses, let us lay aside every weight and the sin which does so easily beset us and let us run with patience the race that is set before us, looking to Jesus the author and perfecter of our faith." Sister Elsie Jungermann, September 21, 1981, KI, DF. Mennonite deaconess Helene M. Bartsch even had her memory verse inscribed on her tombstone. Find A Grave, database and images (https://www.findagrave.com, accessed September 25, 2018), memorial page for Sr Helene M. Bartsch (9 Dec 1894–2 Jul 1966), Find A Grave Memorial no. 24945819, citing Greenwood Cemetery, Newton, Harvey County, Kansas, USA; maintained by Barb (contributor 46494205).

57 Ceremony descriptions compiled from the following: Grant, *Deaconess Manual*; "Form for Consecration of Deaconesses"; and Heffner, *United Brethren Traditions*.

58 "Form for Consecration of Deaconesses," 13.

59 Jens, *Principles of Deaconess Work*, 26.

60 Donovan, *A Different Call*, 104. By contrast, Methodist deaconesses, deacons, and elders all made the promise of obedience last. See Methodist Episcopal Church, *Doctrines and Discipline of the Methodist Episcopal Church* (New York: Methodist Book Concern, 1920), 461, 67, 72.

61 *Self-Examination for Deaconesses* (Protestant Deaconess Conference), 5, 9, 6, 12–13, 15, Consecration Services Folder, DF.

62 *Sixth Annual Report of the Church Training and Deaconess House of the Diocese of Pennsylvania* (Philadelphia, 1897), 8, PP183 acc.92.92, AEC.

63 Aikens, "The Nurse Deaconess and Her Work."

64 Presbyterian Training School [Baltimore, MD], "The Presbyterian Training School [Catalog]" (Baltimore, 1910–1911), Pam. Fol. BV 4176.M31 P7d, PHS.

65 "The Presbyterian Training School of Baltimore: A Bulletin of Information" (Philadelphia), Pam. Fol. BV4176.M31.P7D, PHS.

66 *Sixth Annual Report of the Church Training and Deaconess House of the Diocese of Pennsylvania* (Philadelphia, 1897), 14, PP183 acc.92.92, AEC.

67 Irwin, "Training School for Church Workers."

68 Carter, "The Practical Work of the School."

69 F. B. Meyer, *Their Calling*, 15.

70 This mirrored the common experience of working-class girls before World War I. Tentler, *Wage-Earning Women*, 93.

71 Amelia Kenzler, September 1896, GL, box 2–16, folder 47, CMC.

72 Antonia E. Roediger, August 25, 1909, GL, box 2–17, folder 18, CMC.

73 St. Margaret's House, one of the most successful Episcopal institutions, had a close affiliation with the University of California at Berkeley, even serving as a dorm for women students there. Edwards, "St. Margaret's House."

74 *Philadelphia School for Christian Workers of the Presbyterian and Reformed Churches (Catalogue)* (Philadelphia, 1927–1929), Catalogue 2: TN 1 T25, PHS.

75 *How Will I Spend This Life?* (General Deaconess Board of the Methodist Episcopal Church, ca. 1923), 2, box 2–22, folder 18, CMC. For a more detailed examination of rising educational standards for Methodist deaconesses, consult Brereton's "Preparing Women," 191.

76 Woods, Report of the Personnel Committee to the Annual Meeting of BHHD (February 14–15, 1928), 2085-7-1:03, MAHC.

77 *Would You Like to Be a Deaconess* (Cincinnati: Bethesda Hospital, 1922).

78 Verband Evangelischer Wohltaetigkeits-Anstalten in der Deutschen Evangelischen Synode von Nord America, *Aufforderung an Evangelische Jungfrauen zum Eintritt in Den Dienst Als Diakonissen, Pflegerinnen oder Mitarbeiterinnen in Einer Evangelischen Wohltaetigkeits-Anstalt oder in der Gemeindepflege* (St. Louis: Eden, n.d.), 3. *Rules for Admission of Deaconesses to the Evangelical Deaconess Home and Hospital* (St. Louis, 1921).

79 Sister Henrietta Lutten, October 6, 1981, KI, DF; Sister Flora Pletz, August 3, 1981, KI, DF.

80 Sister Elizabeth Kunze, June 16, 1981, KI, DF; Sister Elsie Jungermann, September 21, 1981, KI, DF.

81 Mergner, *The Deaconess and Her Work.*

82 L. D. Gordon, *Progressive Era*, 2.

83 Rasche, *Deaconess Heritage*, 203; Fritschel, *Milwaukee Hospital*, 54.

84 For a detailed discussion of Methodist training schools, see Brereton, "Preparing Women," and especially, *Training God's Army.*

85 For the Southern Methodist example, "By-Laws for the Government of Deaconess Work."

86 Study Committee of the General Deaconess Board, *Directions and Helps: Course of Study for Deaconesses* (New York: Methodist Book Concern, 1922).

87 Pope-Levison offers corrections to Brereton's argument and further exploration of specifically woman-founded religious training schools in "Biblical, Practical, Vocational: Religious Training Schools," in *Old Time Religion*, chapter 3.

88 Study Committee of the General Deaconess Board, *Directions and Helps: Course of Study for Deaconesses* (New York: Methodist Book Concern, 1922).

89 Sister Ella Loew, June 1, 1981, KI, DF.

90 *Deaconess House and Training School for Christian Workers of the Presbyterian and Reformed Churches (Catalogue)* (Philadelphia, 1909), 6.

91 Heffner, *United Brethren Traditions*, 5.

92 Reid, "How the Home Helps," 26.

93 Pope-Levison, *Old Time Religion*, 112–13; Reid, "How the Home Helps," 27.

94 Vennard, "The Deaconess of Today," box 2–22, folder 7, CMC.

95 Students of the Kansas City National Training School for Deaconesses and Missionaries, *The Shield* (1921), 54.

96 F. Schaub, "The Cultivation of the Deaconess Spirit and the Education of Deaconess Candidates in Our Training Schools," in *The Deaconess and Her Work* (Cincinnati, OH: Bethesda Hospital, after 1924), 3, box 2–14, folder 34, CMC.

97 Sisters Olivia Drusch, Elsie Jungermann, and Pauline Becker all attended Washington University. Jungermann also attended Barnes College, and Becker earned her master's degree. Sister Olivia Drusch, January 26, 1982, KI, DF; Sister Elsie Jungermann, September 21, 1981, KI, DF; Sister Pauline Becker, July 28, 1981, KI, DF.

98 Sister Pauline Becker, July 28, 1981, KI, DF; Sister Elizabeth Lotz, September 14, 1981, KI, DF.

99 Sister Olivia Drusch, January 26, 1982, KI, DF; Sister Frieda Eckoff, June 22, 1981, KI, DF.

100 Report of the Corresponding Secretary of the General Deaconess Board to the BHHD (December 16, 1924), 2085-7-1:02, MAHC.

101 Margaret M. Brooks, *Report of the Personnel Secretary to the Annual Meeting of the Board of Hospitals, Homes, and Deaconess Work for the Year December 1924 to December 1925*, BHHD, Records of Health and Welfare Ministries Division of the General Board of Global Ministries, 2085-7-1:02, MAHC.

102 Julie Mergner to Margaret Frey, January 29, 1925, AELCA.

103 Sister Elsie Jungermann, September 21, 1981, KI, DF.

104 Meyer, "Deaconesses and the Need."

105 To muddy the waters, the Mennonites and sometimes the Episcopalians "ordained" women to the diaconate. I use the more common term "consecration" for admission to the diaconate and reserve the term "ordination" for admission to the priesthood or ministry of the Word and Sacrament.

106 Undated memorandum, Amelia F. Hlavacek File, Biographical Vertical Files, RG414, PHS.

107 Wacker, *Deaconess Calling*, 28–29.

108 Report of the Commission on Adapting the Office of Deaconess to the Present Tasks of the Church (1922), RG 289, box 3, folder 7, AEC.

109 Field-Bibb, "From Deaconess to Bishop," 63.

110 "Woman Pastor of City Church," *Evening Public Ledger*, March 29, 1918, 11.

111 Helm, "What a Deaconess Is," 1.

112 Mary J. Drexel Home and Philadelphia Motherhouse of Deaconesses, *Is Your Life Worth While?*

113 Brekus, *Strangers & Pilgrims*, 201.

114 "Outline of the Work of the General Conference of 1880."

115 Halverson et al., *Women Called*, 8–9. Full clergy rights for Methodist women came in 1956. The United Brethren branch of the Methodist family started ordaining women in 1889.

116 *A Deaconess—Why Not?* 13.

117 Margaret M. Brooks, *Report of the Personnel Secretary to the Annual Meeting of the Board of Hospitals, Homes, and Deaconess Work for the Year December 1924 to December 1925*, BHHD, Records of Health and Welfare Ministries Division of the

General Board of Global Ministries, 2085-7-1:02. This same report lists nineteen deaconesses as "ordained," but I can find no further information on those women. Episcopal deaconess Anna Gray Newell was licensed to preach in California. The only deaconess known to me in the African Methodist Episcopal Zion Church, Florence Spearing Randolph, was also licensed to preach in 1897.

118 Baker, *New York Training School*, 15.
119 Spaeth, "The Chicago Training School."
120 Mellie Perkins, "Our School at Velarde," *WE* 32, no. 5 (1913): 134–35.
121 "A Deaconess as Pastor."
122 Bowie, *Alabaster and Spikenard*, 124.
123 Brekus, *Strangers & Pilgrims*, 182.
124 Bowie, *Alabaster and Spikenard*, 54.
125 Robinson, *Brass to Gold*, 44–49.
126 Dr. J. A. Diekmann, Report to the German Central Deaconess Board of the Methodist Episcopal Church (May 1927), 2085-7-1:02, MAHC.
127 Minutes of the Ninth Annual Meeting of the National Methodist Hospitals and Homes Association in Convention with the Methodist Deaconess Association and the National Deaconess Convention, 1926–1927 (Chicago, February 16–17, 1927), 26, 2079-4-6:05, MAHC.
128 Hall, "Woman and Holy Orders," 20.
129 Amy Blanche Green, "Woman's Work in the Church," *Labors of Love* 25 (1924): 5.
130 Mary P. Truesdell, *The Deaconess Office and Ministry* (New York: National Conference of Deaconesses, 1952), 5.
131 Olive M. Robinson, Margaret M. Jackson, Evelyn E. Seymour, Clara E. Orwig, the Rev. Frances Campbell, Ruth M. Parsons, Agnes R. Bradley, Stella P. Englebert, and the Rev. Dr. Ann Sherman to the Right Rev. John Maury Allin, resolution, August 28, 1974, Records of the Retiring Fund for Deaconesses, RG 288, box 6, folder 14, AEC.
132 Sister Frieda Hoffmeister, October, 27, 1981, KI, DF; Sister Pauline Becker, July 28, 1981, KI, DF; Sister Ella Loew, June 1, 1981, KI, DF.
133 Sister Frieda Hoffmeister, October, 27, 1981, KI, DF; Sister Elizabeth Lotz, September 14, 1981, KI, DF.
134 Catherine Prelinger offers a more sensitive reading of the sources: "Although the deaconess movement contributed to the distinctive character of the male clerical profession, it was not the direct antecedent for the women's ordination movement." The early women priests pointed to "the secular movement for women's liberation" rather than the deaconess movement as their own motivation. Prelinger, "Ordained Women," 291.
135 Brereton and Klein, "Ministry," 180.

CHAPTER 6. DIFFERING VISIONS FOR THE DIACONATE

1 Sister Olivia Drusch, January 26, 1982, KI, DF.
2 USFC 1880.

3 Sister Olivia Drusch, January 26, 1982, KI, DF.

4 *Self-Examination for Deaconesses* (Protestant Deaconess Conference), Consecration Services Folder, DF.

5 Report of the Committee for the Study of the Deaconess Idea and Work (1937), DF.

6 White, *Reforming Sodom*.

7 Ida Marian Swett Treganza to the New England Deaconess Association, March 12, 1921, 2595-7-1:04, MAHC.

8 Annie Raddin French to Sadie Hagen, March 12, 1936, MAHC.

9 "Notes of the Annual Meeting of the New England Conference Deaconess Board" (1936), 2395-7-1:14, MAHC.

10 Martha Bowers Grant to Sadie Hagen, May 24, 1937, MAHC.

11 N. E. Davis to Sadie Hagen, June 26, 1937, correspondence 1937–1938, MAHC.

12 Dougherty, *My Calling*, 230. Jurisson differs and states that the Methodists allowed marriage in 1940, but I cannot substantiate the claim. Jurisson, "The Deaconess Movement," 831.

13 Walkowitz, "Feminine Professional Identity," 1052–55; Wiebe, *Search for Order*, 111–32.

14 Peiss, *Cheap Amusements*, 35, 38.

15 Kessler-Harris, *Woman's Wage*, 22.

16 Leach, *Land of Desire*, xiii.

17 Zelizer, *The Social Meaning of Money*, 30–31.

18 Peiss, *Cheap Amusements*, 57.

19 Herzberger, "Master Is Come."

20 Kreutziger, "Problems Confronting the Deaconess Work," 14.

21 Deaconesses of the Woman's Home Missionary Society, *Present Day Outlook*, 3.

22 Amelia Butler to Deaconess Fuller, April 27, 1931, Amelia Butler folder, National Center for the Diaconate, DF.

23 Records of St. Margaret's House, 1908–1966, RG289, AEC.

24 Bachmann, "Calls for Help Unheeded."

25 Although this book uses the colloquial "Methodist Church" throughout, the earlier body was officially the "Methodist Episcopal Church." The Methodist Episcopal Church, the Methodist Episcopal Church, South, and the Methodist Protestant Church merged in 1939 to form the Methodist Church. Archives and History, General Commission on Archives and History, United Methodist Church, www.gcah.org.

26 S.R.V.K, "Lutheran Motherhouses Face Their Problems."

27 The three precursor groups to the Evangelical Lutheran Church in America all voted in women's ordination between 1970 and 1976 (the Lutheran Church in America and the American Lutheran Church separately in 1970 and the American Evangelical Lutheran Church in 1976). The Lutheran Church–Missouri Synod does not ordain women. For more information on women's ordination, see Olson, Crawford, and Deckman, *Women with a Mission*. This number would be larger

if we included the Episcopal deaconesses, who in 1970 were all assumed into the gender-neutral diaconate. Some of these women deacons did seek ordination in the mid- to late 1970s, around the time of agitation for women's ordination in the Episcopal Church, which became permitted in 1976. See the story of the Philadelphia 11 in the previous chapter.

28 Lee, *As among the Methodists*, 2.
29 Weiser, *To Serve*, 27.
30 As noted, in 1934, the Evangelical Synod became part of the Evangelical and Reformed Church, which in turn became part of the United Church of Christ in 1957. Because almost all of the St. Louis sisters were consecrated as Evangelical Synod deaconesses, I retain that name.
31 Sister Frieda Eckoff, June 22, 1981, KI, DF.
32 Rasche, "The Deaconess Garb," pre-1983, Deaconess Garb Folder, DF.
33 Rasche, *Deaconess Heritage*, 40–45.
34 Zikmund, "Women in the United Church of Christ," 377.
35 Carl Grathwohl, Carl Rasche, and Lee Rockwell, Report to Commission on Benevolent Institutions of the Evangelical and Reformed Church (July 10, 1956), Deaconess Work Folder, DF.
36 "Resolution Honoring the 100th Anniversary of the Deaconess Sisterhood," in *Minutes of the Seventeenth General Synod of the United Church of Christ* (1989).
37 Eden Theological Seminary Luhr Library, "Set Apart to Serve: Evangelical Deaconesses in St. Louis, 1889–2005," DF.
38 *CPC*, 1896, chapter 6.
39 *CPC*, 1914.
40 Presbyterian Church in the USA, *Manual for Church Officers and Members of the Government, Discipline, and Worship of the Presbyterian Church in the United States of America* (Publication of the Department of the Board of Christian Education, 1926); *CPC*, 1920.
41 "Deacon and Deaconess Defined at Assembly," *Presbyterian Advance*, June 3, 1920, 17.
42 *CPC*, 1924.
43 Presbyterian Church in the USA, *Manual for Church Officers and Members of the Government, Discipline, and Worship of the Presbyterian Church in the United States of America* (Publication of the Department of the Board of Christian Education, 1926).
44 Gertrude Ray to Dr. Jacob Long, January 18, 1945, Marie L. Vacek Biographical File, PHS.
45 Anita Hodgkin to E. L. Parsons, December 29, 1924, Records of St. Margaret's House, AEC.
46 Donovan, *A Different Call*, 18.
47 Field-Bibb, "From Deaconess to Bishop," 65.
48 USFC, "Census of Religious Bodies" (1926), 16.
49 Lee, *As among the Methodists*, 66–67. In 1939, the northern and southern branches of the Methodist Episcopal Church, along with the Methodist Protestant Church,

merged to form the Methodist Church. In 1968, another merger with the Evangelical United Brethren produced the United Methodist Church in its current form.

50 Dougherty, *My Calling*, 223.

51 Dougherty, *My Calling*, 61.

52 Dougherty, *My Calling*, 249.

53 Betty J. Letzig to Board of Global Ministries in "Minutes" by the Committee on Diaconal Ministry Annual Meeting, presentation (October 1977), 5, MAHC. This remains true: deaconesses with whom I spoke pronounced the word in varying ways: dī-ˈa-kə-nᵊl, dē-ˈa-kə-nᵊl, or dī-a-ˈkon-əl.

54 Louter and Stephens, "Living the Vision."

55 Kitty Carr Carpenter, "Listen Up, Laity: Hear the Call to Be a Deaconess or Home Missioner?" *News & Views*, the Florida Conference of the United Methodist Church, June 17, 2014, http://www.flumc.org.

56 Johnson, interview.

57 Ridenour, interview.

58 Ryde laughingly explained that she continues to use female pronouns because she is old: "I don't know if I'd remember to use the other [pronouns] myself, [so] I'm not asking anyone else to!" Ryde, interview.

59 The United Methodist Book of Discipline stipulates, "Deaconesses, who are laywomen, and home missioners, who are laymen." United Methodist Church (US), *Book of Discipline of the United Methodist Church* (Nashville, TN: United Methodist Publishing House, 2016).

60 See Barbara Haralson, "Deaconesses at Work in AZ Refugee Crisis," June 23, 2014, http://www.unitedmethodistwomen.org/blogs/deaconess-and-home-missioner/june-2014/deaconesses-at-work-in-az-refugee-crisis; and Tequila Minsky, "United Methodist Women Protest Family Deportations on Capitol Hill," August 1, 2014, http://www.unitedmethodistwomen.org.

61 In addition to Helen Ryde, Rachel Harvey served as associate executive director for Reconciling Ministries Network. Robin Ridenour and Helen Ryde both point to Rachel Harvey's influence in their own discernment of the deaconess and home missioner vocation. This illustrates a pattern in several Lutheran and Methodist deaconesses' stories: that it was another deaconess who first called their attention to their diaconal gifts. Ridenour, interview; Ryde, interview.

62 As an example, in her 1963 book, Elizabeth Meredith Lee was using the United Nations Commission on the Status of Women as a benchmark for social justice and gender equality issues in the United Methodist diaconate. Lee, *As among the Methodists*, 61.

63 Ridenour, interview.

64 Ryde, interview.

65 Sister Edith Baden to Julie Mergner, March 1, 1929, AELCA.

66 Guinther, "Ice Follies."

67 "Topsy-Turvy Party."

68 "New Garb."

69 Sister Mildred Winter, "Recruitment for the Diaconate," in *The Twenty-Eighth Lutheran Deaconess Conference in America* (Omaha, NE, 1948): 21–25.

70 "Policies concerning the Non-Garbed Salaried Deaconess," ed. Archives of the Evangelical Lutheran Church in America (United Lutheran Church in America, [1952]).

71 Weiser, *To Serve*, 22.

72 Weiser, *To Serve*, 27.

73 Weiser, *To Serve*, 15–16, 25.

74 Marc Schogol, "Gladwyne Deaconess Estate Is Saved from Development," *Philadelphia Inquirer*, September 11, 2002.

75 Carolyn Lewis, "ELCA Deaconess Community Moving to Chicago," *News Releases*, Evangelical Lutheran Church in America, May 28, 1998, http://www.elca.org.

76 Evangelical Lutheran Church in America, "Candidacy Manual."

77 Williams, interview.

78 Naumann, *Footsteps of Phoebe*, 17.

79 Herzberger, "The Lord Hath Need of Them."

80 Naumann, *Footsteps of Phoebe*, 436.

81 Naumann, *Footsteps of Phoebe*, 408, 448–49.

82 The Lutheran Church–Missouri Synod Commission of Theology and Church Relations, "Women in the Church: Scriptural Principles and Ecclesial Practice" (1985), 22, 24, 27. This document is listed on the web page of recommended readings for women who are interested in the deaconess ministry. https://www.lcms.org.

83 The Lutheran Church–Missouri Synod Commission of Theology and Church Relations, "The Creator's Tapestry: Scriptural Perspectives on Man-Woman Relationships in Marriage and the Church" (St. Louis, 2009), 12, 10.

84 Concordia Deaconess Conference, "Code of Ethics."

85 Kristin Wassilak, interview by Andy Bates, *Faith and Family*, KFUO, December 7, 2016; The Lutheran Church–Missouri Synod, "In Service to Our Lord: Deaconess Ministry Overview; English" (YouTube, 2011).

86 Rao, interview.

87 Anderson, "Pastoral Care."

88 LCMS "Find a Worker" Locator, Lutheran Church–Missouri Synod (https://lcms.org, accessed February 12, 2019).

89 Lutheran Church–Missouri Synod women can and do still become LDA deaconesses even though the LCMS does not recognize the designation. If an LCMS woman seeks to become a rostered deaconess in her own denomination, she is required to relinquish her participation in the LDA. "Concordia Deaconess Conference" page, https://lcms.org.

90 Webdell, interview.

91 Tinker, interview.

92 Tinker, interview.
93 Webdell, interview.
94 Williams, interview. Williams explained that she adapted these images from Antonia Lynn, "Finding Images," in *The Deacon's Ministry*, ed. Christine Hall (Leominster, UK: Gracewing, 1992), 103–22.
95 Jennifer Clark Tinker, "Receiving Others as Gifts," in "Living Faith," 2013. https://jenniferclarktinker.com, accessed December 5, 2016.
96 Tinker, interview.
97 Phyllis Zagano has studied and written extensively on the possibility of Roman Catholic women deacons. See her works *Holy Saturday: An Argument for the Restoration of the Female Diaconate in the Catholic Church*, and *Women Deacons: Past, Present, Future*, among others.
98 United Methodist Church (US), *The Book of Discipline of the United Methodist Church* (Nashville, TN: United Methodist Publishing House, 2012), paragraph 1314.
99 Wendy Cadge and Michael Skaggs, "Chaplaincy? Spiritual Care? Innovation: A Case Statement." White paper, Brandeis University, September 1, 2018, 15.
100 Johnson, interview.
101 Webdell, interview.

CONCLUSION
1 Anna E. Pfeifer, Sept. 3, 1902, GL, box 2–17, folder 9, CMC.
2 Boyce Bowdon, "Susan Hunt: Embracing Love, Justice, and Service," *Response*, March 2006.
3 Lutheran Church–Missouri Synod, "In Service to our Lord—Deaconess Ministry Overview—English," YouTube video, 17:12, December 12, 2011; Ryde and Tinker interviews.

SELECTED BIBLIOGRAPHY

PRIMARY SOURCES

Archival Sources
Archives of the Episcopal Church, Episcopal Seminary of the Southwest, Austin, Texas
Archives of the Evangelical Lutheran Church of America, Chicago, Illinois
Deaconess Archives, Deaconess Foundation, St. Louis, Missouri
Methodist Archives and History Center of the United Methodist Church, Drew University, Madison, New Jersey
Nippert Collection of German Methodism, Manuscripts 873, Cincinnati Historical Society Library, Cincinnati Museum Center
Presbyterian Historical Society, Presbyterian Church (USA), Philadelphia, Pennsylvania

Interviews by Author
Johnson, Cindy, February 27, 2017
Manns, B. Lee, December 1, 2016
Rao, Grace, February 16, 2017
Ridenour, Robin, March 5, 2018
Ryde, Helen, April 12, 2018
Tinker, Jennifer Clark, March 7, 2018
Webdell, Valerie, December 13, 2016
Williams, E. Louise, September 6, 2018

Published Sources
"A Call to the Young Women of the Church." *Phoebe Home Messenger* 1, no. 4 (July 1916): 1.
"A Deaconess as Pastor." *New England Deaconess Journal* 4, no. 11 (January 1905).
A Deaconess—Why Not? Fourth edition. Buffalo, NY: General Deaconess Board of the Methodist Episcopal Church, ca. 1920.
Aikens, Charlotte A. "The Nurse Deaconess and Her Work." *Our Homes* 11, no. 8 (August 1902): 3.
Anderson, Margaret. "The Distaff Side of Pastoral Care: The Deaconess as Chaplain." *Issues in Christian Education: A Publication of Concordia University in Seward, Nebraska* 39, no. 1 (2005): 5.

Anderson, Sister Henrietta. *A History of the Immanuel Deaconess Institute Compiled in the 75th Anniversary Year*. Omaha, NE, 1962.

"Anna Alexander, Deaconess." *Living Church* 116, no. 4 (January 25, 1948): 22.

Ayres, Anne. *The Life and Work of William Augustus Muhlenberg*. New York: Harper & Brothers, 1880.

Bachmann, E. F. "Calls for Help Unheeded." *Deaconess Messenger*, April 1939, 4.

———. "Some Peculiar Difficulties Confronting the Development of the Deaconess Cause in America." In *Proceedings and Papers of the Seventh Conference of Evangelical Lutheran Deaconess Motherhouses in the United States*. Philadelphia, 1908.

Baker, Gertrude Jean. *New York Training School for Deaconesses*, June 1919, 15.

Bradley, Agnes R. "The Deaconess as Nurse." *New York Training School for Deaconesses*, June 1931, 14.

"By-Laws for the Government of Deaconess Work." *Our Homes* 11, no. 11 (November 1902): 4.

Camp, Rev P. M. "The Importance of Our Deaconess Work." *Woman's Evangel* 34, no. 10 (October 1915): 377–78.

Carter, Clara M. "The Practical Work of the School." *Church Militant* 2 (October 1899): 6.

Chappell, Winifred L. "Embattled Miners." *Christian Century*, August 19, 1931, 1044.

The Commission of Theology and Church Relations, The Lutheran Church—Missouri Synod. "The Creator's Tapestry: Scriptural Perspectives on Man-Woman Relationships in Marriage and the Church." St. Louis, December 2009.

———. "Women in the Church: Scriptural Principles and Ecclesial Practice," September 1985.

Concordia Deaconess Conference. "Code of Ethics," May 18, 2005. https://blogs.lcms.org.

Cooke, Harriette J. *Mildmay; or, The Story of the First Deaconess Institution*. London: E. Stock, 1893.

"Deacon and Deaconess Defined at Assembly." *Presbyterian Advance*, June 3, 1920.

"The Deaconess and the City." *Our Homes* 12, no. 10 (October 1903): 8.

"Deaconess Items." *Our Homes* 13, no. 3 (March 1904): 3.

"Deaconess Margaret Booz." *Living Church*, June 8, 1958.

"Deaconesses." *Christian Recorder*, January 11, 1862.

Deaconesses of the Woman's Home Missionary Society. *The Present Day Outlook on Deaconess Work*, n.d.

Dickey, Mrs. Ida Phillips. "Why Wear the Costume." *Our Homes* 11, no. 7 (July 1902): 5.

"Don't Come to the City, Girls, to Seek Your Fortune." *Message and Deaconess Advocate* 11, no. 6 (1895): 12.

Edwards, Deaconess Frances. "St. Margaret's House, Berkeley, California." *Spirit of Missions*, January 1929, 30–32.

"Einweihung des Evang. St. Lukas-Diakonissenhauses und Hospitals zu Faribault, Minn." *Evangelischer Wohltaetigkeitsfreund* 1, no. 7 (July 1909): 2.

Evangelical Lutheran Church in America. "Candidacy Manual," pdf, November 2015, http://download.elca.org.

Fisk, Josephine S. "Deaconess Home." *Annual Report of the New England Deaconess Association for the Year Ending 1906.* 1906, 5–13.

———. "What the Deaconesses Are Doing." *New England Deaconess Journal,* July 8, 1903.

Fogelstrom, Rev. *The Greatest Need of America; or, Social Christianity at Work by One of the Workers.* Rock Island, IL: Lutheran Augustana Book Concern, 1902.

"Form for Consecration of Deaconesses." *Our Homes* 12, no. 5 (May 1903): 12–13.

Frickey, Minna. "The Deaconess of Today." In *The Deaconess and Her Work,* 8–11. Cincinnati: Bethesda Hospital, n.d., after 1924.

Fry, Susanna M. D. "Ancient and Modern Deaconesses." *Ladies' Repository* 9 (February 1872): 109–12.

Gibson, Miss M. L. "The Ideal Deaconess." *Our Homes* 15 (July 1906): 14–16.

Golder, Christian. *The Deaconess Motherhouse, in Its Relation to the Deaconess Work.* Pittsburgh: Pittsburgh Printing, 1907.

———. *History of the Deaconess Movement in the Christian Church.* Cincinnati: Jennings and Pye, 1903.

Grant, Abraham. *Deaconess Manual of the A.M.E. Church.* Wilberforce, OH, 1902.

Green, Amy Blanche. "Woman's Work in the Church." *Labors of Love* 25 (January 1924): 15.

Guinther, Sister Florence. "Ice Follies Enjoyed by Deaconess Group." *Deaconess Messenger,* February 1946.

Guthrie, Donald. "First Presbyterian Church, Baltimore." *Presbyterian Deaconess Quarterly* 4, no. 1 (March 1909): 15.

Hall, Bishop [Arthur C. A.]. "Bishop Hall to the Deaconesses at the Conference at St. Faith's." *Deaconess,* October 1927.

Hall, Rev. Arthur C. A. "Women and Holy Orders." *American Church Monthly* 10 (September 1921): 12–21.

Helm, Mary. "What a Deaconess Is, and What She Is Not." *Our Homes* 11 (March 1902): 1–2.

Herzberger, F. W. "The Master Is Come and Calleth for Thee, an Appeal to Our Young Lutheran Womanhood for Missionary Deaconess Work." *Lutheran Deaconess* 7, no. 2 (1930): 12–13.

———. "The Lord Hath Need of Them." *Lutheran Deaconess* 1, no. 1 (January 1924): 1–2.

———. "Errichtung Eines Lutherischen Diaconissenheims" [Erection of a Lutheran Deaconess Home]. In *Eingaben fur die Delegatensynode 1911 sur St. Louis, Mo.,* translated by Otto A. Brillinger. St. Louis: Concordia, 1911.

Hodgkin, Anita. *The School for Christian Service: A Statement of Its Plans for Expansion.* Berkeley, CA: St. Margaret's House, 1928.

Holding, Elizabeth E. *Joy, the Deaconess.* Cincinnati: Cranston & Curtis; New York: Hunt & Eaton, 1893. Reprinted by Methodist Episcopal Deaconess Society as *How Hettie Became a Nurse Deaconess.* Chicago: Message Publishing, n.d.

"The Homer Toberman Deaconess House." *Our Homes* 12, no. 12 (December 1903): 3–4.

Horton, Isabelle. *The Builders: A Story of Faith and Works.* Chicago: distributed by the Deaconess Advocate, 1910.

―――. "Womanhood and Service: An Address Given at the Epworth League Convention, Denver, Colorado, July 1905." *Methodist Magazine and Review* 62 (December 1905): 497–505.

―――. *The Burden of the City.* New York: Fleming H. Revell, 1904. Reprinted in *The American Deaconess Movement in the Early Twentieth Century.* Edited by Carolyn De Swarte Gifford. Women in American Protestant Religion, 1800–1930. New York: Garland, 1987.

―――. "The Coming Billionaire." *Deaconess Advocate*, January 1899, 6–7.

Howell, Miss Mabel K. "The Deaconess and Home-Making." *Our Homes* 12 (August 1903): 3, 5–6.

Hurst, J. F. "Charitable Institutions in Europe." *Ladies' Repository* 26, no. 8 (August 1866): 452–55.

Irwin, Agnes. "Training School for Church Workers." *Church Militant* 2 (October 1899): 5.

Jens, Frederick P. *Doctrine of Evangelical Faith for Deaconesses after the Plan Taught in the Evangelical Catechism.* St. Louis, 1920.

―――, trans. *Principles of Deaconess Work, Published by Authority of the Federation of Evangelical Deaconess Associations in the Evangelical Synod of North America.* St. Louis: Eden, 1918.

Jepson, Sister Sophia. *Where Lies the Sacrifice in the Deaconess Work?* N.p., 1916.

Johnston, Mrs. Annie Fellows. *What the Deaconess Does; or, Where the White Ties Lead.* Chicago: Deaconess Advocate, 1899.

Jones, Rev J. Wynne. "Reaching the People." *Presbyterian Deaconess Quarterly* 1 (January 1906): 15–17.

Kaufman, Sister Frieda Marie. *Inasmuch Then as I Am a Deaconess, I Will Glorify My Ministry.* General Conference Mennonite Church, 1947.

Kerr, Rev. Robert P. "What the Pastors Say: The Testimony of Those Who Have Deaconesses in Their Congregation." *Presbyterian Deaconess Quarterly* 3 (December 1907): 22–23.

Krauth, Charles Porterfield. "Woman's Work: The Defects of Protestantism in Regard to It." *Messenger* 2 (1891): 17–18.

Kreutziger, Susie. "Problems Confronting the Deaconess Work and How to Solve Them." In *The Deaconess and Her Work*, 12–17. Cincinnati: Bethesda Hospital, 1924.

Louter, Deaconess Betsy Dodson, and Deaconess Myka Kennedy Stephens. "Living the Vision: How United Methodist Deaconesses and Home Missioners Understand and Embody the Lay Diaconate." Presented at Addressing Our Identity as a Lay Order, Nashville, Tennessee, 2014. http://www.unitedmethodistwomen.org.

Mary J. Drexel Home and Philadelphia Motherhouse of Deaconesses. *Is Your Life Worth While? An Appeal by the Mary J. Drexel Home and Philadelphia Motherhouse of Deaconesses*, [1919].

―――. *A Call to the Female Diaconate Issued by the Mary J. Drexel Home and Philadelphia Motherhouse of Deaconesses.* Philadelphia: Press of Susquehanna Printing, 1908.

McGill, Alexander T. "Deaconesses." *Presbyterian Review* 1 (1880): 268–90.

Mergner, Julie. *The Deaconess and Her Work.* Translated by Mrs. Adolph Spaeth. Philadelphia: United Lutheran Publication House, 1911.

Meyer, F. B. *Deaconesses and Their Calling: A Handbook for the Instruction of Probationers.* Translated by Emma A. Endlich. Milwaukee, WI: Geo. Brumder, 1878.

Meyer, Lucy Rider. *Deaconess Advocate* 29, no. 4 (April 1914): 8.

———. *Deaconess Stories.* Chicago: Hope, 1900.

———. "Deaconesses and the Need." *Message* 5 (February 1890): 9.

———. *Deaconesses, Biblical, Early Church, European, American.* First edition. Chicago: Message Publishing, 1889.

———. *Deaconesses, Biblical, Early Church, European, American.* Third edition. Revised and enlarged. Cincinnati: Cranston and Stowe, 1892.

Miller, Samuel. *Letters on Clerical Manners and Habits: Addressed to a Student in the Theological Seminary at Princeton.* Princeton, NJ: Moore, Baker, 1835.

Mogle, Louella, Deaconess. "Deaconess Work in the South: A Glimpse of Deaconess Work in Augusta, Georgia." *Presbyterian Deaconess Quarterly* 4, no. 1 (March 1909): 21–24.

Moody, Dwight L. "Introduction." *Deaconess Stories.* Chicago: Hope, 1900.

Morris, Samuel Leslie. *At Our Own Door: A Study of Home Missions with Special Reference to the South and West.* New York: Fleming H. Revell, 1904.

"New Garb Gains General Approval." *Deaconess Messenger* (Spring 1948).

"The New Woman." *Message and Deaconess Advocate* 11, no. 11 (1895): 16.

Ohl, J. F. *The Inner Mission: A Handbook for Christian Workers.* Philadelphia: General Council Publication House, 1911.

———. *Lutheran Inner Mission Work in Philadelphia.* Philadelphia: Inner Mission Society of Philadelphia, 1910.

"Opportunities for Deaconess Work." *Woman's Evangel* 31, no. 9 (September 1912): 320–24.

"Outline of the Work of the General Conference of 1880." *Christian Advocate* 55, no. 24 (June 10, 1880): 377.

Perkins, Mellie. "Our School at Velarde." *Woman's Evangel* 32 (May 1913): 134–35.

"Qualifications for a Desireable Deaconess" *Our Homes* 11, no. 12 (December 1902): 6–7.

Radcliffe, Rev. Wallace. "The Presbyterian Deaconess" *Presbyterian Deaconess Quarterly* 1 (1906): 1–4.

"Recent Bequests." *Phoebe Home Messenger* 1, no. 4 (July 1916).

Reid, Ann Townsend. "How the Home Helps." *Presbyterian Deaconess Quarterly* 1, no. 3 (January 1906): 26–28.

Richelsen, John. "Protestant Deaconesses." *Presbyterian Journal* 14, no. 15 (April 11, 1889): 2–3.

Rigg, Rev. Dr. "Rev. Dr. Rigg on the Wesley Deaconess Order." *Our Homes* 11 (April 1902): 5.

Roosevelt, Theodore. *Theodore Roosevelt: An Autobiography.* New York: Macmillan, 1913.

Ross, Edward A. "The Causes of Race Superiority." *Annals of the Institute for Political Science* 18 (1901): 67–89.

S.A. "My Consecration." *Deaconess Messenger*, July 1924, 6.

Scott, Martin J. *Convent Life: The Meaning of a Religious Vocation.* New York: Kennedy & Sons, 1919.

"Selected Deaconesses—or Sister Phebe." *Christian Recorder*, March 9, 1867.

Silver Anniversary Memorial: The Bethel Deaconess Home and Hospital, Newton, Kansas. Newton, KS, 1933.

Sister Anna. "An Open Letter by a Deaconess." *Deaconess Messenger*, April 1923, 7.

"Sister Velma Kampschmidt Wanted to Be a Missionary." *Focus*, August 1989, 5.

Smith, Mary F., Pearl W. Tibbetts, and Minnie Pike. *There Was One Anna.* Kansas City, MO: Brown-White-Lowell, 1948.

Spaeth, A. "Deaconess-Evangelist-Sister." *Messenger* 1, no. 4 (1890): 123–24.

———. "A Review of *Deaconess, Biblical, Early Church, European, American.*" *Messenger* 1, no. 3 (1890): 96.

———. "The Chicago Training School." *Messenger* 1, no. 4 (1890): 125–26.

S.R.V.K. "Lutheran Motherhouses Face Their Problems." *Deaconess Messenger*, July 1945, 5.

Strong, Josiah. *Our Country: Its Possible Future and Its Present Crisis.* Edited by Jurgen Herbst. New York: American Home Missionary Society, 1885.

Students of the Kansas City National Training School for Deaconesses and Missionaries. *The Shield*, 1921.

"Topsy-Turvy Party Held on Friday 13th." *Deaconess Messenger*, Spring 1947.

"Tributes from Deaconesses and Missionaries—Selected from Many." *Missionary Voice* 12 (1922): 308.

Vennard, Iva Durham. "The Deaconess of Today." In *A Report on Deaconess Work*, 10–12. Committee on Co-operation, 1908.

Wacker, Emil. *Deaconess Calling: Its Past and Its Present.* Translated by E. A. Endlich. Philadelphia: Mary J. Drexel Home, 1893.

Warfield, Benjamin B. "Presbyterian Deaconesses." *Presbyterian Review* 10 (1889): 283–93.

Wathen, Edith. *A Gallant Life: Memories of Virginia Custis Young, a Gallant Soul Whose Heart Was Pure, with Courage Steadfast and Purpose Unshaken to the End, Who Lived and Loved and Laughed That Others Might Know Life.* New York: Gorham, 1934.

Wenner, Rev. G. U. *The Office of Deaconess.* Philadelphia: Lutheran Publication Society, 1894.

"The Wesley Deaconess." *Our Homes* 11, no. 2 (1902): 1–2.

"Where Are the Nine?" *Presbyterian Deaconess Quarterly* 1 (June 1905): 25.

Why I Am Glad I Decided to Be a Deaconess. Philadelphia: Literature Headquarters, Women's Missionary Society of the United Lutheran Church in America, n.d.

"Will You Become a Deaconess?" *Messenger* 1, no. 2 (1890): 37–40.

Withrow, Dr. "Dr. Withrow on the Deaconess Costume." *Our Homes* 11, no. 9 (September 1902): 5.

———. "Dr. Withrow on Deaconesses." *Our Homes* 11, no. 4 (April 1902): 5–6.

"Woman Pastor of City Church." *Evening Public Ledger*, March 29, 1918, final edition.

"Women's Record at Home." *Ladies' Repository* 1, no. 3 (March 1875): 266–67.

Woods, Dr. C. S. "The World's Need of Deaconesses." *Deaconess Banner* 7 (March 1928): 2.

———. "Report of the Personnel Committee to the Annual Meeting of the Board of Hospitals, Homes, and Deaconess Work." Board of Hospitals, Homes, and Deaconess Work, Methodist Episcopal Church, February 14, 1928.

Yursik, Bozenka R. "Work for the Immigrant Children." *Presbyterian Deaconess Quarterly* 2 (December 1906): 14–15.

Zimmerman, L. M. "The Glory of Consecrated Womanhood." *Lutheran Church Work*, May 1, 1913, 6–7.

Databases

Ancestry.com Operations, Inc., Provo, Utah

1870 United States Federal Census. 2009. Images reproduced by FamilySearch. https://search.ancestry.com/search/db.aspx?dbid=7163

1900 United States Federal Census. 2004. https://search.ancestry.com/search/db.aspx?dbid=7602

1910 United States Federal Census. 2006. https://search.ancestry.com/search/db.aspx?dbid=7884

1920 United States Federal Census. 2010. Images reproduced by FamilySearch. https://search.ancestry.com/search/db.aspx?dbid=6061

1930 United States Federal Census. 2002. https://search.ancestry.com/search/db.aspx?dbid=6224

1940 United States Federal Census. 2012. https://search.ancestry.com/search/db.aspx?dbid=2442

California, Voter Registrations, 1900–1968. 2017. https://search.ancestry.com/search/db.aspx?dbid=61066

Cook County, Illinois, Marriage Indexes, 1912–1942. 2011. https://search.ancestry.com/search/db.aspx?dbid=2273

Cuyahoga County, Ohio, Marriage Records and Indexes, 1810–1973. 2010. https://search.ancestry.com/search/db.aspx?dbid=1876

Illinois, Marriage Index, 1860–1920. 2015. https://search.ancestry.com/search/db.aspx?dbid=60984

Kansas State Census Collection, 1855–1925. 2009. https://search.ancestry.com/search/db.aspx?dbid=1088

New York, State Census, 1915. 2012. https://search.ancestry.com/search/db.aspx?dbid=2703

New York, State Census, 1905. 2014. https://search.ancestry.com/search/db.aspx?dbid=7364

New York State, Marriage Index, 1881–1967. 2017.

https://search.ancestry.com/search/db.aspx?dbid=61632

Philadelphia, Pennsylvania, Marriage Index, 1885–1951. 2011. https://search.ancestry.com/search/db.aspx?dbid=2536

US City Directories, 1822–1995. 2011. https://search.ancestry.com/search/db.aspx?dbid=2469

US, Evangelical Lutheran Church in America Church Records, 1826–1969. 2015. https://search.ancestry.com/search/db.aspx?dbid=60722

US Passport Applications, 1795–1925. 2007. https://search.ancestry.com/search/db.aspx?dbid=1174

US, School Yearbooks, 1900–1990. 2010. https://search.ancestry.com/search/db.aspx?dbid=1265

Ancestry.com and the Church of Jesus Christ of Latter-Day Saints. Lehi, Utah *1880 United States Federal Census.* 2010. https://search.ancestry.com.

SECONDARY SOURCES

Ahlstrom, Sydney E. *A Religious History of the American People.* New Haven, CT: Yale University Press, 1972.

Allchin, A. M. *The Silent Rebellion: Anglican Religious Communities, 1845–1900.* London: SCM Press, 1958.

Bendroth, Margaret Lamberts, and Virginia Lieson Brereton, eds. *Women and Twentieth-Century Protestantism.* Urbana: University of Illinois Press, 2002.

Bowie, Mary. *Alabaster and Spikenard: The Life of Iva Durham Vennard, D.D., Founder of Chicago Evangelistic Institute.* Chicago: Chicago Evangelistic Institute, 1947.

Boydston, Jeanne. "Gender as a Question of Historical Analysis." *Gender and History* 20, no. 3 (November 2008): 558–83.

Brekus, Catherine A. *Strangers & Pilgrims: Female Preaching in America, 1740–1845.* Gender & American Culture. Chapel Hill: University of North Carolina Press, 1998.

Brereton, Virginia Lieson. *Training God's Army: The American Bible School, 1880–1940.* Bloomington: Indiana University Press, 1990.

———. "Preparing Women for the Lord's Work: The Story of Three Methodist Training Schools, 1880–1940." In *Women in New Worlds: Historical Perspectives on the Wesleyan Tradition.* Edited by Hilah F. Thomas, Rosemary Skinner Keller, and Louise L. Queen, 1:178–99. Nashville, TN: Abingdon, 1981.

Brereton, Virginia Lieson, and Christa Ressmeyer Klein. "American Women in Ministry: A History of Protestant Beginning Points." In *Women in American Religion.* Edited by Janet Wilson James, 178–80. Philadelphia: University of Pennsylvania Press, 1980.

Brown, Irva Colley. *In Their Time: Lucy Rider Meyer (1849–1922) and Josiah Shelley Meyer (1849–1926): One Hundredth Anniversary, Chicago Training School, 1885–1985.* Chicago: Garrett-Evangelical Theological Seminary, 1985.

Brumberg, Joan Jacobs, and Nancy Tomes. "Women in the Professions: A Research Agenda for American Historians." *Reviews in American History* 10, no. 2 (June 1982): 275–96.

Bushman, Richard L. *The Refinement of America: Persons, Houses, Cities.* New York: Vintage, 1993.

Butler, Anthea D. *Women in the Church of God in Christ: Making a Sanctified World.* Chapel Hill: University of North Carolina Press, 2007.

Carroll, Bret E. *The Routledge Historical Atlas of Religion in America.* New York: Routledge, 2000.

Cetina, Judith G. "In Times of Immigration." In *Pioneer Healers: The History of Women Religious in American Health Care.* Edited by Ursula Stepsis and Dolores Liptak, 86–117. New York: Crossroad, 1989.

Clapp, Elizabeth J. *Mothers of All Children: Women Reformers and the Rise of Juvenile Courts in Progressive Era America.* University Park: Pennsylvania State University Press, 1998.

Coburn, Carol, and Martha Smith. *Spirited Lives: How Nuns Shaped Catholic Culture and American Life, 1836–1920.* Chapel Hill: University of North Carolina Press, 1999.

Collier-Thomas, Bettye. *Jesus, Jobs, and Justice: African American Women and Religion.* Philadelphia, PA: Temple University Press, 2014.

Cook, Sir Edward Tyas. *The Life of Florence Nightingale.* 2 vols. London: Macmillan, 1914.

Crist, Miriam J. "Winifred L. Chappell: Everybody on the Left Knew Her." In *Women in New Worlds: Historical Perspectives on the Wesleyan Tradition.* Edited by Hilah F. Thomas and Rosemary Skinner Keller, 1:362–78. Nashville, TN: Abingdon, 1981.

Deweese, Charles W. *Women Deacons and Deaconesses: 400 Years of Baptist Service.* Brentwood, TN: Baptist History and Heritage Society, 2005.

Donovan, Mary Sudman. "Paving the Way: Deaconess Susan Trevor Knapp." *Anglican and Episcopal History* 63, no. 4 (1994): 491–502.

———. *A Different Call: Women's Ministries in the Episcopal Church, 1850–1920.* Wilton, CT: Morehouse-Barlow, 1986.

Dorsey, Bruce. *Reforming Men and Women: Gender in the Antebellum City.* Ithaca, NY: Cornell University Press, 2002.

Dougherty, Mary Agnes. *My Calling to Fulfill: Deaconesses in the United Methodist Tradition.* New York: Women's Division, General Board of Global Ministries, the United Methodist Church, 1997.

———. "The Social Gospel according to Phoebe: Methodist Deaconesses in the Metropolis, 1885–1918." In *Women in New Worlds: Historical Perspectives on the Wesleyan Tradition.* Edited by Hilah F. Thomas and Rosemary Skinner Keller, 1:200–216. Nashville, TN: Abingdon, 1981.

———. "The Methodist Deaconess, 1885–1918: A Study in Religious Feminism." PhD diss., University of California–Davis, 1979.

Douglass, Paul. *The Story of German Methodism: Biography of an Immigrant Soul.* New York: Methodist Book Concern, 1939.

Ewens, Mary. *The Role of the Nun in Nineteenth-Century America.* New York: Arno, 1978.

Field-Bibb, Jacqueline. "From Deaconess to Bishop: The Vicissitudes of Women's Ministry in the Protestant Episcopal Church in the USA." *Heythrop Journal* 33 (January 1992): 61–78.

Fischer, Gayle V. "Dressing to Please God: Pants-Wearing Women in Mid-Nineteenth-Century Religious Communities." *Communal Societies* 15 (1995): 55–74.

Fitch, Catherin A., and Steven Ruggles. "Historical Trends in Marriage Formation: The United States, 1850–1999." In *The Ties That Bind: Perspectives on Marriage and Cohabitation.* Edited by Linda J. Waite, 59–87. New York: de Gruyter, 2000.

Fitzgerald, Maureen. *Habits of Compassion: Irish Catholic Nuns and the Origins of New York's Welfare System, 1830–1920.* Urbana: University of Illinois Press, 2006.

Franchot, Jenny. *Roads to Rome: The Antebellum Protestant Encounter with Catholicism.* Berkeley: University of California Press, 1994.

Fritschel, Herman L. *A Story of One Hundred Years of Deaconess Service: By the Institution of Protestant Deaconesses, Pennsylvania, and the Lutheran Deaconess Motherhouse at Milwaukee, Wisconsin, 1849–1949.* Milwaukee, WI: Lutheran Deaconess Motherhouse, 1949.

———. *The Story of Milwaukee Hospital "The Passavant" during Four Score Years, 1863–1943.* Milwaukee, WI: Milwaukee Hospital, 1945.

Gaustad, Edwin Scott, and Philip L. Barlow. *New Historical Atlas of Religion in America.* New York: Oxford University Press, 2001.

Gedge, Karin E. *Without Benefit of Clergy.* New York: Oxford University Press, 2003.

Gibson, J. W., and W. H. Crogman, eds. "Florence Randolph." In *[The New] Progress of a Race*, 423. Naperville, IL: Nichols, 1920.

Ginzburg, Lori D. *Women and the Work of Benevolence: Morality, Politics, and Class in the Nineteenth-Century United States.* Yale Historical Publications. New Haven, CT: Yale University Press, 1990.

Goldstein, Eric L. *The Price of Whiteness: Jews, Race, and American Identity.* Princeton, NJ: Princeton University Press, 2006.

Gordon, Beverly. "Fossilized Fashion: 'Old Fashioned' Dress as a Symbol of a Separate, Work-Oriented Identity." *Dress* 13 (1987): 49–59.

Gordon, Linda. *The Great Arizona Orphan Abduction.* Cambridge, MA: Harvard University Press, 1999.

Gordon, Lynn D. *Gender and Higher Education in the Progressive Era.* New Haven, CT: Yale University Press, 1990.

Griffith, R. Marie. *God's Daughters: Evangelical Women and the Power of Submission.* Berkeley: University of California Press, 1997.

Grindal, Gracia. *Sister Elisabeth Fedde: "To Do the Lord's Will"; Elisabeth Fedde and the Deaconess Movement among the Norwegians in America.* Minneapolis, MN: Lutheran University Press, 2014.

Halverson, Delia, Kabamba Kiboko, Laceye Warner, and M. Lynn Scott. *Women Called to Ministry: A Six-Session Study for the United Methodist Church.* [Nashville]: General Commission on the Status and Role of Women, The United Methodist Church, 2015.

Hatch, Nathan O. *The Democratization of American Christianity.* New Haven, CT: Yale University Press, 1989.

Heffner, Dee Dee. *Called to Serve: A Survey of the Deaconess and Home Missionary Movements in the Former Evangelical United Brethren Traditions.* Espanola, NM: Self-published, 1976.

Helsinger, Elizabeth K., Robin Lauterbach Sheets, and William Veeder. *The Woman Question: Society and Literature in England and America, 1837–1883.* New York: Garland, 1983.

Hoy, Suellen M. *Good Hearts: Catholic Sisters in Chicago's Past.* Urbana: University of Illinois Press, 2006.

Jacobson, Matthew Frye. *Whiteness of a Different Color: European Immigrants and the Alchemy of Race.* Edited by American Council of Learned Societies. Cambridge, MA: Harvard University Press, 1999.

Joselit, Jenna Weissman. *The Wonders of America: Reinventing Jewish Culture, 1880–1950.* New York: Holt, 2002.

Jurisson, Cynthia A. "The Deaconess Movement." In *Encyclopedia of Women and Religion in North America.* Vol. 2, edited by Rosemary Skinner Keller, Rosemary Radford Ruether, and Marie Cantlon. Bloomington: Indiana University Press, 2006.

Keller, Rosemary Skinner. "Lay Women in the Protestant Tradition." In *Women and Religion in America: The Nineteenth Century.* Edited by Rosemary Radford Ruether and Rosemary Skinner Keller, 1:242–93. San Francisco: Harper and Row, 1981.

Keller, Rosemary Skinner, Gerald F. Moede, and Mary Elizabeth Moore. *Called to Serve: The United Methodist Diaconate.* Nashville, TN: United Methodist General Board of Higher Education and Ministry, 1987.

Kessler-Harris, Alice. *A Woman's Wage: Historical Meanings and Social Consequences.* Lexington: University Press of Kentucky, 1990.

Kraman, Carlan. "Women Religious in Health Care: The Early Years." In *Pioneer Healers: The History of Women Religious in American Health Care.* Edited by M. Ursula Stepsis and Dolores Liptak, 15–38. New York: Crossroad, 1989.

Ladd-Taylor, Molly. "Toward Defining Maternalism in U.S. History." *Journal of Women's History* 5 (Fall 1993): 110–13.

Lagerquist, L. DeAne. *From Our Mothers' Arms: A History of Women in the American Lutheran Church.* Minneapolis, MN: Augsburg, 1987.

Leach, William R. *Land of Desire: Merchants, Power, and the Rise of a New American.* New York: Pantheon, 1993.

Lears, T. J. Jackson. *Rebirth of a Nation: The Making of Modern America, 1877–1920.* New York: HarperCollins, 2009.

———. *No Place of Grace: Antimodernism and the Transformation of American Culture, 1880–1920.* Chicago: University of Chicago Press, 1981.

Lee, Elizabeth Meredith. *As among the Methodists: Deaconesses Yesterday, Today, and Tomorrow.* New York: Woman's Division of Christian Service, Board of Mission, Methodist Church, 1963.

Lindley, Susan Hill. *You Have Stept out of Your Place: A History of Women and Religion in America.* First edition. Louisville, KY: Westminster John Knox Press, 1996.

McDannell, Colleen. *The Christian Home in Victorian America, 1840–1900*. Religion in North America. Bloomington: Indiana University Press, 1986.

Morgan, Alda Marsh. "'The Spiritual Motive': Vocational Formation at St. Margaret's House (1928–1936)." In *Deeper Joy: Lay Women and Vocation in the 20th-Century Episcopal Church*. Edited by Fredrica Harris Thompsett and Sheryl A. Kujawa-Holbrook, 104–19. New York: Church Publishing, 2005.

Naumann, Cheryl D. *In the Footsteps of Phoebe: A Complete History of the Deaconess Movement in the Lutheran Church–Missouri Synod*. St. Louis, MO: Concordia, 2008.

Nelson, Sioban. *Say Little, Do Much: Nurses, Nuns, and Hospitals in the Nineteenth Century*. Philadelphia: University of Pennsylvania Press, 2001.

Olson, Jeannine E. *Deacons and Deaconesses through the Centuries*. Rev. ed. St. Louis, MO: Concordia, 2005.

———. *One Ministry, Many Roles: Deacons and Deaconesses through the Centuries*. St. Louis, MO: Concordia, 1992.

Olson, Laura R., Sue E. S. Crawford, and Melissa M. Deckman. *Women with a Mission: Religion, Gender, and the Politics of Women Clergy*. Tuscaloosa: University of Alabama Press, 2005.

Peiss, Kathy Lee. *Cheap Amusements: Working Women and Leisure in Turn-of-the-Century New York*. Philadelphia: Temple University Press, 1986.

Pope-Levison, Priscilla. *Building the Old Time Religion: Women Evangelists in the Progressive Era*. New York: NYU Press, 2014.

———. "A 'Thirty Year War' and More: Exposing Complexities in the Methodist Deaconess Movement." *Methodist History* 47 (2009): 101.

Prelinger, Catherine M. "Ordained Women in the Episcopal Church: Their Impact on the Work and Structure of the Clergy." In *Episcopal Women: Gender, Spirituality, and Commitment in an American Mainline Denomination*. Edited by Catherine M. Prelinger, 285–309. New York: Oxford University Press, 1992.

———. *Charity, Challenge, and Change: Religious Dimensions of the Mid-Nineteenth-Century Women's Movement in Germany*. New York: Greenwood, 1987.

———. "The Female Diaconate in the Anglican Church: What Kind of Ministry for Women." In *Religion in the Lives of English Women, 1760–1930*. Edited by Gail Malmgreen, 161–92. Bloomington: Indiana University Press, 1986.

Prelinger, Catherine M., and Rosemary Skinner Keller. "The Function of Female Bonding: The Restored Diaconessate in the Nineteenth Century." In *Women in New Worlds: Historical Perspectives on the Wesleyan Tradition*. Edited by Hilah F. Thomas, Rosemary Skinner Keller, and Louise L. Queen, 2:318–37. Nashville, TN: Abingdon, 1982.

Rasche, Ruth W. *The Deaconess Heritage: One Hundred Years of Caring, Healing, and Teaching*. St. Louis, MO: Deaconess Foundation, 1994.

———. "The Deaconess Sisters: Pioneer Professional Women; A Centennial Commemorative." In *Hidden Histories in the United Church of Christ*. Edited by Barbara Brown Zikmund, 95–109. New York: United Church Press, 1984.

Robert, Dana Lee. *American Women in Mission: A Social History of Their Thought and Practice.* Macon, GA: Mercer University Press, 1996.

Robinson, Kenneth L. *From Brass to Gold: The Life and Ministry of Dr. D. Willia Caffray.* University Park, IA: Vennard College, 1971.

Roebuck, David G. "Limiting Liberty: The Church of God and Women Ministers, 1886–1996." PhD diss., Vanderbilt University, 1997.

Ruether, Rosemary Radford. *Christianity and the Making of the Modern Family.* Boston: Beacon, 2000.

Ruether, Rosemary Radford, and Eleanor McLaughlin. *Women of Spirit: Female Leadership in the Jewish and Christian Traditions.* New York: Simon and Schuster, 1979.

Satter, Beryl. *Each Mind a Kingdom: American Women, Sexual Purity, and the New Thought Movement, 1875–1920.* Berkeley: University of California Press, 1999.

Schmidt, Jean Miller. *Souls or the Social Order: The Two-Party System in American Protestantism.* Chicago Studies in the History of American Religion, vol. 18. Brooklyn, NY: Carlson, 1991.

Schmidt, Leigh Eric. *Hearing Things: Religion, Illusion, and the American Enlightenment.* Cambridge, MA: Harvard University Press, 2000.

Schnorrenberg, Barbara Brandon. "Set Apart: Alabama Deaconesses, 1864–1915." *Anglican and Episcopal History* 63 (1994): 469–90.

Scott, Anne Firor. *Natural Allies: Women's Associations in American History.* Urbana: University of Illinois Press, 1991.

SenGupta, Gunja. *From Slavery to Poverty: The Racial Origins of Welfare in New York, 1840–1918.* New York: NYU Press, 2009.

Tentler, Leslie Woodcock. *Wage-Earning Women: Industrial Work and Family Life in the United States, 1900–1930.* New York: Oxford University Press, 1979.

Thuesen, Peter J. *In Discordance with the Scriptures: American Protestant Battles over Translating the Bible.* New York: Oxford University Press, 1999.

Walkowitz, Daniel J. "The Making of a Feminine Professional Identity: Social Workers in the 1920s." *American Historical Review* 95 (October 1990): 1051–75.

Warner, Laceye C. "Methodist Episcopal and Wesleyan Methodist Deaconess Work in the Late Nineteenth and Early Twentieth Centuries: A Paradigm for Evangelism." PhD diss., Trinity College, University of Bristol, 2000.

Weiner, Lynn Y., Ann Taylor Allen, Eileen Boris, Molly Ladd-Taylor, Adele Lindenmeyr, and Kathleen S. Uno. "Maternalism as a Paradigm." *Journal of Women's History* 5, no. 2 (Fall 1993): 95–131.

Weiser, Frederick Sheely. *To Serve the Lord and His People, 1884–1984: Celebrating the Heritage of a Century of Lutheran Deaconesses in America.* Gladwyne, PA: Deaconess Community of the Lutheran Church in America, 1984.

———. *Love's Response: A Story of Lutheran Deaconesses in America.* Philadelphia: Board of Publication, United Lutheran Church in America, 1962.

———. *Serving Love: Chapters in the Early History of the Diaconate in American Lutheranism.* Philadelphia: United Lutheran Church in America Board of Deaconess Work, 1960.

Welter, Barbara. *The Woman Question in American History*. Hinsdale, IL Dryden, 1973.

White, Heather R. *Reforming Sodom*. Chapel Hill: University of North Carolina Press, 2015.

Wiebe, Robert H. *The Search for Order, 1877–1920*. New York: Hill and Wang, 1967.

Willard, Frances Elizabeth. *Writing Out My Heart: Selections from the Journal of Frances E. Willard, 1855–96*. Edited by Carolyn De Swarte Gifford. Urbana: University of Illinois Press, 1995.

Winston, Diane H. *Red-Hot and Righteous: The Urban Religion of the Salvation Army*. Cambridge, MA: Harvard University Press, 1999.

Wuthnow, Robert. *Poor Richard's Principle: Restoring the American Dream by Recovering the Moral Dimension of Work, Business, and Money*. Ewing, NJ: Princeton University Press, 1996.

Yohn, Susan M. "'Let Christian Women Set the Example in Their Own Gifts': The 'Business' of Protestant Women's Organizations." In *Women and Twentieth-Century Protestantism*. Edited by Margaret Lamberts Bendroth and Virginia Lieson Brereton, 213–35. Urbana: University of Chicago Press, 2002.

Zelizer, Viviana A. *The Social Meaning of Money*. Princeton, NJ: Princeton University Press, 1997.

———. "The Social Meaning of Money: 'Special Monies.'" *American Journal of Sociology* 95 (September 1989): 342–77.

Zikmund, Barbara Brown. "Women in the United Church of Christ." In *Encyclopedia of Women and Religion in North America*. Edited by Rosemary Skinner Keller, Rosemary Radford Ruether, and Marie Cantlon. Bloomington: Indiana University Press, 2006.

INDEX

Addams, Jane, 22

African American deaconesses, 5–6, 26, 35–38

African Methodist Episcopal Church, 26; deaconess membership, 19; diaconate establishment, 18

Albertsen, Anna Dorothy, 139

Alexander, Anna, 36

allowance: ambiguity, 109, 112–114; defenses, 109; by denomination, 110; denominational regulations on, 111; and diaconal integrity, 114–115, 116, 165–166; gendering of, 111–113, 115–116; as needs based, 112–113; shifts to salary, 110, 173; socio-economics of, 110–111, 113–114, 116–118

Anderson, Margaret, 183

Andros, Mary L., 51

Anglicans, 10–12

Auld, William, 41

Ayres, Anne, 21

Bachman, E. F., 45, 136, 166

Baden, Edith, 177

Baker, Gertrude Jean, 157

Baptist Training School (Philadelphia), 107, 148

Baptists, 26, 129, 197n4; deaconess membership, 19

Barnwell, Mary Lou, 173

Bay, Clara, 34, 138

Bechtler, Mary Amanda, 84fig

Bennett, Belle Harris, 55

Benz, Anna, 34–35

Bethel Deaconess Home and Hospital (Newton, KS), 125–126

Bethlehem Children's Home, Immanuel Deaconess Institute (Omaha, NE), 32fig

Bible, 145; American approach to, 18; and celibacy, 49–50; in curriculum, 23, 147–149; in daily life, 72, 141; deaconess embodiment of, 21; "deaconess" origins in, 7–9; ecumenical use of, 106; Greek language in, 8; King James version, 7–8, 157; Luther translation, 7; New Testament, 3, 7–8. *See also* scripture

Blanchard, Hazel, 53

Booz, Margaret, 103

Brekus, Catherine, 153–155, 156

Briggs, Charles, 43

Brookes Bible Institute (St. Louis), 150

Brown, Irva Colley, 129

Buchanan, Bessie, 153, 154fig, 157

Cadge, Wendy, 187

Caffray, Willia, 156–157

call, divine, 131, 138–139, 156–157

Camp, Rev., 133

capitalism, 119–120

Catholicism, anti-, 20, 22, 78–79; and celibacy, 48, 49, 102–103; and deaconess garb, 86–87, 88–90, 92, 95; and lifestyle, 96–99, 101; and Mildmay, 12; misrepresentations of Catholics, 79, 81, 95–96, 101; *Our Country* (Strong), 78; and Protestant womanhood, 99, 103–104; and vows, 11, 101–103

ABOUT THE AUTHOR

Jenny Wiley Legath is Associate Director of the Center for the Study of Religion at Princeton University. An expatriate Texan, she lives in New Jersey with her husband, three sons, and two dogs.